and this book shows how the pandemic changed us all and most importantly how we all must lead in times of crisis to persevere over extreme adversity."

James Balda, president and CEO, Argentum

"The COVID-19 pandemic constituted the leadership challenge of a generation. Cindy Baier's book chronicles the impressive response by Brookdale Senior Living with their partners at Vanderbilt University Medical Center. Its examples of everyday heroism movingly demonstrate the power of empathy, dedication, and commitment to a common purpose."

Daniel Diermeier, Chancellor, Distinguished University Professor of Political Science, College of Arts & Science, and Management, Owen School of Management, Vanderbilt University

"Cindy Baier has written a must-read guide for today's leaders. Her real-world experience as CEO of Brookdale during the global pandemic is an exceptional example and playbook for executive teams and organizations to model."

Jonathan Flack, US Family Enterprises leader, PwC LLP

"Superbly reported and written with clarity, *Heroes Work Here* chronicles the courageous actions taken by Brookdale Senior Living under the bold leadership of its CEO, Cindy Baier, during the COVID-19 pandemic. Their team's outstanding emergency response undoubtedly saved lives—and you'll learn how they did it in this important book."

Robert A. Frist Jr., CEO, HealthStream

"*Heroes Work Here* provides a powerful example of the courage required when faced with great uncertainty. In the early days of the global pandemic, not much was known for sure other than the potentially disastrous effect on the seniors served by Brookdale Senior Living. How that challenge was met is characterized by heroic commitment, fierce resolve, and extraordinary teamwork."

Kathy Green, managing partner, Executive Coaching Connections

"This book takes the idea of 'caring' to a whole new level. Brookdale excelled in every vertical as they helped protect America's seniors—the most vulnerable population—during the COVID-19 pandemic. Cindy's story is personal, humble, and touching, and the Brookdale team are the truly extraordinary ordinary leaders we needed to help seniors through the crisis."

Sam Hazen, CEO, HCA Healthcare

"Working with Cindy and Brookdale to ensure the government supported the senior living industry during the pandemic was often 24/7. She was always there to strategize and act on a moment's notice. The Brookdale organization responded passionately and urgently in this war to help save lives. This is their story!"

Bob Hillis, CEO, Direct Supply

"This book is a *must-read* for business leaders and their teams across the senior living and aging services field—as well as for leaders in any business that seek a road map for how to turn crisis into opportunity by unleashing creativity and innovation through teamwork. The 'lessons learned' shared by Cindy Baier and her colleagues at Brookdale Senior Living are priceless insights into what it means to lead at a time of fear and uncertainty, to inspire in the face of an unimaginable outside threat, and to harness the power of teamwork to accomplish the seemingly impossible."

Bob Kramer, founder and fellow, Nexus Insights; cofounder and strategic advisor, NIC

"Cindy Baier and her team at Brookdale have been at the forefront of senior housing's response to COVID-19 and the emergence from the industry's toughest days."

Vincent Mellet, Deerfield Management Company

"The care Brookdale has provided in the buildings, including to my own mother-in-law, has been terrific. And the care Brookdale has provided during the pandemic has been exceptional. Heroic. Every positive adjective you can come up with. Thanks and congratulations."

Governor Mark Parkinson, president and CEO, American Health Care Association and National Center for Assisted Living

"Absolutely brilliant book! I taught Dale Carnegie classes twenty-five years ago on how to weave a narrative between two stories—Cindy has completely mastered that! Her story brought a tear to my eye. I've read well over a thousand business books, and *Heroes Work Here* is an outlier among them. It is so real, so vibrant, and so important for today's leaders."

Robert Reiss, CEO, the CEO Forum Group

LUCINDA M. BAIER

Heroes

WORK HERE

AN EXTRAORDINARY STORY OF
COURAGE, RESILIENCE, AND HOPE
FROM THE FRONT LINES OF COVID-19

ForbesBooks

Published by ForbesBooks, Charleston, South Carolina.
Member of Advantage Media Group.

ForbesBooks is a registered trademark, and the ForbesBooks colophon is a trademark of Forbes Media, LLC.

Printed in the United States of America.

10 9 8 7 6 5 4 3 2 1

ISBN: 978-1-95588-405-1
LCCN: 2021924777

Cover design by David Taylor.
Layout design by Wesley Strickland.

This custom publication is intended to provide accurate information and the opinions of the author in regard to the subject matter covered. It is sold with the understanding that the publisher, Advantage|ForbesBooks, is not engaged in rendering legal, financial, or professional services of any kind. If legal advice or other expert assistance is required, the reader is advised to seek the services of a competent professional.

Advantage Media Group is proud to be a part of the Tree Neutral® program. Tree Neutral offsets the number of trees consumed in the production and printing of this book by taking proactive steps such as planting trees in direct proportion to the number of trees used to print books. To learn more about Tree Neutral, please visit **www.treeneutral.com**.

Since 1917, Forbes has remained steadfast in its mission to serve as the defining voice of entrepreneurial capitalism. ForbesBooks, launched in 2016 through a partnership with Advantage Media Group, furthers that aim by helping business and thought leaders bring their stories, passion, and knowledge to the forefront in custom books. Opinions expressed by ForbesBooks authors are their own. To be considered for publication, please visit **www.forbesbooks.com**.

Safe Harbor Statement

Certain statements in this publication may constitute forward-looking statements within the meaning of the Private Securities Litigation Reform Act of 1995. These forward-looking statements are subject to various risks and uncertainties and include all statements that are not historical statements of fact and those regarding the intent, belief, or expectations of Brookdale Senior Living Inc. (the Company) and its management. These forward-looking statements are based on certain assumptions and expectations, and the Company can give no assurance that such assumptions or expectations will be attained. Actual results could differ materially from those projected. Factors that could cause events or circumstances to differ from the forward-looking statements include, but are not limited to, the risks detailed from time to time in the Company's filings with the Securities and Exchange Commission, including those set forth under "Risk Factors" contained in the Company's Annual Report on Form 10-K and Quarterly Reports on Form 10-Q. Readers are cautioned not to place undue reliance on any of these forward-looking statements, which reflect management's views as of the date of this publication. The Company cannot guarantee future results and, except as required by law, it expressly disclaims any obligation to release publicly any updates or revisions to any forward-looking statements to reflect any change in the Company's assumptions or expectations.

To my husband and soul mate, Dave,
whose love, encouragement, and guidance mean everything to me;
my mother, Sheryl, whose advice influences me every day;
my sister, Lisa, whose courage and passion for life inspire me;
and my Brookdale family, the extended family that
I wish I had found sooner.

We will always remember
those we have lost.

*May their memory be
a blessing.*

CONTENTS

ACKNOWLEDGMENTS

Words cannot express my gratitude for my husband, Dave. He is my perfect partner in life and the person most important to me. Dave is my trusted mentor: the person I turn to with problems I can't solve alone, the individual whose opinion matters more than any other, the man who helps me see the big picture, and the one who gives me the strength to move forward when my energy is depleted. Dave is also the person who believes in me more than I believe in myself; he is my greatest champion. During the pandemic, Dave devoted himself to using his research skills as a former litigator to conduct extensive research on all things COVID-19. He was a sounding board as I worked through Brookdale's pandemic strategy and provided thoughts on our execution.

I wouldn't be the person I am today without the lessons that I learned from my mom and my grandparents. They taught me the value of hard work and how to overcome adversity. Most importantly, they helped me develop a servant's heart.

My sister, Lisa, taught me how to win the fight of your life.

We wouldn't have reacted to the pandemic as quickly and effectively as we did without the early warning from former board member Jim Seward. Jim has been an important mentor to me. The entire board of directors at Brookdale devoted considerable time and effort to work side by side with management and helped create a successful path forward through the most difficult situation imaginable. I have learned so much from our board members (current and former) and remain eternally grateful for their support.

It is impossible to overstate my deep appreciation for the leaders at Brookdale. I have never met so many people who are willing to sacrifice so much for the benefit of others.

Brookdale associates are the true heroes of this story. Their bravery, dedication, resilience, and positive outlook helped protect tens of thousands of residents and patients from a dire threat to their lives. My hope for this book is to capture the story of our Brookdale associates, the everyday heroes called to duty beyond anyone's imagination. I have learned so much from them. They have my sincere and ongoing thanks. In honor of our associates, all net proceeds from this book will be donated to Brookdale's Associate Compassion Fund, a nonprofit organization Brookdale established more than a decade ago to support associates during times of need. Together, Brookdale leaders and associates have become my extended family.

Every time I visit one of our communities, I learn so much from our residents. I am deeply grateful for them, their families and loved ones, and their continued trust in Brookdale.

I am extremely appreciative for Brookdale's shareholders who supported the company during an incredibly difficult time. They understood the need to focus on the health and well-being of our residents, patients, and associates despite significant disruption in the value of their investment during the early days of the pandemic.

I am thankful for Brookdale's capital providers, business partners, industry trade associations, and members of the healthcare community who worked together to help save lives and our industry.

I am grateful for the Brookdale board members and leaders who helped tell our story in this book. I am also deeply appreciative of Julie Davis, Erin Vargo, Bree Barton, and the team at ForbesBooks for their help in developing the manuscript.

always enjoyed waking up early, even before the roosters. When someone says the early bird gets the worm, I take that as a personal challenge.

My grandparents owned a farm in central Illinois and gave my parents six acres of their land, so my sister and I grew up among corn and soybean fields with endless rows of glorious green stalks that disappeared into the horizon.

Lisa is my only sibling, a year older than I am. She was the gregarious one, and people were naturally drawn to her magnetic personality. Whereas I, "Cindy," was a homebody who enjoyed cooking and helping out around the house, Lisa loved the outdoors. During middle school, she joined the track team and became one of the fastest runners in Illinois—second in the state in the eighth grade!

Lisa wore her hair long, often in pigtails, and my mom (a former beautician) styled mine in short cuts. Our dark hair contrasted with the amber waves of hay that we would haul in bales to the horses before school. I remember waking up early every day, wiping the sleep from my eyes before pulling on my cowboy boots and heading out the door to help take care of our small herd of horses.

Farm life was peaceful in the morning. All was quiet while the air was still, and I took pleasure in the wondrous scents ushered in by the rain or the change in seasons. The calm of the morning didn't last long; the horses quickly stirred from their sleep when they heard me turn on the water from the hose that was connected to a well on the property.

Feeding the horses was an important job. Each hay bale weighed somewhere between forty-five and fifty pounds, and each horse ate fifteen to twenty pounds of hay a day. Every morning, the horses would run toward the gate as it opened. Considering they were around a thousand pounds each, you can imagine the mayhem that ensued as they vied to be the first to eat, shoving their way to the hay we were bringing them. Needless to say, the breakfast routine required a lot of hay, and it was a challenge to separate the bales into flakes so that all the horses could eat at once.

Life was predictable yet strenuous.

I was an imaginative child, constantly reading books that gave me a window into a different world. Many mornings I found myself getting lost in my imagination, thinking about the stars in the sky. The universe seemed so big, and the twinkling stars seemed to beckon with endless possibility, slowly fading with the light of dawn. The night sky above the farm was a canvas where I could get lost in my thoughts and dreams.

The occasional jolt from the hose water connecting to the electric fence zapped me back to reality. Little did I know, I would experience a similar sense of shock as an adult.

I still enjoy waking up early.

One day in mid-January 2020, I started my usual morning routine without a hitch. I was up at 3:00 a.m. to get some exercise before starting my workday. As the president and chief executive officer (CEO) of Brookdale Senior Living, I make it a habit to take off with a bold start. I've held the position since early 2018 after serving as the company's chief financial officer (CFO) for more than two years prior, and every day is a challenge I'm happy to take on.

Since the start of my tenure as CEO, we had implemented several new strategies that resulted in community-specific revenue growth each year. Importantly, we were gaining momentum on our turnaround plan and would soon report that our 2019 net profit had improved by more than $250 million in just one year. Brookdale is a publicly traded company with a mission to serve seniors, and I am honored to be its CEO. In my book, life doesn't get any better than being able to make a difference in another person's life every day.

Life as a CEO was always challenging; I had learned that my daily priorities could change quickly. That morning, I read the news and worked through my email to prepare for another day at the helm of an organization overseeing seven-hundred-plus communities and almost eighty home health and hospice agencies and eighty-four outpatient therapy clinics across more than forty states. Nothing struck me as particularly unusual.

But then I talked with former Brookdale board member and my trusted mentor, Jim Seward. I felt a pit forming in my gut as I thought about the possibilities behind what he was saying. I was determined that, whatever lay ahead, we would prevail.

Failure was not an option. This was a lesson I'd learned well in my youth.

* * *

Like most of the children in farming communities, we learned a lot at an early age, because farmers are usually looking for extra hands to help during the growing season.

While we had to take care of the horses year round, Lisa and I were tasked with even greater responsibilities during the growing season: first helping in my grandfather's cornfields and later earning extra cash through backbreaking work as day laborers helping local soybean farmers. We'd hand-weed acres and acres of fields as early as possible in the day before the sun's rays rendered us useless.

Timing is critical in farming, and during certain seasons, we were prepared for the messy, sweaty, bedraggled affair, the reward of which would be a cheeseburger lunch with fries and a small wad of cash. I never questioned our lifestyle, and if I did, one glimpse of my sister two soybean rows over reminded me that we were in this together. We would compete to see who could finish their row fastest, racing to grab a cool drink of water that waited at the edge of the field.

We didn't have a choice in helping on the farm, and if we had, we wouldn't have had it any other way.

In adulthood, I would feel this same sense: we don't choose our circumstances, but we control our response.

* * *

Jim Seward is a trusted mentor of mine. When he speaks, I listen. A conversation with Jim in mid-January 2020 offered an early, important insight into the situation developing in China. It wasn't broadly reported in the news at that point, but it was unusual enough to give him pause.

I took a moment to process the new information about a novel coronavirus emerging from a wet market in Wuhan, and I tried to discern what he was really telling me. It was too early to know then that we were on the verge of a global disaster.

As he described the events taking place, and I thought about the potential ramifications for our industry, a cold current of electricity moved up my spine. I felt compelled to increase our preparedness. I glanced at the trees just outside my window, their roots holding firmly to the earth. The sight of them reminded me to stay strong and grounded.

It would be several weeks before I would fully understand just how much life was about to change—we wouldn't have much of a say in the matter.

The good news was I already had experience in absorbing shock, starting from a young age.

* * *

Both my parents were only children, so I didn't grow up with the aunts, uncles, and cousins who make up a traditional extended family. When my grandparents' health began to fail, they sold the farm and moved to a city not far away. With my parents' separation and ultimate divorce, we would leave the farm too.

I did everything in my power to make sure I didn't add to Mom's troubles. I was a good student and gladly followed the rules.

I missed the short walk up the hill to see Grandma and Grandpa. I also missed my dad; when he moved away, I wouldn't see him again for the better part of twenty-five years. My small family had become even smaller. I was thirteen years old and grateful for the lessons I had learned from the farm, but life only became harder.

On the day my parents' separation began, my mom had already arranged a move to a new house in a small town (population 2,750).

The plan was for me to wait for her after school so she could give me a new house key. I would walk home from school and wait with Lisa until Mom came home from work.

As I waited, I sensed something was terribly wrong, but I didn't know what. I did as I was told and waited, shivering in the cool winter air. Soon I would learn the cold reality.

Mom wasn't coming.

It didn't take long for my shock to turn to resolve. The same reaction showed up when I first considered the magnitude of the pandemic's effects within Brookdale's communities.

* * *

During January 2020, thanks to Jim's early suggestion, I started watching the concerning events going on in China. After an initial review of the facts, I thought the novel coronavirus might have the impact of a bad flu season, and I felt Brookdale was prepared. We knew how to manage the flu. We'd developed strong infection prevention protocols, and while I kept my finger on the pulse, I didn't anticipate the worst. All of the early cases were in China or seemed to be related to people who had traveled there. Regardless, in January we started reinforcing our strong infection control protocols.

Then, in February, we started to see cases with local transmission in Europe and the United States, including the rapid proliferation of cases at a skilled nursing facility operated by another company in the state of Washington. We started to transform Brookdale in order to help protect those we serve.

By mid-March, Brookdale's executive team knew that the novel coronavirus, now known as COVID-19, was spreading quickly, no longer limited to isolated outbreaks. We also knew that the population

Brookdale serves would be among the most vulnerable to the virus because of age and chronic conditions.

We would get ready to move heaven and earth. Thankfully, my experiences in childhood prepared me for this very thing.

* * *

My childhood was over when Mom didn't come to meet me at school on that fateful day.

After what seemed like hours, one of Mom's coworkers (she had worked as a bus driver at the time) emerged from inside the school, walked over to me, and told me that my mom had been in a bad car accident.

Mom was in her car alone, driving her forest-green Thunderbird on Highway 150 heading back for her afternoon school bus run. She lost control when she hit a patch of ice, causing her car to spin around and hit a beer truck. The damage to the car was hard to fathom. It was crumpled around her like a crushed can. When the rescue squad arrived at the scene, another of Mom's friends was in the crew. He recognized her distinctive dark-green car with a white roof and prepared for the worst, convinced that no one could have survived the carnage that he saw.

He had underestimated Mom.

They worked feverishly to extract her from the wreck with the "jaws of life" and rushed her to the hospital. She was as badly mangled as the car she was driving. Thankfully she had been wearing her seat belt, but she suffered major soft tissue damage and a crushed femur. They would need to put her leg back together like a jigsaw puzzle, using rods and pins to hold it together while it healed, her heart stopping twice before she stabilized.

She fought hard for her life and remained in the hospital for weeks, returning home in a wheelchair. We were so grateful when Mom could be carried up the stairs to continue her recovery at home. She was bedridden for months while her leg healed enough to support her weight again, but she was home with her children whom she loved dearly.

My sister was busy with basketball, track, and other activities, and because of our limited resources, I became the primary caregiver for my mom and left my childhood behind virtually overnight. I was involved in all aspects of Mom's care, including preparing meals, helping her eat, bathing her, and managing her bedpan. Mom was physically and emotionally broken. The combination of her pending divorce and the accident was all too overwhelming. I desperately wanted to make her happy, seeing her so sad and in such pain. I was determined to help her put her life back together.

Unfortunately the accident and divorce had taken a heavy financial toll, and it didn't look like she would be headed back to work for many months. It's a sad fact that school bus drivers didn't make a lot of money even under the best of circumstances.

After Mom recovered from her accident, she worked hard to try to support us with her wages as a bus driver and part-time credit associate at Sears, Roebuck and Co. There simply weren't enough resources for the family to survive, so I started coming up with solutions to help support us. I was fourteen years old when I got a job as a cook in a nice restaurant near our home. It was a wonderful opportunity—for starters, because I always liked to cook, and moreover, because I was able to order a meal off the menu during every shift.

I am not sure how I was able to get the job at my age. Times were tough, but I knew I was tougher because I was my mother's daughter. I had to make it work so I could help my family survive. Several months into the job, the manager of the restaurant was shocked to learn my age but kept me on. I had the right skills, showed up on time, and did my best every shift.

Throughout high school, I worked in the restaurant and other odd jobs, including "walking beans" (a form of weed control in soybean fields), detasseling corn, cleaning houses, teaching swimming, and serving as a lifeguard. I was always in motion, doing everything I could to help our family. It was the only way.

I revisited this same sense of duty and service at the start of the pandemic.

* * *

Growing up in a small town where you knew all your neighbors, I never expected to find myself in a pivotal role that would ultimately impact the health and well-being of tens of thousands of people during a pandemic. I've always seen myself as an ordinary person, but I rose through the ranks of corporate America because of my willingness to work hard and my keen passion for solving the toughest, most challenging problems that lay before me.

Yet the looming public health crisis surrounding COVID-19 was on a level I'd never imagined.

In the early months of 2020, an avalanche was forming. We came to understand that we would have to source supplies that weren't readily available, put additional protocols in place to help protect against a virus that we had never seen before, and communicate quickly to tens of thousands of associates who would care for the tens of thousands of precious lives we were tasked with helping to protect.

What we didn't know was how often the situation would shift. Each time, we'd have to do the same things—find available supplies, define protocols, and manage care on the granular level—over and over and over again in hundreds upon hundreds of locations every day.

This was a continuously evolving task no one could have predicted nor prepared for.

When COVID-19 hit the United States, everything changed—and Brookdale had to change as a result. With the good fortune we had experienced in the months prior, we braced for impact and—by the grace of wise counsel, board members, leadership teams, exemplary associates, and incredibly adaptable residents, patients, and loved ones—we helped save lives and weathered the storm.

I'm only one person, but my position was unique: I stood at the center of the largest senior living operator in the country as we experienced the greatest public health crisis in over a hundred years.

Because COVID-19 was truly a novel coronavirus, there were times when it felt like we were wearing blinders. As an organization, we focused on learning quickly and nimbly incorporating new knowledge into our protocols. In hindsight, as they say, we see 20/20.

As it happens, this was a familiar scenario for me early in my life.

* * *

I finished high school when I was sixteen years old, and I was excited about college. I was proud to be the first person in my family to attend and believed that a good education would improve my life. At the same time, my family needed me; my grandfather lost his eyesight, and my grandparents needed my help.

I answered the call. Instead of moving away to college, I moved in with my grandparents to help out. This was another intense period in my life. I was taking classes full-time at Illinois State University, working nearly full time, and helping my grandparents at home.

My college years were, like my childhood, burdened with inordinate responsibility yet filled with love and gratitude.

At the onset of his blindness, my grandfather's vision was blurry, but he could see shadows; his world was essentially only light and dark. My grandparents had moved into a two-bedroom apartment, so my grandpa needed help learning to navigate it safely. Grandpa enjoyed listening to the radio, and we found that books on tape were a way to engage him during the day. He loved telling stories and talking about our old life on the farm and was always interested in what was currently happening in our lives. Being together kept his spirits high.

Grandpa needed to have all of his meals prepared for him. Luckily, I loved to cook! He could make his way to the table, and we would explain what was on his plate, describing each position like the hands of a clock: peas and carrots at two o'clock, pork chop at six, potatoes at nine. He also needed help with his medication, especially preparing his insulin shots to manage his diabetes. I became his favorite caregiver, helping him with all of this and more, including grooming and getting dressed, and managing all housekeeping duties for my grandparents.

Grandpa liked to get out of the house, so we would go for walks in the neighborhood; he'd hold my arm on one side and his white cane with a red tip on the other. We'd smell the air and guess whether rain was on the way, which kept him connected to nature. His life was filled with meaning and joy.

So was mine. It was through these experiences that I cultivated a servant's heart.

I wouldn't say I would have chosen that path. By the time I graduated high school, I was looking forward to an easier life—that's why I went to college. I'm not sure that I actually found an easier life, but every step of the way, I found fulfillment. With my college education, I was able to put food on the table and ensure that I would have a roof over my head. Meanwhile, I managed to care for my family, whom I loved and cherished with all my heart.

I wouldn't have had it any other way.

* * *

This book isn't about me. It's about a brave team of leaders, colleagues, and heroes surrounding me that went through an extraordinary experience together alongside me. With the oversight of the board and the assistance of the leadership team, I charted the course; and together we weathered the storm and started our journey to a bright future.

It would be hard to overstate the grit and determination demonstrated by my team, which included my mentors and the board and leadership team, along with the tens of thousands of associates who were heroic in helping to save lives during the COVID-19 pandemic by containing illness, mitigating risk, and enriching seniors' lives as much as possible. Not to mention the tens of thousands of residents and patients who remained steady, adaptable, and resilient throughout.

This is not my story. It is *our* story: it deserves to be celebrated, and it needs to be told. The Brookdale Senior Living response to the pandemic has been nothing less than extraordinary.

The lessons we learned are universal, and I hope that hearing it told from our insiders' perspective inspires you. We felt the need to pause and memorialize our experience: we united around a common mission; sought out the best counsel we could find; relied on each associate to bring their best skills to the table; and responded boldly to a once-in-a-century pandemic, ultimately navigating what might have been a cataclysmic event.

We learned that everybody has a role to play—everybody. If each person had not done their part to achieve the mission, we most certainly may not have succeeded.

My goal in writing this book is twofold: One, to recognize and celebrate the achievements of Brookdale's associates. Our associates, many of whom consider themselves to be "everyday" people, have demonstrated time and again that they are truly the heroes of today. They have helped save lives, comforted those in distress, and transformed the way Brookdale embraces the six dimensions of our residents' Optimum Life®,[1] including the emotional, physical, social, spiritual, intellectual, and purposeful. The last dimension relates to how having purpose provides motivation and improves well-being.

Two, I wanted to highlight the leadership skills and processes that have made an impact on our communities in an effort to inspire and encourage other leaders and businesses facing challenges. The COVID-19 pandemic has affected people and businesses around the country and across the world, albeit in different ways. We have learned to cope with the challenges and the effects of an invisible threat. For some, this is a time of new growth and opportunity.

Through the course of this book, we share insights gleaned from various leaders—including my mentors, board members, and others—and the critical thinking behind these actions. We have clarified early warning signs and notes on teamwork, financial preparedness, strategic communications, and the many leadership lessons we learned along the way. I hope you'll see that the lessons we learned apply to many other businesses and industries in times of crisis.

Looking back, I can say with confidence and humility that Brookdale's response was extraordinary.

---

1   Optimum Life is a registered trademark of American Retirement Corporation.

OUR MISSION

Enriching the lives of those we serve with compassion, respect, excellence, and integrity

OUR VISION

To be the nation's first choice in senior living

OUR CORNERSTONES

 ## MORE THAN A JOB, A **PASSION**

Have fun and celebrate life every day

 ## DOING THE RIGHT THING TAKES **COURAGE**

Provide meaningful rewards for associates, residents, and shareholders

WE SUCCEED THROUGH **PARTNERSHIP**

Work together as one team

 ## BUILT ON A FOUNDATION OF **TRUST**

Listen, understand, partner, and solve

PART I

ALL HANDS ON DECK

---— CHAPTER 1 ---—

Benefiting from the Brilliant Foresight of the Board

Celebrating Leaders Who Prompted Early Action

B*rilliance* is defined as exceptional clarity. It can be viewed as the ability to shine light on an event before its time. Brilliant leaders are forward thinking, always seeking to stay ahead of both opportunities and threats. In a world more interconnected than ever, with global travel linking our lives together in a complex web of interdependence, modern teams must seek leaders with broad perspectives and keen perceptions to navigate turbulent waters.

Thankfully, in the months before the pandemic reached the United States of America, the brilliant board at Brookdale Senior Living was buoyed by smart leaders (both former and current members) who prompted the senior leadership team to take early action.

Exceptional Insight That Prompted Early Action

Jim Seward was a member of Brookdale's board from 2008 until October 2019. We missed his leadership but remained grateful for his long-standing service.

Jim had been the chairman of two important committees of the board—both the Investment and Audit Committees, which oversee a wide range of financial matters for the company, including a review of our financial statements before they are released to the public. Because Jim and I worked so closely together when I was CFO from 2015 to 2018, and because one of a CFO's primary responsibilities is financial reporting, we had built a really strong relationship, and he helped me refine my ability to spot and analyze macroeconomic trends and their potential ramifications. He excelled in grasping trends in the global landscape and understanding their implications on a company level.

Jim became aware of COVID-19 from different public sources before it was discussed widely as a threat, and he made a concerted effort to follow the events occurring in China. In mid-January 2020 he notified me of his concerns with the intent to educate and inform— not in any official capacity but as a friend, colleague, and key mentor.

Influenza is of primary concern in the senior care industry, and Brookdale prepares every year to help mitigate the effects of seasonal flu. A pandemic, however, is a black-swan event—unexpected and unpredictable when it arrives.

Around this time, the "expert" opinion, from both international and domestic institutions, was that the virus posed little to no threat to the United States. The dominant narrative was that the virus originated in a "wet market" and was isolated to that area. Raising a red flag at this time would have been seen as absurd.

Yet the consensus narrative did not add up.

> ## Stay Alert for Unexpected Threats and Unique Opportunities for Your Business.

By mid-January 2020 Jim concluded—fully aware that he could be wrong—that the virus posed a huge risk, particularly to the senior care sector. Nobody could be certain, but he believed that COVID-19 could play out as a large-magnitude, medium-probability event and would need to be addressed. He explained the implications to me and allowed me to exercise my independent judgment to assess the risk early despite the consensus views.

I trusted his keen sensitivity and judgment and immediately began focusing on increasing our preparedness. Jim's early insight prompted me to take decisive action weeks before the government made any official statements or recommendations.

HERO HIGHLIGHTS FROM JIM SEWARD

Brookdale Senior Living board member from November 2008 to October 2019

SOUNDING THE FIRST ALARM

During times of crisis, ordinary people rise to the occasion to do extraordinary things. I certainly qualify as an ordinary person. I'm not sure my COVID-19 warning with Cindy Baier was extraordinary, but it was early—

early enough to go against consensus at the time—and made a positive impact.

Looking back, I would identify three components of leadership—caring, awareness, and independent thinking—that remained at the forefront of our thinking at the time. These core values led Brookdale to take the early action steps upon concluding that significant risk was imminent.

Caring is a central part of the Brookdale philosophy: it is ingrained in the culture at the highest level in its overarching mission to perform with genuine compassion for Brookdale's residents and at the ground level through the commitment that Brookdale associates make to the residents via thousands of daily acts of kindness.

Awareness can be defined as focusing on the external environment with as little ego, judgment, and bias as possible. It is simply an effort to see things as they are— and not how we want them to be—in other words, getting out of one's own way.

The third component is *independent thinking*. Everyone is capable of viewing the news objectively, but it is not always easy, given the pressure to accept "expert" consensus as the safe and comfortable view. Consensus, importantly, may be correct. But it isn't necessarily the truth. If one is wrong in going with the consensus, it is certainly a safer position because you are in the midst of "expert" company. If one goes against consensus, it is a lonely place, and there is personal risk involved.

The ability to cultivate an independent-thinking mindset enables leaders to reach the best conclusion regardless of personal agenda and risk.

Alas, history is replete with famous consensus expert opinions that turned out to be wrong.

I had no certainty my concern was correct, but I had done enough research to know it was more than just a hunch, and that the risk was real. *There are many components of leadership, but caring, awareness, and independent thinking were key in the early stages of COVID-19, prompting Brookdale's leadership to take proactive steps that made a critical difference.* These components enabled Brookdale to navigate one of the most challenging crises ever and remain part of Brookdale's DNA and culture.

No Ordinary Matter

My job as CEO is to run the company. A company's board of directors is responsible for governance and oversight and, as a rule, helps a CEO look for opportunities and threats.

In other words, the board's job is to oversee my role and to ensure the corporate leadership team is running the company in a manner that's consistent with the strategy that the board has approved. That's standard corporate governance.

Keep Informed of Current Events to Understand Your Operating Environment.

In early 2020, we had an existing operating strategy and budget for the year that the board had approved, but by the middle of March, the pandemic changed virtually everything. Immediately we knew our revenues were at risk and that we needed to incur substantial additional expenses to cover additional labor, personal protective equipment (PPE), supplies, and other essential needs. The budget we had prepared and initially presented to the board in December was no longer applicable, because the fundamental assumptions about the impact of COVID-19 were wrong.

The board is also responsible for making sure the corporate leadership team is adequately addressing quality issues for the residents. Given the extent to which the pandemic could affect the health and well-being of our residents, the board needed to understand the changes that we were making to Brookdale to help keep our residents safe.

In ordinary times, a board has a cadence that is pretty consistent from year to year. Each member knows about how many hours a year they are expected to spend overseeing the company. Prior to the pandemic, all board members would have had a relatively clear idea of how much work was required of them and what they could expect for their service.

Usually a public company board meets together as a full board six or fewer times a year in order to discuss the company's performance and measure its progress against the strategic objectives it has set. A board also discusses any significant risks to the company and considers possible risk mitigation efforts. Given these responsibilities, it's vital that board members are routinely scanning the horizon for risks and opportunities and thinking about the impact on a company.

When the pandemic hit, every board member at Brookdale answered the call and performed at an even higher level than what otherwise would have been expected of them in normal times. Some people may envision a position on a corporate board as a luxurious role that requires little effort or sacrifice, but that's a misconception.

The level of oversight involved when managing more than seven hundred communities, almost eighty home health and hospice agencies, and eighty-four outpatient therapy clinics across forty-plus states is extraordinarily intense and ordinarily happens at a very broad strategic level. But the pandemic was no ordinary matter. Each member's expertise was called upon in a way that had never happened before. During the most intense part of the pandemic, board members were engaged with Brookdale on a daily basis. Their engagement included activities such as reading and analyzing a daily update from me, having one-on-one conversations with management, or participating in board or committee meetings, which occurred more frequently than in a "normal" year.

Because of the highly specialized skill sets of our board members, they quickly became strategic advisors in various areas of importance to the company-wide effort. In ordinary times, a board generally directs from above, but the pandemic required an all-hands-on-deck approach, which saw the board members directly collaborating with various members of the corporate leadership team.

Relying on a Robust Board of Directors

It's essential for a CEO to work with the Nominating and Corporate Governance Committee and board as a whole to nominate a slate of potential board members. Ultimately a shareholder vote determines who serves on the board. It is also essential for a CEO to advocate for a robust board of directors with a wide range of backgrounds and perspectives. I believe that the most effective boards have a diverse set of skills and experiences with which to analyze the company from many different perspectives.

> ## Build a Diverse Board of Directors with a Wide Range of Critical Skills.

Early in my tenure as CEO, I recommended to our Nominating and Corporate Governance Committee that we add healthcare and hospitality experience as well as someone with public company CFO experience to our board of directors. During the pandemic, we were grateful that we had such broad experience on our board, as each of our directors would play an important role in monitoring that we were responding appropriately to the public health crisis and that we were taking the steps necessary to help protect Brookdale.

Guy Sansone joined our board in October 2019 and became chairman of the board on January 1, 2020. The chairman of the board has broad responsibilities: he (or she) is the key contact who works most closely with the CEO and all of the other board members and sets the agenda for each board meeting. Guy had spent more than twenty-five years optimizing the performance of healthcare companies, previously serving as the chairman of Alvarez & Marsal's Healthcare Industry Group. As an experienced veteran working with both healthcare and senior living companies, he had a leadership profile that was the perfect fit to lead our board. His background was incredibly helpful as we thought through the relationship with our landlords and the critically important lease restructurings.

HERO HIGHLIGHTS FROM GUY SANSONE

Joined Brookdale Senior Living Board of Directors October 2019, currently nonexecutive chairman of the board; currently cofounder, chairman, and CEO of H2 Health

VISIONARY LEADERSHIP, PASSIONATE TEAM MEMBERS, AND OPERATIONAL EXCELLENCE

Almost twenty years ago, I was thirty-seven years old when my business partners and I were thrust into what seemed to be the most insurmountable scenario imaginable: We were tasked with saving HealthSouth Corporation from the threat of a Chapter 11 filing that would have destroyed the company altogether in the aftermath of one of the largest corporate fraud scandals in United States history. Almost twenty people from senior management pled guilty and ultimately served time in prison; countless others resigned from guilt or embarrassment from the ordeal.

Our chances of success were bleak, but we had several key advantages: we had the support of passionate employees who maintained a strong belief in the organization, and we had a series of strategic contingency options in the event our plan was derailed by factors beyond our control.

By setting a clear vision, leveraging our employees' passions, and implementing a flexible restructuring plan that addressed the needs of regulators, the Justice Department, lenders and banks, shareholders, and ultimately our employees, HealthSouth emerged from that process and has thrived for most of the last two decades under the name of Encompass Health.

This experience came to the forefront of my mind during the COVID-19 pandemic, as I had not seen such a confluence of events—visionary leaders, passionate team members rising to the occasion, and strategic insights for optimal operational and financial planning—until I had the fortune to work with the senior leadership team at Brookdale, led by Cindy Baier.

While Brookdale's challenges were not brought on by unscrupulous actions, the obstacles faced were arguably worse than those faced by HealthSouth, particularly given the storm of events at play: in addition to an unprecedented global pandemic, Brookdale's communities faced wildfires, tornadoes, ice storms, and other natural disasters.

I hadn't witnessed this level of passionate leadership, contingency planning, and operational performance in almost twenty years. *It was an extraordinary feat by the board, the corporate leadership team, and all associates who kicked into high gear for the health and well-being of the residents and patients across the communities.*

Long before the pandemic, I believed strongly that our board should include a physician, given the healthcare focus at Brookdale along with the age and chronic conditions of the residents we serve. Happily, Dr. Jordan Asher joined our board in February 2020, just before the pandemic reached a critical state. He was a key partner who would contribute his valuable medical perspective to the board and at the same time share keen insights as a licensed MD leading the COVID-19 response in his own healthcare system.

Little did we know when we first invited him to join, Jordan and I would be spending a lot of time together on 5:00 a.m. phone calls talking about the threat the pandemic posed and conducting scenario planning around the various situations we might face: How would we respond to the community at large? What happens if a resident gets infected? Could associates use bandanas if masks were unavailable? Was it possible to use goggles for eye protection?

We had typically transferred residents and patients to the hospital when they got sick and required medical supervision, but Jordan was the first to highlight that such a routine solution would likely no longer be an option. He gave us important insights about the state of hospital systems, even before the limitations were visible within the industry.

HERO HIGHLIGHTS FROM
JORDAN ASHER, MD, MS

Joined Brookdale Senior Living Board of Directors February 2020; currently chief physician executive and executive vice president, Sentara Healthcare

EMOTIONS FLOWED AND CREATIVITY ABOUNDED

In the face of so much uncertainty at the start of the pandemic, I was here to help in any way I could—as a board member, as a physician (leading Sentara's COVID-19 response), and as a colleague and friend.

The emotions were overwhelming—so was the fear of the unknown. Yet I was struck by the forthrightness and forethought that Brookdale and its leadership undertook.

In the beginning, any and all solutions were laid on the table. *Throughout an admittedly nightmarish set of circumstances, the conversations remained creative, productive, and forward thinking.*

In the early stages, I heard about other organizations that were sticking their heads in the sand out of fear and denial. Not Brookdale.

We worked through every scenario imaginable. Boldly, we stretched the limits of our thinking. Painstakingly, we considered how the virus might spread. We participated in countless conversations about resource management when supplies were difficult to obtain and family engagement options when restrictions commenced. *Creativity abounded—followed by rapid implementation.*

We also embraced the human element in our roles as members of the board. We leaned on one another for added support. We opened up and shared our human emotions. On top of addressing the monumental task of helping to protect tens of thousands of residents and associates, we were all dealing with our own COVID-19 situations. I wondered, How would I explain to my kids the severity of the situation? How could I be sure I was doing everything in my power to help protect the lives of the people I was stewarding, as well as my own family and loved ones?

Engaging with my fellow board members through daily conversations aided me in my own situation. A shared burden is lighter than carrying it alone. Being vulnerable as a leader is never easy, but sharing my fears helped.

I began to develop even greater strength than I ever imagined by virtue of such heightened collaboration.

Thinking back to the early days of the pandemic brings back so many emotions. The anxiety was palpable, and fear of the unknown was gripping. The greatest challenge for us as leaders was to manage all of these emotions while maintaining clarity of thought. *We had to allow ourselves to feel, identify the feelings, and then process them so we could move forward; otherwise, we would have been paralyzed.*

Oliver Wendell Holmes once said, "A mind stretched by a new idea never returns to its original shape." Over the course of the pandemic, we as leaders were tasked with complexities beyond our previous experiences, but this led us to a new appreciation of our own humanity. For me, the pandemic reinforced the notion that I was not alone in my fears.

By embracing our humanness and vulnerability, I believe we reached the next level in our evolution as leaders.

Likewise, Denise Warren brought critical insights about hospital systems: she was not only the chief operating officer of WakeMed Health and Hospitals at that time but also a former public company CFO. Denise understood the need for both mission *and* margin within our business: she quickly processed the financial implications of the decisions we were making. Having an Audit Committee chair with a skill set in both finance and operations was a blessing.

Jordan and Denise each exercised exceptional judgment, cluing us in to scenarios we hadn't considered.

Notably, Rita Johnson-Mills brought healthcare experience from the private sector along with experience working with federal and state officials. Rita maintained a strong focus on quality, regularly asking probing questions about management's plans and helping us think through the challenges that various members of our workforce would face.

Vicki Freed holds a critical role overseeing sales and customer service in the cruise line industry, which experienced the impact of the pandemic very early on. The cruise line industry has many parallels to senior living, because they provide lodging, fine dining experiences, and engaging activities for customers around the clock. The demographics are also very similar between our industries.

> ## Adapt Best Practices from Other Industries to Improve Your Business.

Further, Royal Caribbean—the company Vicki works for—had an exceptional track record in crisis management. Given her special understanding of customer satisfaction and firsthand experience addressing the challenges of COVID-19, Vicki became a key ally as we contemplated troubling scenarios and weighed our options for keeping residents, patients, and associates engaged when our communities were closed to visitors.

We were also lucky to have seasoned board member Frank Bumstead, whose heroic service during the Vietnam War shaped his extraordinary perspective. Throughout our strategic planning sessions,

Frank lent precious insights on leadership as the board weighed life-and-death decisions and oversaw the troops on the ground. During the darkest days of the pandemic, Frank shared how he survived the war and how he felt to have his life on the line with enemy soldiers trying to kill him. He explained how he focused on the lives that his actions would save. Frank did what needed to be done. He overcame his fear and returned home safely to his family. Frank's words of wisdom and hope helped me cultivate deeper personal strength during our harshest trials.

Additionally, Frank spends several hours each morning following current events in order to help his clients manage their investments. He is quick to identify emerging trends and assess their impact. During the pandemic, Frank shared his insights nearly every day and balanced the delivery of tough feedback with words of encouragement. This meant a lot to me on a personal level.

And finally, Lee Wielansky and Marc Bromley each brought a measured understanding of the real estate industry that became vitally important as we prepared for the impact of the global pandemic on our capital structure. Before the pandemic, both Lee and Marc had spent a lot of time working with management as we shifted the ownership structure of the assets in our portfolio to have more of our communities owned by Brookdale and to lease fewer of them.

Owning assets gives the company more strategic flexibility than it has with leased assets. The financial impact of the pandemic meant that we would need to restructure a significant portion of our leased portfolio. Being able to tap into their deep well of real estate knowledge was of enormous advantage as we considered our options. In addition, Lee has a strong historical relationship with representatives of our largest landlord. Accordingly, he was able to provide guidance based on his personal experience. Marc helped me to view our real estate decisions through the lens of an investor, often sharing relevant articles and publications.

A Timeline of the Crisis

To put our story into perspective, allow me to review what was happening in the world in the early days of the pandemic.

Prior to the start of the pandemic, Brookdale was demonstrating positive operational momentum. We were delivering on targets we had set for ourselves and were expecting 2020 to result in continued growth for Brookdale. Based on the turnaround strategy we introduced in 2018, which led to a shift in our strategy from a national to a local strategy that capitalized on the benefits of being the largest senior living operator in the United States, we had wind in our sails and every reason to believe our growth would meet or exceed our expectations.

On December 31, 2019, the first outbreak of COVID-19 was reported, coming from Wuhan, China.

In mid-January, Jim Seward notified me of impending events in China even before consensus reports took them seriously. Prompted by Jim's early insights, I began monitoring the global health situation and began to increase our preparedness by reinforcing our already-strong infectious disease protocols. By the end of January, Brookdale was analyzing how to prepare our communities and agencies.

On January 30, 2020, the World Health Organization (WHO) issued a global health emergency due to a worldwide death toll of 200 and an exponential jump to more than 9,800 cases. It was only the sixth time in its history that the WHO had taken such an action. By February 3, the United States had declared a public health emergency.[2]

---

2   "A Timeline of COVID-19 Developments in 2020," AJMC, published January 1, 2021, https://www.ajmc.com/view/a-timeline-of-covid19-developments-in-2020; "WHO Timeline—COVID-19," World Health Organization, published April 27, 2020, https://www.who.int/news/item/27-04-2020-who-timeline---covid-19.

During our earnings call on February 19, we informed our shareholders that the safety of our residents and associates would always be of the utmost importance at Brookdale. We explained that our teams across the country had been placed on high alert, that we had strong protocols for contagious viruses such as the flu, and that associates had been trained to look for signs of infection early in order to take appropriate action.

In the weeks after our earnings call, the threat to our company grew quickly. It was clear that we were entering a storm, the intensity of which was building rapidly.

On February 25, the Centers for Disease Control and Prevention (CDC) announced that COVID-19 was heading toward pandemic status.

On February 26, the CDC confirmed the first case of COVID-19 in the United States suspected of local transmission.[3] This patient had not traveled to an area with a known outbreak and was not aware they had come into contact with any COVID-19 case. This was an important development, because it meant COVID-19 was no longer an issue in a faraway land; it was an issue within the United States, and transmission was close to our communities.

Around this time, we decided we needed dedicated cross-functional leadership to address this emerging health crisis, and we created our Emergency Command Center (ECC), which later transitioned into an Emergency Response Center (ERC). The first meeting of the ECC happened on February 28.

On March 2, we announced cessation of all nonessential corporate travel and shortly thereafter canceled our in-person leadership conference.

---

3   "CDC Confirms Possible Instance of Community Spread of COVID-19 in US," CDC, published February 26, 2020, https://www.cdc.gov/media/releases/2020/s0226-Covid-19-spread.html.

On March 11, the WHO declared COVID-19 a pandemic.[4] This was the day we closed our communities to visitors, including all loved ones of our residents as well as in-person prospective resident tours and in some cases new resident and patient admissions.

We made the decision to restrict access to our communities in an effort to help protect our residents, patients, and associates and further slow the spread of the virus. We knew that this would be hard for residents and patients and their loved ones, because one of the precious components of the senior living lifestyle is the time spent with family and friends.

> ## Seek to Understand All Financial Aspects of Your Business and Potential Impacts.

Limiting access to our communities was a crucial decision and a turning point. In addition to the direct impact on residents and their loved ones, we had to consider the impact on Brookdale, because our residents live in our communities for an average of approximately two years. In order to maintain occupancy and cash flow, we needed to attract roughly half of the community population each year. The pandemic made it very difficult to encourage a prospective resident to move into a community that they would not be able to view and visit in person before moving in—further, knowing that they would not be allowed visits from their loved ones for an unknown period of time.

---

4   Domenico Cucinotta and Maurizio Vanelli, "WHO Declares COVID-19 a Pandemic," *Acta Biomedica* 91, no. 1, March 19, 2020, https://www.ncbi.nlm.nih.gov/pmc/articles/PMC7569573/.

On March 13, President Trump declared COVID-19 a national emergency.[5]

On March 17, we updated our investors. We communicated that our highest priority was then and would continue to be the health and well-being of our residents, patients, and associates. We discussed the fact that we had proactively initiated our preparation efforts prior to the first confirmed case suspected of local transmission within the United States and had begun to implement precautionary measures throughout our communities.

Those measures included Brookdale's established flu and other infectious disease prevention and control protocols, which had been and continued to be enhanced based on recommendations and requirements by the CDC and other federal, state, and local public health authorities. Brookdale's care associates had already been trained in infectious disease prevention and control, and Brookdale reinforced existing protocols during this time. We also informed investors that Brookdale had restricted or limited access to its communities for visitors, in-person prospective resident tours, and, in certain cases, new resident and patient admissions.

During our investor update, we noted that, in addition to facing a material revenue impact, we would likely incur significant costs to help protect against the virus and address transmission within our communities. We explained that the situation was extremely fluid and that we were carefully monitoring the financial impact of the COVID-19 pandemic, modeling scenarios of what could happen and how we might respond.

---

5   "Proclamation on Declaring a National Emergency Concerning the Novel Coronavirus Disease (COVID-19) Outbreak," Trump White House, published March 13, 2020, https://trumpwhitehouse.archives.gov/presidential-actions/proclamation-declaring-national-emergency-concerning-novel-coronavirus-disease-covid-19-outbreak/.

> ## Take Decisive Action in a Crisis, Even If You Don't Have All the Answers.

We knew the impacts of the pandemic on revenue, expense, and cash flow were dependent on numerous factors, including how the virus spread, how regulators responded, the effectiveness of our infectious disease prevention and control efforts, and the demand for our services. To make a long story short, there were innumerable possible outcomes.

Needless to say, we knew that we were in the most challenging situation imaginable. We immediately took aggressive steps to preserve our liquidity. Out of an abundance of caution, in mid-March the company drew the full available balance on its revolving line of credit. We also suspended our share repurchase program and reduced capital expenditures to essential needs only.

To understand the magnitude of the impact these decisions had on Brookdale, take a look at the stock market implications. Our February 19, 2020, stock price of $8.39 reflected our positive momentum. As the pandemic developed around the world, our stock traded down as the market factored in what was happening with the pandemic and assessed its likely impact on our business. It was disheartening to watch our stock price decline around 80 percent in about a month—from $8.39 on February 19 to $1.89 on March 20, 2020.

At the same time, the demands on our corporate leadership team and board had never been more intense. Our lives revolved around the battle against COVID-19 to help protect our residents, patients, associates, and Brookdale itself. Many of our corporate leaders and

I developed a rhythm of work, eat, sleep, and repeat—day after day, seven days a week, for months on end.

Lessons Learned

Thanks to the sound judgment of key advisors, Brookdale leadership recognized the threat of COVID-19 before official sources alerted us. Weeks before it was accepted in the consensus, our corporate leadership team took decisive steps to communicate with the board, reinforce our already-strong infectious disease protocols to help curb transmission, and communicate our current knowledge of the evolving situation. Every board member had a unique role to play as we navigated the unprecedented and unpredictable events, and each person leaned into their specialized skill sets, culminating in a harmony of voices and talents that the corporate leadership team could rely on as we stood at the helm of our battleship.

Looking back, it's still hard to believe how dramatically our operating environment changed in the mere twenty-seven days from our earnings release on February 19 to the public announcement that we were withdrawing our public earnings guidance on March 17. The world changed in what felt like the blink of an eye. Less than one month after we first reported the emerging threat to our company, it was clear that COVID-19 would have a significant impact on our residents, patients, associates, and on Brookdale itself, and we began taking increasingly aggressive actions to avert the crisis. This wasn't merely a storm; we were in the equivalent of a Category 5 hurricane that wouldn't be over in a few days or even weeks.

Within days, it would be clear that all had changed for the country as well. In fact, just two days after we provided our update, California issued a statewide stay-at-home order on March 19. All California residents were required to stay home unless they were going out to shop for essential needs or to work in an essential job. Soon thereafter, the majority of the country began sheltering in place.

For Brookdale, staying home wasn't an option. Our residents depended on us for meals; support with activities of daily living; emotional, purposeful, and social connections; and help managing their healthcare needs. We were most certainly essential. We would serve on the front lines of the pandemic for as long as it took, and we prepared to batten down the hatches.

CHAPTER 2

Establishing Our Emergency Response

Designating Leaders to Batten Down the Hatches and Helm the Command Center

B rookdale's North Star is always the health and well-being of our residents, patients, and associates.

With the threat of COVID-19 looming, we expected it would have a disproportionate impact on our residents compared to America's general population, because of their age and chronic conditions. In January 2020, our top two clinical leaders—Senior Vice President of Clinical Services Kim Elliott and, at the time, our division president of Brookdale Health Care Services (overseeing home health, hospice, and outpatient therapy) Anna-Gene O'Neal—were tasked with our initial preparations for COVID-19. We began community preparations for COVID-19 by reinforcing our already-strong flu and other infectious disease prevention and control protocols.

Guided by the insights of our board and other advisors, we took early action to care for our communities, exercising an abundance of caution and following the prescribed guidelines of local and state health authorities, state licensing agencies, and the CDC and WHO.

Kathy MacDonald, our senior vice president of Investor Relations, had the astute idea to create a website dedicated to keeping residents, associates, and prospects informed of Brookdale's preventive actions and publish a COVID-19 tool kit as a resource for the general public. Beginning in the early days of the pandemic, we led our industry by regularly updating our website, leading industry panels, and sharing knowledge with a robust network of peers within the senior living and healthcare industries.

Our early actions included implementing social distancing protocols; wearing masks; reinforcing handwashing guidelines (using soap and water for at least twenty seconds); emphasizing our standard policy of staying home when sick; routine sanitization of communities; monitoring resident temperature and oxygen levels; symptom screening of associates (temperature, cough, etc.); and promoting education and reminders about flu vaccines and taking flu antivirals as prescribed.

However, even as we maintained our focus on the day-to-day operations of Brookdale, we continually contemplated what more we could do.

Organizing Our Emergency Response

As the risk from COVID-19 grew, we created a leadership structure that would guide the pandemic response for the entire company. Given our extensive experience responding effectively to hurricanes, wildfires, and other natural disasters, we created an Emergency Command Center (ECC) that began meeting on February 28, 2020—later changing the name to the Emergency Response Center (ERC), reflecting its ultimate operational function as a support team that assisted our communities and field team on issues relating to COVID-19.

> ## During a Crisis, It Is Important to Have a Command Center That Operates 24/7.

This battle felt like a war, and we initially needed a top-down strategy to help prepare the troops on the front lines of all of our seven-hundred-plus communities and almost eighty home health and hospice agencies and eighty-four outpatient therapy clinics for COVID-19. The ECC quickly became the central organizing force, developing protocols and providing support for all pandemic-related issues.

Having an expert emergency response team in place enabled our corporate leadership team (the C-suite and other staff at the headquarters and in the field) to remain focused on our three everyday business strategies: 1) attracting, engaging, developing, and retaining the best associates; 2) earning resident and family trust by providing valued, high-quality care and personalized service; and 3) winning locally and leveraging scale effectively. Establishing the ECC also enabled our leadership team to ensure we remained true to the culture, mission, and cornerstones that keep a battleship strong.

We envisioned the relationship to perform like a symphony. The ECC (and later, ERC), as conductor, sought knowledge (through connections with outside resources) and made or helped facilitate global decisions that had to be communicated with precise timing, clear signals, and swift action. In turn, the field, communities, and corporate functional leaders acted as the members of an orchestra, executing on the internal response in as harmonious a manner as possible.

The ECC guided the "performance," providing feedback and making adjustments to ensure people were on the same page—and answering questions, solving problems, and helping to clear pathways for those responsible for execution.

Designating the Leadership Team

Mary Sue Patchett had over thirty years of senior living experience and had worked her way up in the industry from executive director (top leader in a senior living community) to Brookdale's executive vice president of Community and Field Operations. She had helped lead the crisis meetings for hurricanes and wildfires expertly and had demonstrated her ability to lead her fellow associates during these natural disasters through her good judgment and genuine empathy for the community associates. Given Mary Sue's breadth and depth of experience in senior living operations and because of her ability to convey a calm confidence to the field and community leaders, we tapped her to lead the ECC.

HERO HIGHLIGHTS FROM
MARY SUE PATCHETT

Joined Brookdale Senior Living February 1998; was serving as executive vice president of Community and Field Operations and

---

commander of Brookdale's Emergency Response Center when she departed in June 2021

STAY INFORMED, BE PREPARED, AND LEAD

Planning for seasonal events such as flu and hurricanes requires a rapid and effective assembly of resources that spans from a few days to a few weeks—preparing for and managing the event and then performing an after-action report. These events normally impact a select number of communities at a time, but never seven-hundred-plus communities at once.

Brookdale leadership quickly recognized the unique challenges posed by COVID-19. Hence the formation of the first-ever longer-term Emergency Response Center team (including Operations, Clinical, Customer Experience, and Human Resources) to fast-track and manage the resources necessary to support our corporate, field, and community leaders.

As prolonged pandemic management became necessary, the ECC established A, B, and C teams to provide a 24/7 response. Revised CDC guidelines often triggered state regulatory guidance to be updated, which meant coordinating our rollout across over forty different states at once. *Centralizing our efforts within the ECC enabled a seamless and effective response to the changing conditions in real time.*

However, we also recognized the fight against a pandemic would require experience beyond our team, so we identified additional, outside consultants to assist. In order to be proactive in helping to keep our residents, patients,

> and associates as safe as possible, we developed new platforms for analysis, decision-making, and execution in addition to our normal channels of information, regulatory direction, and communication. *This represented a multi-tiered communications strategy that enabled associates at all levels to stay informed, be prepared, and lead, establishing a clear and timely response throughout our communities.*

Sara Terry is another senior leader with multiple decades of industry experience and an intense focus on the resident, family, and associate experience within a crisis. She was an integral part of the seasonal crisis meetings for hurricanes and wildfires. At the time, she was serving as our senior vice president of Resident and Family Engagement, which meant she was already overseeing the Centers of Excellence for dining, resident engagement, resident and family experience, environmental services (cleaning and housekeeping), fleet management, and dementia care. Her experience helped to provide a comprehensive response to COVID-19.

Additionally, Sara had developed strong relationships with the leaders across functions and at many levels within Brookdale, so she had the clarity and credibility to gain support and initiate quick action throughout the organization. Sara was known for her ability to execute skillfully and quickly. She became our immediate pick as the ECC's chief of staff. (In recognition of the tremendous contribution that Sara made, she was later appointed to Brookdale's executive leadership team, which is composed of my direct reports.)

> ## Cross-Functional Teamwork Is Critical to Move Quickly.

Given that the pandemic was at its core a public health crisis, we wanted to include our top senior living clinician to oversee clinical services and infection control, and at the time, Kim Elliott had been Brookdale's senior living clinical leader for over five years. Clinical aspects of hurricanes and wildfires are less prominent than what we found with COVID-19, so it was a conscious decision to include Kim, given her clinical knowledge as well as her connections with the CDC and our pharmacy partner (a key factor when the vaccine started becoming a reality). With more than twenty-five years of clinical leadership in the post-acute space, Kim is passionate about developing and implementing high standards to help keep our residents safe and healthy. Since the early signs were showing the pandemic was particularly difficult for adults over sixty-five, there was a heightened alert to act quickly and prepare for what was to come. Ultimately, the frontline clinicians who would be providing care directly to our communities would need top-notch protocols, training, and support.

Kim's connections and expertise were vital, so she was added to the command center. (As a reflection of her outstanding work and the importance of clinical services to Brookdale, Kim was later promoted to senior vice president, chief nursing officer.)

Our mission hinges on the human element. We are a service-based business of people serving people, and we suspected that we needed a strong change-management leader in order to prepare and support our associates, establish the necessary steps for change, and partner with operations to ensure proper implementation.

Jaclyn Pritchett was serving as vice president of Human Resources at the time, so we asked her to join the ECC. Jaclyn would focus on revising protocols and procedures (such as a ban on nonessential work-related travel); upgrading the Associate Compassion Fund to account for pandemic-related needs; aligning associate guidelines with CDC updates; and adding special resources for our associates to our intranet, including information about combating compassion fatigue and materials to help associates with virtual learning at home for their kids. Throughout her duties, Jaclyn concerned herself with change-management principles to help associates better absorb new information and follow through with appropriate action.

(Jaclyn was later promoted to senior vice president of Human Resources, having demonstrated her exceptional service in this regard.)

These four leaders formed the core leadership team of the ECC, which was tasked with coordinating our pandemic response on a day-to-day basis. This structure allowed other key leaders to continue their focus on the business and other critically important initiatives. Naturally, the ECC had access to all company resources and retained the authority to add more team members to grow the effort as needed.

At the same time, we designated additional leaders to help organize our internal response. We knew that it was critically important to glean best practices from leaders within the broader healthcare community on top of the minimum standards provided by the CDC and state and local departments of health.

Anna-Gene O'Neal was chosen to assist with this effort based on her outstanding clinical expertise and network. As a fellow with the Nashville Health Care Council, Anna-Gene had cultivated deep, meaningful relationships within the healthcare community and was well positioned to solicit best practices that could be communicated to Kim Elliott as she led the ECC's clinical efforts.

Critical Communications

Communication is critically important to any emergency response effort, and we increased the frequency and clarity of our communications with residents and their appointed family members or loved ones, as well as with our associates. Communicating both expectations and protocol adherence was particularly important as we moved from building upon our strong infection control protocols to limiting access to our communities to the rollout of COVID-19 vaccines among our residents and associates.

> **Communicate, Communicate, and Communicate—Both Clearly and Frequently.**

The ECC operated like a virtual war room, scheduling and leading multiple lengthy meetings every day to address various aspects of the COVID-19 response. They were dialed into virtually all verticals within Brookdale and served as a central clearinghouse for supporting our communities as they responded to the threat posed by the virus. As the central hub for any questions that arose, they researched the appropriate responses, and if they didn't know the answer, figured out who did and then shared the information throughout the system for consistency. Through this process, virtually every department in Brookdale leaned in to figure out how to help.

HERO HIGHLIGHTS FROM
KATHY MACDONALD

Joined Brookdale Senior Living January 2018; currently senior vice president of Investor Relations

SMALL GROUPS OF THOUGHTFUL, COMMITTED CITIZENS CAN CHANGE THE WORLD

Throughout my career, I've been inspired by Margaret Mead's quote, "Never doubt that a small group of thoughtful, committed citizens can change the world. It's the only thing that ever has." This story is one of Brookdale's many examples of living by this quote.

On an early morning in February, the Brookdale leaders of key functional areas huddled in a small conference room. Each leader shared how their teams were taking actions against the novel coronavirus based on what we knew at that time. This small group built on each other's ideas and, as a group, decided on the day's priorities. I was in awe of the talent and knowledge displayed and by the generous offers of support despite each already bearing a heavy workload. At that moment, I realized that this was Brookdale's culture in action.

As I moved through the day, there was a small voice inside that told me Brookdale was ahead of the curve and

---

that we had a responsibility to help beyond our senior living communities and agencies. *Based on what I heard from the key functional leaders, I handwrote a website layout with key elements about the actions Brookdale was taking to help protect seniors from the coronavirus. The intent was for our website to be a place to share our ideas with other senior living operators and the public at large.* I am so thankful for the openness of our CEO Cindy Baier, who spent ten minutes with me so I could share this new idea. With my handwritten layout, pencil, and eraser, I pitched the vision for a unique Brookdale website. She was immediately excited about the idea and helped me enhance the concept document. She closed the meeting by asking me to present at the following morning's leadership huddle.

With an overnight conversion to PowerPoint, we shared my website vision and asked the other leaders' feedback to make it even more robust. They suggested providing downloadable tool kits for other senior housing operators, and Cindy added that we should create short, executive-led videos to keep associates and residents and their loved ones informed. Cindy then did a "call to action" for the Marketing and Communications leaders to designate the right people to build the website as quickly as possible.

I am so thankful for the small but thoughtful team of leaders that stepped up and innovated as we decided how to communicate important messages during the largest public health crisis any of us had ever known. Through the leadership and heavy lifting of Heather Hunter in the Communications Department, this website became a foundation for the Communications team efforts to share our actions and advice. Michael McCamish, Shelly Riera, and Kristin Puckett in the Marketing Department created the website, collected and posted all the tool kit materials, and distributed the content to our already-strong social media platforms.

Based on the positive feedback from trade associations and the public, we believe we were the first in our industry to create a COVID-19 website to share our best practices. Early on, we developed and posted videos about every three days to inform seniors, loved ones, prospects, and associates about actions that could be taken to help prevent the spread of COVID-19. We continued producing a regular cadence of informational and motivational videos. We developed tool kits that demonstrated the expertise of Brookdale in effective infectious disease controls; we cared about helping to protect the nation's seniors, so education was of utmost importance.

We learned many leadership lessons from this story: as an executive, encourage new ideas from unexpected people in your organization, and empower small groups from diverse backgrounds to execute projects about which they are passionate and that support the organization's greater good.

Chief Information Officer Tara Jones presented herself as a true leader during this phase as she drove mission-critical projects across the goal line. Although the moment had the urgency of hair on fire, she led calmly. There wasn't time to finesse relationships, but she nevertheless forged strong, productive partnerships across the company. She was under constant stress to deliver, and throughout, Tara exemplified a positive "we can figure this out" attitude that was quickly adopted by her entire team. They did figure it out—and they constantly went above and beyond the call of duty in their efforts.

The End User Services (EUS) group—led by senior director of End User Services Hank Reimer—was ready, willing, and able to support associates throughout the crisis. For instance, at the beginning of the pandemic, pivoting to work from home practically overnight was an enormous challenge (for example, virtual meeting software, networking, hardware, VPN, telecom readiness, setup, training). EUS rose to the occasion.

The monstrous task of gathering pandemic data related to associates and residents—and then translating that data into actionable information—fell to Senior Director of IT Financial Applications Frank Di Tirro and Vice President of Human Resource Systems Lisa Hoffmann. This partnership—along with their teams' support—exceeded expectations time and time again. For example, they built a user-friendly, custom app for tracking and reporting resident vaccination doses ("VaxTrax"), which became an extraordinary, reliable tool for the efficient rollout of our vaccine clinics.

Additionally, our Information Technology team members provided superb support as our community leaders and associates assisted residents to ensure everyone who wanted to communicate with friends and loved ones outside of our communities remained connected.

The team of policy experts—including Senior Director of Clinical and Policy Management LuAnne Leistner, Vice President of Clinical Operations Angela Haley, and Senior Director of Optimum Life® Carol Cummings Selander—worked tirelessly to keep up with changes so these could be communicated clearly and in a timely manner. Furthermore, the Legal Operations team, led by Vice President of Legal Kirstin Sumner, and the Labor and Employment team, led by Vice President of Legal Marti Downey, reviewed new and adapted policies for accuracy with applicable laws, regulations, health orders, and standards in each of the forty-plus states and local jurisdictions in which we operated. To say it was a lot of work and responsibility is an understatement!

HERO HIGHLIGHTS FROM SARA TERRY

Joined Brookdale Senior Living November 2003; currently senior vice president of Resident and Family Engagement and member of Brookdale's Emergency Response Center

PIVOTING FOR INNOVATIVE COMMUNICATIONS

Staying informed in order to make timely decisions was one of the most challenging issues for the ECC. Information from national and government sources was initially inadequate or not clear enough to establish all protocols and guidelines needed to help protect our residents, patients, and associates. We established a process to gather, report, and evaluate information from various sources, which enabled us to develop protocols on top of the standards set by government sources. At critical points, we were able to share important insights with federal, state, and local agencies in the fight against COVID-19. We enhanced our existing state regulatory communication and established state coordinators in each state in which we operated in an effort to communicate information centrally for support planning.

Brookdale leaders developed multiple channels for communication with our residents and patients (and their loved ones) and our associates. We also specifically developed and distributed ongoing information to senior living and healthcare associations and organizations and the public at large (via webinars, video updates, news bulletins and letters, and resident/family meetings on a virtual meting platform). Our online newsroom became an important source of information for our constituencies: www.BrookdaleNews.com.

Pivoting became a leadership action strategy. Communication channels pivoted to video conferencing interactions so that residents and their loved ones could communicate as communities closed their doors to outside visitors. Technology became more important than ever, and we distributed additional iPads' and Google Chromebooks®[6] to our communities.

Timeliness, clarity, and urgency (with calm confidence) were the goals of every communication. Diligent reviews of multiple information sources were established before protocol changes and actions could be taken.

Often, regulatory guidelines needed to be interpreted at a state level in addition to the overall federal directions. Decision frameworks were designed to provide guidance and empower actions as close to the community level as

---

6   Chromebook is a US registered trademark of Google LLC.

possible. Public guidance changed routinely—sometimes within twenty-four hours—reinforcing our mantra: stay informed, be prepared, and lead! Key to these efforts were our company-wide communications and alignment on plans. We worked diligently as the ECC, along with the entire company, to provide needed information and protocols as well as emotional support.

The Communications team supported community leaders by providing letters to send to residents and patients and their loved ones, tailored to reflect experiences at individual communities. The ECC reviewed the initial drafts, weighed in on revisions to templates as needed, and provided the Communications team with information as situations changed. Individual community managers began hosting scheduled virtual meetings for loved ones (or email communications), updating both our preparation and prevention efforts and remaining transparent about COVID-19 cases within our communities. We developed a protocol for sharing COVID-19 transmission information to loved ones of residents as well, which included individual emails and letters.

Our goal was to communicate broadly. At the start of the pandemic, Brookdale posted new videos to our online newsroom, updating our company response approximately every three days. Community leaders also regularly posted photos of activities that were taking place in our communities. We received numerous compliments about the practical information contained in our videos.

Our response to the COVID-19 pandemic relied heavily on social media, led by Senior Director of Social Media and Brand Kristin Puckett. The investment in technology and content we had made over the years prior to the pandemic equipped our local communities to use social media to communicate effectively. Because of our comprehensive and strategic approach, Facebook also recognized Brookdale as an exemplary social media leader for our COVID-19 response.

Julie Davis and Heather Hunter were outstanding in handling crisis communications and media relations in support of our communities, working around the clock to address questions and issues that arose. Thanks to their exceptional efforts—along with the contributions of the entire Communications team, which handled thousands of documents related to information for residents and loved ones—Brookdale received several local and regional awards from the Public Relations Society of America (PRSA) and the International Association of Business Communicators (IABC).

HERO HIGHLIGHTS FROM JULIE DAVIS

Joined Brookdale Senior Living in March 2013; was serving as vice president of Communications when she transitioned to a consultant role in April 2021

LIGHTS, CAMERA, AND A LOT OF ACTION!

I remember vividly the early days of the pandemic. We had to handle whatever needs were identified. We had to keep our residents and associates as safe as possible. We had to succeed, even if we didn't know how!

As members of the Communications Department, we always felt we were a small but mighty team. We were small in number and mighty because we impacted the perceptions, trust, and engagement of tens of thousands of associates. We also impacted the public through our work managing issues and promoting positive stories in the media.

Stepping up to meet the increased need for accurate, compassionate, and speedy messages during the early pandemic days was the biggest challenge any of us had faced in our careers. Without hesitation, we took responsibility for supporting community leaders in regularly updating residents and family members about the impact of COVID-19 in individual communities. We were determined to deliver the information they wanted and needed, which entailed twelve- and fourteen-hour days, seven days a week. As a crisis communications expert, Communications project manager Heather Hunter was a natural to lead this effort. She put her whole heart and soul into developing materials for our team members' use, providing resources to them, and becoming the team's primary liaison with other corporate departments to help facilitate the work. She also was instrumental in our response to hundreds of local, regional, and national media inquiries.

As the director of Communications, Sandy LaFave suddenly found herself building dedicated sections of our intranet with COVID-19 information, with Communications project manager Sara Grunwald partnering to update thousands of procedural documents related to all aspects of our company. Together they were like Atlas holding the weight of the world on their shoulders— ensuring documents were accurate, timely, and easy to find in a crisis so that our communities could succeed in helping to keep people as safe as possible. They handled development of almost two hundred COVID-19-related internal company messages throughout the pandemic. Sandy suddenly became the in-house virtual meeting expert, figuring out how to host meetings with hundreds (and sometimes thousands!) of participants from across the country and working to present all information and updates in as clear and compelling a manner as possible. This was far more than a standard slideshow.

We discovered quickly that producing videos was effective for reaching so many of our stakeholders: residents, family members, associates, shareholders, the media, and the general public. Fortunately, we already had internal capabilities that included video equipment and a recording studio. We also had two team members on hand well versed in writing video scripts. And we had a team of executives who were willing to step in front of the camera and engage viewers with solid informa-tion and genuine sincerity. In the month of March 2020 alone, we professionally produced and distributed nine videos of a few minutes each about important topics like proper handwashing, the importance of social distancing, adjustments in resident programing, and reassurances to associates. We even created a game show–type true/false format for sharing new information.

Cindy Baier also kept an eye on Brookdale's commu-nications efforts, even as she was focused on leading the company. We established a rhythm for posting new videos, and as CEO, Cindy was our main on-camera talent. It was important to keep our rhythm going, and Cindy made herself available as necessary.

I felt so fortunate to work with such an extraordinary team through the pandemic. If I am ever called on to help lead through a world-changing, life-altering crisis again, these are the folks I want on my side!

Strengthening Standard Protocols

The ECC also took immediate action to address protection for our associates and to strengthen our existing infectious disease protocols.

Within a matter of weeks, we went from reinforcing personal and community hygiene protocols to implementing social distancing guidelines and procuring personal protection equipment for everyone in our communities, both staff and residents. We started with proper hand hygiene and the use of alcohol hand sanitizer that contained a minimum of 60 percent alcohol. Associates began wearing masks shortly thereafter.

Upon the arrival of COVID-19 to the United States, every healthcare provider, direct-to-consumer business, and soon, the general public were scrambling for PPE—but supplies were simply not available to meet this level of demand. With tens of thousands of residents and home health, hospice, and outpatient therapy patients, plus associates spanning hundreds of communities, agencies, and outpatient therapy clinics, we were desperately in need of additional supplies.

We couldn't wait for the Federal Emergency Management Agency (FEMA) or others to solve the problem. We had to mobilize our purchasing, so the ECC directed the Procurement, Financial Planning and Analysis, and Information Technology teams to develop a system for centrally tracking critical, par-level inventory items—evaluating current levels, securing supplies, and planning for distribution. Our Procurement team became experts in N95 versus KN95 masks and various testing kits. In record time, the system was established.

To meet the PPE requirements, the Procurement team—led by Vice President of Procurement Jen Nolan and clinical consultant Martie Moore (who had previously been involved with FEMA and other pandemics)—identified the need to set up an entirely new supply chain. This was needed because our historical vendor partners couldn't supply even our historical requirements, as the government diverted supplies to hospitals to prepare for the pandemic. By the end of April 2020, we had amassed an arsenal of 2.8 million N95 and KN95 masks, 14.1 million surgical masks, 1.5 million isolation gowns, more than half a million cloth masks, and more through our new supply chain.

Our newly established reporting system could even track the source of supplies (for example, FEMA) in order to comply with new government documentation requirements.

We engaged associates and vendors throughout the organization to identify potential supply vendors and fast-track the supplies to our communities. Field leaders traveled to distribution sites to pick up supplies for communities, and one community partner flew a personal plane to deliver supplies overnight in support of our associates. Even our primary printing companies, Fidelity and Bell Litho, pivoted their supply warehouses and shipping platforms so they could serve as central distribution centers for us.

Additionally, the ECC encouraged our functional Centers of Excellence and field teams (associates who support and have oversight of communities but do not themselves work within a community) to enhance our already-strong clinical protocols, vastly increasing our volume of health screenings conducted for residents, patients, and associates. During the month of March 2020 alone, our residents and patients underwent approximately four million temperature and pulse oximeter readings—a measure of blood oxygen saturation. (Oxygen desaturation was found to be an early symptom of COVID-19 for many seniors.)

HERO HIGHLIGHTS FROM KIM ELLIOTT, RN, MSN

Joined Brookdale Senior Living July 2014; currently senior vice president, chief nursing officer, and member of Brookdale's Emergency Response Center

IDENTIFYING EARLY WARNING SIGNS AND ENHANCING CLINICAL COMPETENCY

As the clinical lead during the COVID-19 pandemic, I faced what I saw as the ultimate challenge of leadership. Leadership is difficult even when facing familiar situations and situations where some team members have experience combating an illness and need to train others on short notice—but leading through a pandemic where no one fully understands the virus is another story altogether.

When the virus first hit the United States, I focused my attention on what we did know rather than the unknowns.

Every moment not spent with my team providing guidance, answering questions, and supporting execution

I spent reading and absorbing every bit of information I could find, researching how the virus impacted seniors in China, and learning about how the earliest-affected, congregate-living settings managed prevention and minimized outbreaks. Lessons from other countries helped us avoid early missteps and informed our plan moving forward.

The symptoms that were showing up in the general public were not necessarily the same as the symptoms most prevalent in seniors: fever and loss of taste and smell were not as common among seniors as increased confusion or decreased appetite (evidenced by refusing meals).

While researching, I stumbled across information that an early sign of COVID-19 in seniors was a potential oxygen desaturation from normal baseline. I remember staying up late to dig into the topic and then sending an email to Cindy Baier in the wee hours of the night. She immediately replied, and within hours we started procuring pulse oximeters for every community to begin monitoring baseline oxygen saturations. This enabled us to detect one of the earliest signs of COVID-19 in seniors in order to help prevent further transmission of the virus. We had minimal access to COVID-19 testing at this time, because testing was tightly restricted by government agencies, so many of our earliest cases were first identified by drops in blood oxygen levels.

We focused on three main priorities: First, prevention. We needed to do everything in our power to help keep

COVID-19 out of our communities. We reinforced extensive training protocols to our associates regarding infection prevention and control measures, including sanitization, symptom screening, and proper use of PPE. Each protocol required analysis and regular updates. For example, training for PPE included detailed protocols on what to use and when, and how to apply and remove (don and doff) without cross contamination. Every time a protocol was updated, we updated our written policies, charts, and guidelines, and we worked closely with procurement to secure needed supplies for our associates. Our clinical teams never stopped: team members worked sixteen- to eighteen-hour days, seven days a week, in support of the communities as we established our strategy to help prevent COVID-19 from entering our communities.

Our second priority was containment. If the virus were to enter our community, our goal was to help contain it as quickly as possible in order to limit transmission. We had read stories of massive outbreaks at competitors where 90 percent of a skilled nursing facility's patients tested positive early in the pandemic, and we knew we needed a solid plan to help prevent it from happening in our communities.

Once we had a positive case, we took immediate action to help prevent further transmission and managed containment so well that some of our communities with a single case of COVID-19 had no other cases identified. With a lower case count, your risks are drastically reduced, so our nurses and community teams saved lives by containing the virus.

Our third priority was managing our clinical response in order to promote the full recovery of any resident who did contract the virus. The virus was relentless on individuals over the age of seventy-five with multiple chronic conditions. The risk for severe illness with COVID-19 increases with age, and older adults are at the highest risk. While younger adults often had no symptoms or minor symptoms like loss of taste and smell, the virus that affected our population was a different story. Our residents would often have severe symptoms that frequently required skilled nursing care or hospitalization. If they remained in the community, they were isolated or stayed in an area with other COVID-19-positive residents to help prevent the spread of the virus, and they would frequently have a longer recovery period after diagnosis. It was not uncommon to see residents needing thirty days or more to recover from the virus.

Yet the incidence of transmission, duration of symptoms, and impact on the individual were difficult to predict.

With many viruses, the first three to four days are usually the worst, and individuals improve and recover with each additional day. COVID-19 was different. We often saw sharp declines as late as day eight or ten. We had to remain vigilant with each case, as we quickly learned an individual's status could rapidly decline and present completely different signs and symptoms within a one-to two-hour time frame.

Next we had to determine when a higher level of care was needed. In some cases, even finding hospitals that could admit our residents as patients was a challenge, and certainly one we had never encountered prior to COVID-19. We engaged with external healthcare providers, such as physician groups, and focused on enhancing competency levels as we learned more about the virus.

As an example, we reinforced protocols on how to properly wash hands, and communities completed observations to validate handwashing was being done correctly. Once we learned that COVID-19 was transmitted via respiratory droplets, we spent time researching filtration capabilities of different types of masks and training on proper mask use, including how to put a mask on, covering the nose and mouth, and removing it without spreading the virus and touching the mask. We had to process new information quickly with every new medical finding about testing, treatment, and medication options.

During this time, the clinical team also grew in areas other than competency: they grew into remarkably resilient, heart-driven leaders. They loved our residents as if they were their own family members. While many Americans were sheltering in place at home, our associates were showing up to work day after day to help others. As nurses, we entered the profession to care for those who could not care for themselves and to do everything in our power to compassionately assist in restoring health. Many healthcare professionals will never see their chosen profession in the same light post-pandemic. Disease, surgery, aging, and injuries are a normal part of healthcare; we are taught to manage these conditions. Few were prepared for such a powerful adversary: a novel coronavirus characterized by changing variables and unpredictable outcomes.

It has been a great privilege to lead the Brookdale Clinical team through the pandemic. A leader learns the most during times of pressure, and there are many lessons I will carry with me from this experience. Our teams were simply amazing. Although there were many nights we felt completely broken, we maintained our focus on our residents. They needed us, and so did their loved ones. The daughters, sons, grandchildren, and siblings were depending on us to help protect their loved ones. We always kept this top of mind and never ceased giving all we could to deliver on this promise.

Moreover, the need for social distancing soon became evident. We would close all communities to visitors to help reduce the risk of transmission to our residents and associates. We also quickly revised our approach to resident meals. Within a week's time, we transitioned from serving residents in our beautiful, large-capacity dining rooms to providing dedicated room service to residents and patients within our communities.

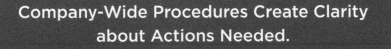

Company-Wide Procedures Create Clarity about Actions Needed.

This was a massive undertaking. During March 2020, our first month implementing this change, we served approximately two million room service meals company-wide. This required many communities to staff a dedicated room service attendant (a brand-new position) to deliver meals to resident apartments. We also had to leverage our partnerships to source large quantities of disposable food service supplies for room service delivery. Given the need for social distancing, we promoted more frequent engagement between residents and loved ones through video conferencing and engaging room service efforts by staff.

Although we have always had strict cleaning and sanitation protocols, with the guidance of Senior Director of Environmental Services Jeannine Monteleone, we immediately enhanced our efforts to help ward off COVID-19. Our initial arsenal of sanitation agents included 1.9 million ounces of hand sanitizer and 1,448 gallons of yellow peroxide multi-surface cleaner and disinfectant (affectionately called "the yellow") for use in our communities.

In the early stages of the pandemic, neither the CDC nor leading healthcare institutions realized that even people without symptoms could spread COVID-19. As scientists discovered that asymptomatic and pre-symptomatic individuals were able to spread the virus, the challenge increased exponentially. This new knowledge prompted Brookdale to launch a nationwide baseline-testing program for our communities' residents and associates.

Unfortunately, testing methods were not well developed or available at scale, and a nationwide provider had not yet been established in the early stages of the threat. Nevertheless, we were able to source sufficient testing capabilities for every one of our communities. In July 2020, we reached a milestone of more than a hundred thousand COVID-19 tests administered to residents and associates. In August 2020, we completed baseline testing for residents and associates at all of our seven-hundred-plus communities across more than forty states. Given that asymptomatic residents could be COVID-19 positive, we used the test results to assess our protocols and continued to make enhancements, when necessary, to help protect our residents, patients, and associates.

Identification of COVID-19-positive residents, patients, or associates through testing enabled us to promptly isolate individuals to help prevent the spread of the virus. Our goal was to facilitate the best care setting for treatment of individual residents, whether that meant transporting them to a hospital or skilled nursing facility or allowing them to remain in our communities. For COVID-19-positive residents within our communities, residents would isolate within their apartments or within special resident care areas (where warranted).

At a minimum, our standard was to comply with the CDC, state, and local health guidelines throughout our emergency response efforts. In addition, we would engage with leading medical centers for recommendations and guidance to complement our clinicians' expertise. This innovative, multi-tiered approach led us to be an early adopter of using pulse oximeters to monitor the health status of our residents.

HERO HIGHLIGHTS FROM ANNA-GENE O'NEAL, RN, MS

Joined Brookdale Health Care Services in August 2019; was serving as BHS division president when the sale of a majority stake in BHS to HCA Healthcare was completed in July 2021

I began my clinical and professional career as an emergency department nurse in a very busy Level 1 trauma center. Preparing for the worst and then hoping for the best was how I lived every day professionally for almost ten years—first as a nurse, then as a department leader. Understanding the art of triage, allocation, and then reallocation of resources came naturally to me. Infection control practices were paramount because we never knew what infectious diseases or blood and bodily fluids we might be exposed to on a daily or even hourly basis. Foundational to our approach was the expectation that we based patient care on the SOAP process: (s)ubjective data, (o)bjective data, (a)ssessment, and (p)lan. Having achieved clinical certifications (then becoming an instructor of the same certification courses) was an essential part of my training that prepared me for the pandemic.

I learned personally that my only fears in the emergency room stemmed from that which I did not know. The more information I could gather at the patient level or the disease process level, the more I could maintain a sense of control in an environment with few controls. This enhanced my ability to ensure an adequate assessment, knowing what objective data to search and what questions to ask from the subjective perspective.

As leaders at Brookdale, we knew that helping to protect our residents and patients as well as our associates was paramount while this virus preyed disproportionately on those most vulnerable: the elderly. The tsunami effect of this virus across the entire world—a virus without a clinical protocol for treatment and one that depleted resources worldwide—was frightening. *We had no beacon to guide us. What we had was the commitment to the clinical process: subjective, objective, assessment, and plan.*

We knew subjectively what was happening around the world and in our communities. We needed to gather the objective data from a comprehensive system assessment in order to develop a plan. What we were experiencing was unfortunately not unique to Brookdale; all of us in the healthcare industry were in the same position. Fortunately, even in an industry as competitive as ours, the walls came down as healthcare professionals came together to leverage knowledge about the virus as well as insights and access to resources in a collective attempt to help protect our respective communities. We all yearned for the newest detail, statistic, product, supply chain update, latest CDC update, and more. *We had to arm ourselves with the very best knowledge and intelligence possible: information was a life preserver—a beacon of hope in an ocean of ever-changing high seas.*

Daily, if not hourly, we reached out to our professional colleagues to share, to listen, to learn, to plan, and to support. We kept each other on speed dial. We leveraged connections in both the public and private sectors. As the pandemic flooded our health systems, Brookdale needed to know what was happening in the acute care environment to best prepare and respond for the protection of our residents and patients. Further, as the hospitals exceeded capacity, they needed to know and impress upon senior living communities (as well as the post-acute provider space) the need to innovate at warp speed to help decompress the hospital patient load—leaving room only for those with the highest clinical acuity. Brookdale's plan A—to move COVID-19-positive residents from our assisted living communities to acute care or skilled nursing settings—became almost immediately obsolete for some communities. We had to pivot; we had no choice.

In addition to this peer network and sharing, the Nashville Health Care Council (a consortium of healthcare providers) brought together—for the purpose of responding to COVID-19—small groups of leaders, including those in acute care, public health, government policy, supply chain, diagnostic laboratories, post-acute providers, and senior living. While this group started small, it quickly expanded as we met on a regular basis to share best practices with each other while also engaging in Q&A. Again, as a healthcare community, we were all bonded by a shared sense of purpose: the protection of human life.

Whether for individual patients I had the privilege of serving in my early clinical days within the emergency department or for the communities of patients I have the responsibility of helping to protect now, the same lesson holds true for me: (s)ubjective, (o)bjective, (a)ssessment, and (p)lan. There is a system we can use with every problem we face; this helps us create order when chaos surrounds us.

By June 2020, Brookdale began planning a phased approach to reopen communities to loved ones. Around this time, the Emergency Command Center (ECC) transitioned into an Emergency Response

Center (ERC) and communicated standards and provided oversight as communities opened again.

Communities had to assess their COVID-19 infections relative to the infection rates in the metropolitan areas in which they operated. Typically, local health departments provided parameters for reopening, whether that meant implementing outdoor-only visits; limiting touching (so no hugs); or restricting eating and drinking together because masks were required at all times.

Scheduling these visits was a tremendous undertaking, since plans had to be coordinated and communicated in advance, but it was well worth it. It was beyond heartwarming to see loved ones reuniting in person after months of uncertainty at the start of the pandemic. As vaccinations rolled out, restrictions during visits eased up and brought loved ones even closer.

Vaccine Rollout

By fall 2020, the prospect of a COVID-19 vaccine was on the horizon, and the ERC and our corporate leadership team did everything in our power to remain informed and ahead of the curve. We knew that once a vaccine was approved, there would be significant competition for access to whatever vaccines became available.

With the help of wise counsel and enhanced communications with local and national decision makers, Brookdale urgently advocated for prioritized access to vaccines for our residents and associates. Given the age and chronic conditions of senior living residents, which rendered them among the most vulnerable to the disease, I worked with our government affairs team to make a concerted effort to this end, and it paid off.

It would be impossible to capture the excitement and applause that erupted when we found out our residents and associates were included by the federal government in the very first phase of the vaccine prioritization. The vaccines were shots of hope with the potential to save lives and help return our communities to some semblance of normalcy.

We quickly learned that federal prioritization was necessary but not sufficient for our needs. The federal government made the prioritization recommendation, but when the vaccines were distributed, the states ultimately determined how they would prioritize the vaccines. So after gaining prioritization federally, we immediately shifted our efforts to the state level in order to gain priority access to vaccines in all the states in which we operated at this time. Some states prioritized our residents and associates without delay. In other states, we would educate and advocate with officials to gain prioritization for our residents.

At Thanksgiving, the prospect of a vaccine was one of the many things for which we would give thanks. The corporate team spent the rest of the year (including foregoing December holiday celebrations) and the early part of the next year to focus on these earnest efforts, so our residents and associates could receive prioritized status for vaccine access; simultaneously, we began planning and facilitating vaccine clinics within our communities.

As a result of these proactive efforts, we accelerated the execution of vaccine clinics that dramatically changed the course of the pandemic. We held our first clinics on December 18, 2020—one week after the FDA approved the first vaccine for Emergency Use Authorization. We would continue our advocacy efforts until our residents and associates were prioritized in every state and we had been able to host our community clinics. In just under four months, we completed the implementation of at least three vaccine clinics in each of our communities.

In total, during this time, we facilitated over 120,000 vaccine shots within our communities. By April 2021, the last COVID-19 vaccination clinics were held, 93 percent of our residents had been inoculated, and our COVID-19 caseload had dropped by 97 percent. Our community leadership teams went above and beyond to make these clinics a time of celebration. They created themes, decorated and featured complementary music, and conducted all-day clinics with appointments in order to maintain proper social distancing. Our residents had been greatly anticipating these clinics, and our leaders made them special.

We accomplished all of this thanks to an ongoing positive relationship with CVS Health®,[7] longtime administrator of our community-based flu clinics as well as our efforts to communicate with (and sometimes implore!) federal and state officials, local health departments, and many others. I will always look back on this time with gratitude for the efforts of Mckenzie Mack, strategic account executive with Omnicare®,[8] a CVS Health® company. Mckenzie was a fierce advocate for Brookdale and was involved in all of the planning for the vaccine clinics. Mckenzie worked around the clock to support us. Brookdale's weekly calls with Mckenzie and Derek Darling (at the time vice president for Strategy and Internal Operations at Omnicare®) were key in keeping the momentum as we pushed hard for our vaccination clinics to happen as quickly as possible.

Additionally, we clearly recognized that these monumental achievements with our clinics were the direct result of our associates' dedication to do what they could to effectively lead all of the preclinic education, obtain consents from residents (or from the designated family member for memory care residents), and other essential tasks, which enabled teams to move quickly as soon as access to the COVID-19 vaccine was granted.

---

7   CVS Health is a registered trademark of CVS Pharmacy, Inc.

8   Omnicare is a registered trademark of Omnicare, Inc.

It's important to note that throughout this time, the entire leadership team knew well that the heavy lifting of Brookdale's COVID-19 response was happening in our communities. As servant leaders, we considered the impact on the field with every decision made. The executive directors and health and wellness directors who were leading our communities had nonstop questions from residents and loved ones, and the ERC had to arm them with the knowledge and protocols necessary to manage the virus and provide reassuring answers. After almost a year of this pandemic, the day-to-day life in the community hadn't been business as usual for quite a while. Our teams were putting PPE inventory on shelves and preparing for ongoing difficulties. The days were long and often stressful, and our leaders and associates were remarkably resilient.

Lessons Learned

Throughout our emergency response, we acted humbly, leaning into our strengths in research and execution and nimbly remaining ready to pivot on a moment's notice as conditions and business requirements changed. We set bold goals and measured our progress regularly to be certain we stayed on track.

Moreover, we clearly identified the steps we needed to take in order to move quickly, and we thought ahead as we formed alliances with fellow industry leaders and potential partners. We focused on developing strong partnerships with key suppliers, which enabled us to build a reliable supply chain to meet the needs of our communities and associates.

We also felt a special obligation as thought leaders to share our success models with society at large, so we committed to sharing our knowledge with the world through our COVID-19 website, online newsrooms, and participation in industry working groups and seminars.

CHAPTER 3

Securing Resources for Financial Flexibility

Taking Bold, Preemptive Action to Ensure Liquidity

When Lehman Brothers filed for bankruptcy in the fall of 2008, it set off a global financial crisis. They had been a blue-chip investment firm—the fourth largest in the world at the time—after being in operation for over 150 years. Lehman ended up liquidating because they required more cash than they could secure when they needed it. They'd been operating with instruments like subprime mortgages and other, less liquid assets, and the destabilizing effect sent an otherwise deeply rooted institution into a tailspin—followed by the rest of the country—all because they were short on liquidity. In other words, they ran out of cash.

Managing liquidity in business is like managing your personal bank account. If you don't have the cash to pay your mortgage, you'll eventually lose your house, because the creditor (your bank) will repossess it. It's a business truism that "cash is king." This is especially true when times are uncertain.

It's important for the CEO of a company to understand both cash flow and liquidity. You can be at the helm of an amazing business (good growth, improving profitability, and strong assets), but if you don't have the cash to pay your obligations when the time comes, your business will not survive. This is why it's important to ensure that revenue growth outpaces cost growth and that profit margins are healthy. It's also why it's important for businesses to have cash, or assets that are liquid enough to convert them to cash quickly, in order to pay obligations as they come due.

This is Corporate Finance 101.

So why do we need cash? It's not just sitting in the bank. Cash is what fuels all operations. Cash pays your associates. Cash pays your suppliers. Cash pays your lease and debt obligations. Cash is the fuel that keeps the engine running in any business.

Securing Liquidity

On January 31, 2020, we had just completed the sale of our majority stake in our Entry Fee venture. This Entry Fee business was a grouping of elite properties with a model different from the rest of the company: residents would pay an "entry fee" investment, part of which would be refundable to their heirs in future years. We had two goals in selling our stake in our Entry Fee communities: 1) to simplify and streamline our overall business, since Entry Fee was so different from the rest of the company; and 2) to provide liquidity for our operational turnaround.

When we planned the transaction back in 2019, no one could have anticipated the major shock of a pandemic, and therefore no one could have predicted just how important this transaction would become. Call it luck or perfect timing, but this transaction, unrelated to our pandemic planning, set us up with additional resources and the gift of time to address the challenges that COVID-19 would create.

COVID-19 was a black-swan event that created significant uncertainty about the impact the pandemic would have on our financials. Quantifying the potential impact seemed impossible.

Never, Ever, Ever Run Out of Cash.

Nevertheless, liquidity would be one of our top priorities, and securing it would require bold steps. As Warren Buffett has stated, "Cash combined with courage in a time of crisis is priceless."

In February 2020, I asked Brookdale's CFO Steve Swain to lead our efforts to calculate the potential business impact of the pandemic and to help maintain the liquidity needed to weather the storm. Taking steps to ensure we maintained liquidity would be Steve's first, second, and third priorities!

Like many other companies, our first step was to borrow against our credit line to have more cash in the bank. Steve then assisted Executive Vice President of Finance and Treasurer George Hicks to quickly refinance our near-term debt maturities. Steve also instructed the Financial Planning and Analysis team to model several different scenarios with low, medium, and high impacts from COVID-19. These scenarios helped Steve and me gauge the COVID-19 threat.

This analysis prompted additional immediate action. We paused our share repurchase program and delayed or canceled a number of our elective capital expenditure projects. All of these steps would help maintain our liquidity, even though there was no way of predicting the size and duration of the storm at this point.

We were building a war chest for the ensuing battle.

HERO HIGHLIGHTS FROM STEVE SWAIN

Joined Brookdale Senior Living September 2018; currently executive vice president and chief financial officer

PLANNING EARLY AND RAISING MONEY WHEN IT'S NOT NEEDED

Cash is king, and a CFO's job is to never run out of it. Liquidity, covenants, and mitigation: these were just some of the words that rang in my head throughout 2020 loudly and often—countless times between 3:00 and 5:00 a.m.

I learned my first lessons in liquidity with a former employer as part of the Investor Relations and Treasury Departments. We learned—the hard way—the importance of planning early, raising money even when it's not needed, and proactively selling noncore assets.

The price of raising money when it's desperately needed costs a lot more than money raised in advance. The price of must-have liquidity is the usury rate; some bonds at my former company carried 13 percent, 13.5 percent, and 14 percent interest coupons. Ouch! Within the company, these notes were not so affectionately referred to as our "credit card" debt.

Needless to say, repeating these hard lessons at Brookdale was not an option. In order to maintain our

---

financial resources to survive the pandemic, I had the responsibility of both developing our financial plan in advance and executing it seamlessly.

Managing through the pandemic was stressful, so I tried to infuse a little levity in order to break the tension. For instance, I liked to tell the following "joke." Question: What was most important to me in 2020? Answer: my back, arms, and hands. My back because it was always supporting me, my arms because they were always by my side, and my hands because I could always count on them. *Every now and then, stop, laugh, and take a deep breath before continuing the drive forward!*

The truth is it wasn't any of those things that got us through. More than anyone, it was Cindy Baier who supported me throughout the ordeal. Cindy had been Brookdale's CFO before me and was uniquely qualified to have financial conversations with me, and these conversations made all the difference. Although I engaged in lively debates with my peer group throughout the pandemic, at the end of the day, Cindy and I walked side by side. I credit her for helping me maintain a steady focus throughout.

I also knew I could always count on the financial team— oars in the water pulling hard each and every day. I am truly blessed to help support and lead such a dedicated and capable group of professionals. As the initial pandemic phase fades from the rearview mirror, I am working to maintain our team spirit. *An experience like this changes your perspective, because now you know you can accomplish anything together.*

> We are grateful for this chance to reflect, take a deep breath, and continue the drive forward.

Additionally, before COVID-19 hit, we had been working with the board on a plan to renegotiate our largest lease. This lease restructuring became another critical action as we began to measure the dramatic effects of the pandemic on cash.

As we entered into early negotiations on refinancings and lease restructurings, our lenders and landlords needed to understand the actions we were taking to help protect our residents, patients, and associates, along with the financial impact of the pandemic. In other words, what were we doing to batten down the hatches? Our creditors were willing to refinance our communities to weather the storm—our boats, if you will—but they needed assurance that there were no leaks in the ship's bottom.

We had to communicate a plan in stormy, ever-changing conditions.

During any crisis, the need for information expands exponentially—both internally and externally. Even after we completed refinancing our near-term maturities, our lenders had a vested interest in the impact of the pandemic on Brookdale and wanted additional reporting.

Because other borrowers in the industry had not been able to make their required mortgage payments, lenders became very focused on the performance of all mortgaged communities in their loan portfolio—including ours. We made a concerted effort to share robust updates about the pandemic and its material effects with our capital providers, along with our comprehensive plan to help protect our residents, patients, and associates. We were transparent about what we knew and what we didn't. As a result of our diligent reporting, relationship building, and information sharing, we were able to build additional trust with our creditors.

Roosevelt Davis, senior director, MF Customer Engagement Fannie Mae, shared the following perspective: "When the pandemic hit, Brookdale contacted Fannie Mae to share its plan of action to protect their residents and staff. Their foresight gave us a measured level of assurance that they were proactively managing safety issues and taking steps to mitigate the financial impact of the pandemic. We've worked with Brookdale for a long time, and we really value that relationship."

Planning Early and Raising Money

Scenario planning, developing risk mitigation strategies, and revising plans became a way of life.

> ## Scenario Planning Is Key.

With March 2020 results just finalized, Adam Voss and Ben Korb in Brookdale's Financial Planning and Analysis group submitted the first 2020 COVID-19-impaired projection (a.k.a. the March Scenario). To say there was incalculable uncertainty would be an understatement. Nonetheless, the March Scenario was our first effort to quantify the possible financial impact of COVID-19 on Brookdale. It helped us understand how much extra liquidity we might need under a range of potential outcomes and assumptions.

Looking back, the impact that COVID-19 had on Brookdale was massive. In 2020 alone, lost revenue plus what we spent on incremental pandemic-related costs was over $400 million—that was effectively equivalent to nearly twice our entire 2019 cash flow from operations—a gargantuan impact, all thanks to a virus that no one could see! Given the impact, we needed to "variable-ize" our cost structure: that is, decrease costs while still focusing on our number one priority of helping to keep residents, patients, and associates as safe as possible and continuing to provide high-quality care to our residents.

Steve and his team looked up and down every line item in our budget for opportunities. Across the company, associates tightened their belts and delivered, mitigating the majority of the pressure. Committed teams lowered operating costs, restructured leases, reduced elective capital expenditures, cut general and administrative expenses, and lowered interest expense with the directive of not compromising the level of quality service we provided or straying from our commitment to legal and regulatory compliance.

Of particular note, we needed to remember that we were a business of people taking care of people. Therefore, it was important that associate-related cost reductions during the pandemic come from reassigning individuals whose jobs were impacted by COVID-19 (such as community bus drivers) to activities that had incremental demands for which they had the appropriate skills—and being careful only to backfill open positions when necessary.

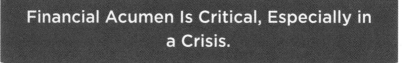

Financial Acumen Is Critical, Especially in a Crisis.

We also knew we had to raise money even when it wasn't immediately needed. Brookdale's executive vice president of Finance and treasurer George Hicks often remarks, "If we wait to do something until we are clearly needful, it will be too late."

In 2020, George astutely planned treasury actions that assumed the "downside" liquidity scenario. He proactively closed over $1 billion of debt transactions, the majority against the backdrop of a worldwide pandemic. For instance, in late summer and early autumn 2020, and without a vaccine even on the horizon, George managed to refinance our bank line of credit and substantially all of our 2021 maturities. Even more remarkable, the terms of the new debt were in line with or better than historical terms.

George's credibility with Freddie Mac and Fannie Mae were absolutely instrumental in getting the deals over the finish line. We were told later by Steve Schmidt, national director of Freddie Mac Multifamily, that they continued to have confidence in Brookdale as COVID-19 impacted all aspects of the economy, noting, "Brookdale is a pillar of the senior housing community, and their commitment to transparency, candor, and a 'get it done' approach have been the foundation of our relationship for the past two decades."

HERO HIGHLIGHTS FROM GEORGE HICKS

Joined Brookdale Senior Living April 1985; currently executive vice president of Finance and treasurer

REFINANCING OUR DEBT MATURITIES AND PULLING OUR CREDIT LINE

Brookdale entered 2020 engaged in an already active financing program during the first part of the year. As

---

of December 2019, we had a significant amount of debt due in 2020. Moreover, we had recently signed two major purchase agreements, agreeing to acquire twenty-six communities from two lessors.

In order to finance the acquisition transactions and retire some of our near-term maturities, we closed on one financing in January and two more in mid-March.

In order to prepay our 2020 debt maturities, we then closed on a fourth financing at the end of the first quarter. At this point, we had closed on $445 million in the first thirteen weeks of the year and had retired essentially all of our 2020 maturities.

Each of these financings had been initiated four to five months before their respective closings. In other words, they were all initiated pre-COVID-19, but each one closed a little further into the COVID-19 maelstrom than the one before. *By the time of our April closing, COVID-19 had become a major complicating element in the underwriting process, creating delays and uncertainty.*

Although we were pleased and relieved to put these transactions behind us, we also knew that we had over $300 million of debt due in 2021. Occupancy had already begun to suffer from the pandemic, and everything took a back seat to our number one priority of the health and well-being of our residents, patients, and associates.

Adding further concern, as occupancy began to suffer, we began to appreciate that access to the company's revolving line of credit might become impaired as a result of financial covenants that were heavily dependent upon our ability to move in new residents.

Despite the strong temptation to relax after having closed on so much new debt in the first quarter, the management team quickly realized that we needed to tend to both our 2021 maturities as well as our revolver. Accordingly, in early April, we initiated efforts to refinance both. We knew that it would not be a typical underwriting process: for one, it would be complicated by new processes designed to determine that a borrower was doing its best to help mitigate the effects of COVID-19 and maintain the health and well-being of its residents; and two, lenders would be modifying their loan structures by requiring reserves and lowering leverage.

However, we persevered and managed to refinance most of our revolver assets and complete the acquisition of a lease buyout, and we retired our 2021 debt maturities by means of two financings that closed in August and September in the aggregate amount of $487 million.

At this point, we had closed on approximately $930 million of new debt in 2020, most of it under severe pressure from the impact of COVID-19. However, we weren't quite done, because we had now eliminated our revolver. We decided to address that issue by putting a smaller revolving credit facility in place, so we assembled a collateral pool sufficient to support a new $80 million revolving line of credit, and we closed it out on December 11, 2020.

Our ability to respond to the COVID-19 crisis by completing all of these transactions can be attributed largely to the excellent relationships we have built over the years—chief among them Freddie Mac and Fannie Mae, as well as with our Delegated Underwriting and Servicing (DUS) Program lenders who support the mortgage financing process.

Securing Government Aid

A pandemic is, by definition, a public health crisis: it affects the broader population and not just those in our care. Yet we were bearing disproportionate costs—significant expenses and exorbitant losses—as we responded to the crisis. Business ownership in the private sector and government stewardship have different roles, and it was vital for all Americans that the government step in to support senior living as part of its work to help protect the public.

We were not looking for a handout; we were looking for help keeping the population under our care as healthy as possible so we could help save as many lives as possible. We recognized the unique danger of COVID-19 to the particular population we serve; senior living residents were among the most vulnerable in the country due to their age and the prevalence of chronic conditions among this demographic. Our response—and the response by government— could mean the difference between life and death for many Americans.

We needed financial support, and we needed prioritization of resources, including PPE, testing, and ultimately, vaccines for those in our care. We needed acknowledgment from the government that this population mattered. Importantly, many of our residents are veterans who had risked their lives to help protect our country. Now it was time for the government to help protect them.

Senior living is primarily regulated at the state level and remains a largely private-pay business. As such, our industry historically didn't have enough established relationships with federal government officials who would be making critical decisions on support and resource prioritization. Given the importance of senior living to the overall healthcare system, we had previously recognized the need to broaden Brookdale's exposure to members of Congress and other federal officials. We conducted an initial series of introductory meetings on Capitol Hill in July 2019. Although we had just started the process of introducing Brookdale and building these important relationships, by the time the pandemic arrived, our industry was still lagging far behind in this area. As a result, there was a very high probability that our industry could be left out of government aid altogether.

Unified Voices Are a Force Multiplier.

Within weeks of forming an ECC at Brookdale, we mobilized an industry-wide government affairs program to secure resources such as PPE, testing, and financial relief for Brookdale and for others within the senior living industry. I contacted trade associations and other CEOs within our industry, and I charged Brookdale's nascent internal government affairs team to join forces with these outside contacts. If we were going to pursue government relief, we would have to work collectively to multiply our chances of securing resources. Brookdale took the lead by drafting a senior living stabilization package. By March 20, 2020, members of a leading trade organization, Argentum, aligned around a proposal to stabilize the senior living industry and began their legislative outreach efforts.

Brookdale's federal government affairs team included John Herzog of Kimbell & Associates; Chad White, our general counsel; and Dan Huffines, our associate general counsel. The Honorable Jackie Clegg, a former board member with vast experience in government, helped us develop our strategy; we added Matt Gallivan—a government affairs consultant who had previously served as the head of the Nashville Health Care Council—to the team; and we later added Tim Trysla of Alston & Bird as an advisor. With losses escalating and significant costs climbing by the day, government funding was necessary not only for the maintenance of Brookdale's cash liquidity but for the health and survival of our industry.

> ## Always Be Ready with a Quick and Effective Message.

Our federal government affairs team worked tirelessly, educating legislators and government officials about our industry in an effort to preserve senior living's vital role in the healthcare continuum. In many cases, our meetings highlighted the fact that many government officials and others in the general public thought of senior living as nursing homes. We needed to reinforce the message that senior living is largely a private-pay industry, as compared to skilled nursing facilities, which receive significant payments from Medicare or Medicaid. We underscored the fact that our private-pay industry provided such vitally important services to seniors and that we served the population that was among the most vulnerable to the virus because of age and chronic conditions.

Making our case was all the more challenging, because the vast majority of government contacts were remote: many had difficulty remotely accessing their work from home, which presented additional hurdles in the beginning. Over many months, our team made an incredible number of points of contact with legislators, political appointees, and civil servants during this process.

Nevertheless, we succeeded in reaching the right people, and our team did an outstanding job advocating on behalf of our residents, patients, and associates. We saw this as another success to celebrate.

HERO HIGHLIGHTS FROM DAN HUFFINES

Joined Brookdale Senior Living August 2014; currently vice president, associate general counsel, and assistant secretary

CAMPAIGN TO SECURE THE PROVIDER RELIEF FUND

The unprecedented reality of the pandemic, including its disproportionate impact on senior living residents and patients, brought along many opportunities for the problem solvers of the company.

Quickly we realized that our industry would need government support to help protect our seniors. We did not have a dedicated federal government affairs team in house, so we built one overnight. In March 2020, we scrambled to gain an audience with anyone in Washington who would listen. Our message at the time was simple: *the pandemic would take an early and disproportionate*

---

toll on our nation's seniors, and companies like ours would play an instrumental role in helping to protect seniors from the virus.

The work in the first few weeks was grueling: dialing, emailing, and updating our message day and night. We were competing with other industries for the ear of policymakers, and many had preexisting relationships and strong federal trade organizations. As a primarily state-regulated industry, senior living lacked these relationships. It was clear our industry was an underdog.

In March 2020, Friday the thirteenth no less, we received the first sign that the federal government was open to hearing our plea for financial aid. That night around 6:00 p.m., John Herzog received a call from the office of Treasury Secretary Mnuchin, who had led relief negotiations with congressional leaders. The secretary wanted to speak with Cindy Baier about the pandemic's financial impact on the senior living industry. This provided our first concrete opportunity to help educate a critical policymaker about the necessity of our industry and the unique challenges we faced. *The secretary's call amounted to an early win, galvanizing our team for what would become an all-out, six-month push to obtain relief for our industry.*

The CARES Act became law two weeks later and contained two major avenues for relief: the Paycheck Protection Program (PPP) and the $100 billion Provider Relief Fund (PRF). The former would help some senior living providers but was limited to businesses with five hundred or fewer employees and wasn't based on reimbursement of losses. The PRF option held promise as a grant program to reimburse losses attributable to COVID-19. However, senior living wasn't specifically mentioned in the bill's text. In fact, soon after passage of the CARES Act, the PRF was repeatedly referred to as the Hospital Fund.

We worked diligently to make sure the Department of Health and Human Services (HHS) knew the intent of Congress—that senior living providers were initially intended to be eligible for PRF grants. Within three weeks, we reached another milestone with the support of our industry partners. Bipartisan groups of senators and representatives sent letters to HHS to positively express their intent that senior living would qualify for PRF relief.

Ultimately, the state-level regulatory environment was the most challenging aspect of advocating for our industry. Unlike Medicare and Medicaid providers, those in the senior living industry operate in divergent state regulatory schemes, and most senior living providers had no payor relationship with federal payment systems. Quite simply, HHS didn't know how to validate state-licensed senior living providers or their financial records.

To overcome this challenge, we persisted—again, alongside our industry partners—by offering potential validation frameworks to HHS. The dedication of HHS to find a validation solution was apparent, and eventually one idea stuck. The HHS staff member working on the validation challenge called Tim Trysla and me on a Friday night. HHS's validation plan would require our industry's trade associations to promptly set up a portal so senior living providers could match state-level licensure numbers with federal tax numbers within less than a week. This step was necessary so that HHS could help prevent disbursing funds to applicants who weren't operating assisted living communities. Tim and the Alston & Bird team were very pleased that HHS decided to pursue this particular path. Cindy and her leadership team would work with Argentum to convince the industry to participate. Resolving the validation challenge was one of the more critical inflection points, and it turned out to be the final hurdle to obtaining PRF relief for our industry. It was a lifeline to the industry and would not have happened without Cindy's leadership. We had finally achieved financial relief as occupancy and revenue losses mounted.

Throughout the pandemic, our internal team continued their day jobs while feverishly working for government relief. Our team fought earnestly for Brookdale, knowing that our success would ultimately bring tremendous financial help to our industry. *We broke down the seemingly impossible into milestones that would be manageable, and we secured wins along the way that motivated our team to persist.*

One of my most vivid memories from the pandemic occurred on March 19, 2020, when I received a call on my cell phone from

Treasury Secretary Steven Mnuchin. I was in my kitchen at home, making dinner. We had been trying to reach him for days and would have only a few minutes to plead our case. In a matter of about two seconds, I turned off the stove and launched into an explanation of our industry and the issues we were facing and asked him for help. He assured me that he understood the significance of our industry's role in the pandemic and the importance of supporting us in the government relief package. Then he gave me his cell phone number so I could reach him for any necessary follow-up. I was so grateful for his time and impressed by his quick mind and leadership style.

Relationships Matter.

After several weeks of uncertainty at the start of the pandemic, our government relations team and I finally had great hope that our industry would be included in the government relief packages that were being disbursed.

The final step in the process was the application itself. Because the government planned to validate application data by matching it to IRS records, financial information needed to be submitted at the federal tax identification number (TIN) level. Pulling, validating, and submitting our financial and operational data at this granular TIN level required heavy lifting. In fact, the foundation of our Phase 3 application alone required a data pull of over a quarter million measurement points. This herculean effort was led by Director of Corporate Accounting Mike Scott, Senior Vice President and Chief Accounting Officer Dawn Kussow, Senior Vice President of

Shared Services Mary Kay O'Dea, and Senior Vice President of Tax Joanne Leskowicz.

Over the coming months, our government affairs efforts would experience a roller coaster of progress and setbacks, hopefulness and frustration. In the end, we counted our blessings as we received some Provider Relief Fund grants in 2020 to reimburse a portion of our losses as well as assistance with a small amount of PPE and testing supplies. Importantly, it was through these ardent efforts that we also received prioritization for our residents and associates to receive the COVID-19 vaccine.

It's important to note that it took significant effort and dedication from many senior living CEOs and other leaders, as well as our trade associations—including Argentum, American Seniors Housing Association (ASHA), and the American Health Care Association (AHCA)—to receive government funding, support for testing, and some PPE, as well as to prioritize assisted living residents and associates to receive the vaccine.

I am particularly grateful to Bob Hillis and his team at Direct Supply, an important vendor for Brookdale, because they used their long-standing government affairs efforts to help our industry deliver our critical message. I am also grateful to president and CEO of Argentum James Balda, president of ASHA David Schless, president and CEO of AHCA Mark Parkinson, and their dedicated teams.

Lessons Learned

Some of the unrelated actions we had taken in the months prior to the start of the pandemic would prove to be enormously helpful during the crisis. This illustrates the power of trusting your gut instincts, even outside of a crisis.

The same applies to the people you entrust as advisors. In 2019, we had engaged John Herzog to assist with government affairs. John turned out to be one of the most valuable players in our efforts to secure funding for our industry because of his relationships with individuals at the US Department of Health and Human Services.

Relationships, as it turns out, can be as good as gold.

CHAPTER 4

Mastering Preparation and Protocols

Fighting an Invisible Enemy through Enhanced Infection Control

A t this turning point in Brookdale's history, we were fighting an invisible enemy. This was a monumental challenge. Our corporate leadership team could create the framework, but only our front lines—tens of thousands of amazing associates across our communities, home health and hospice agencies, and outpatient therapy clinics—would be able to deliver the support our residents and patients needed every day.

We knew we needed to balance actions to help keep our residents safe with their need for engagement. We focused on a three-prong strategy: 1) keep COVID-19 *out of* our communities as much as possible; 2) limit the spread of COVID-19 *within* our communities as much as possible; and 3) help facilitate care for COVID-19-positive residents in the best setting for their condition, including right where they lived, when appropriate. And we increased our communications to keep residents and their loved ones connected as much as possible.

Safety as the Top Priority

When the pandemic hit, we had over forty years of experience practicing and refining our already-strong infection protocols. We pride ourselves on helping to keep our residents safe, effectively stewarding our communities when the seasonal flu inevitably descends upon us every year. In January 2020, we started reinforcing our strong infection prevention and control protocols.

In March 2020, we tailored our strong infection prevention policies, procedures, and best practices in order to help reduce or eliminate exposure of COVID-19 among our residents, patients, and associates. We added social distancing, the widespread use of PPE, health screenings, isolation, and quarantines. Communities were provided with COVID-19 health screening logs by mid-March, and we began conducting health surveillance that included having associates and visitors complete health screenings prior to entering the communities. Training was critical to the task: Even though many of the enhancements were not new, we needed to focus our efforts as CDC guidance evolved so that we were all on the same page. Associates had to be trained (or retrained) on infection control, hygiene, reporting, and appropriate use of PPE.

We began sourcing additional PPE for our associates in order to help reduce or eliminate possible exposure to COVID-19. In mid-April, top community and field leaders were informed that all associates were required to wear masks, regardless of active COVID-19 cases in the surrounding area, and all residents and patients were strongly encouraged to wear masks.

CEO Cindy Baier (as a child) rides her pony Ginger at her family's farm; the electric fence can be seen in the photo.

The remnants of CEO Cindy Baier's childhood family car after her mother's devastating auto accident.

Brookdale Glen Ellyn (Illinois) welcomes residents to its spacious apartment homes.

CEO Cindy Baier makes an appearance on Bloomberg Live in 2019; prior to the pandemic, Brookdale was experiencing positive operational momentum.

Former Commander of Brookdale's Emergency Command Center Mary Sue Patchett celebrates an incoming shipment of sanitization wipes weeks before the pandemic hit the United States.

CEO Cindy Baier served as the main video talent during Brookdale's pandemic communications.

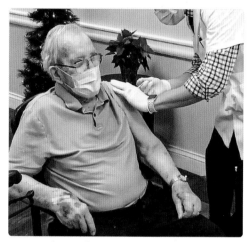

A couple at Brookdale Niskayuna (New York) poses for photos to send to loved ones during social isolation.

Frank Hoerrle in Brookdale Westlake Village (Ohio) became one of the first Brookdale residents vaccinated on December 18, 2020.

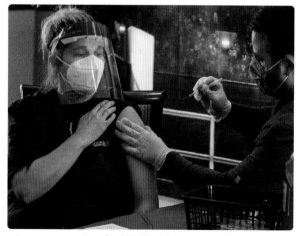

An associate receives the COVID-19 vaccine in February 2021.

A resident at Brookdale Tamarac Square (Colorado) poses for a photo during a vaccine clinic.

Brookdale Carriage Club Providence (North Carolina) offers a virtual wonderland of forestry and lakeside views for its residents.

Brookdale Lake Shore Drive (Illinois) features a picturesque private dining room absent COVID-19 restrictions.

Brookdale Chambrel Roswell (Georgia) offers a unique outdoor shuffleboard court for resident engagement.

Brookdale Carriage Club Providence (North Carolina) hosts a full bar for events and happy hours absent COVID-19 restrictions.

Brookdale West Ashley (South Carolina) features a beautiful front drive with a portico.

Brookdale Lake Shore Drive (Illinois) offers stunning views of both the Chicago skyline and Lake Michigan.

CEO Cindy Baier visits with associates at Brookdale Green Hills Cumberland (Tennessee) prior to the pandemic.

Brookdale Woodward Estates Maintenance Manager Andre Wallace dresses up as a boxer for a vaccine clinic themed "We're gonna knock COVID-19 out!"

Brookdale associates exemplifying the mantra, "Heroes work here!"

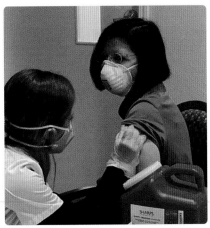

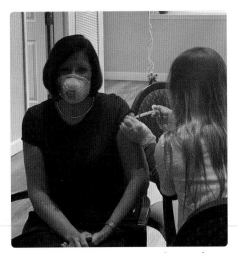

CEO Cindy Baier receives the COVID-19 vaccine.

CEO Cindy Baier receives the second dose of the COVID-19 vaccine.

Cindy Kent, former executive vice president and president of Senior Living.

Cindy's sister, Lisa, in the hospital before her liver transplant.

CEO Cindy Baier with associates at Brookdale Berkeley Boulevard (North Carolina).

CEO Cindy Baier presents the Cornerstone Awards virtually to recipients in 2020.

Barbara Flynn, a nurse at Brookdale Canton (Ohio), reviews resident information to deliver quality care.

Linda DeVault, executive assistant to CEO Cindy Baier, leads the Nashville office fundraising effort for the Alzheimer's Association's Walk to End Alzheimer's®.

Resident Amanda Henderson receives flowers from Kimberly Farmer and Emma Newman at Brookdale Sumter (South Carolina).

Window visits became an important way for families to connect during the pandemic.

*A resident at Brookdale Sandy Springs (Tennessee)
enjoys a window visit and phone call with loved ones.*

A resident at Brookdale Pinehurst (North Carolina) celebrates his 100th birthday party with the help of a community parade.

Brookdale Franklin (Tennessee) resident Carlotta Summers enjoys a "window visit" with her family.

Loved ones wave to residents of Brookdale during a car parade.

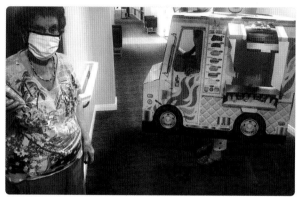

Residents enjoy snacks distributed from a pedestrian-powered, themed food cart.

Associates at Brookdale Sandy Springs (Tennessee) share snacks and drinks with residents on a themed cart.

Brookdale Glen Ellyn (Illinois) features a stunning indoor pool and jacuzzi for year-round recreation absent COVID-19 restrictions.

ENGAGEMENT
ROOM SERVICE

Please fill out this tag, and leave on your
door handle. An associate will pick up and
return needed items.

NAME

ROOM NUMBER

Check off what you need:

☐ Crossword Puzzles
☐ Word Find
☐ Sudoku
☐ Adult Coloring
☐ Colored Pencils
☐ Markers
☐ Deck of Cards
☐ Books - Areas of interest _____

☐ B-Fit Exercise Handout
☐ Notecards/Stationary
☐ Video Call to Family/ Friend
☐ Pastoral Virtual Support

Any other in-room idea not listed?

BROOKDALE
SENIOR LIVING

*Residents enjoyed the option to receive
special attention to their needs by way of
the Engagement Room Service door hanger.*

*CEO Cindy Baier teases resident "Dr. Ed" at
Brookdale's Celebrate Aging Film Festival in 2018.*

*CEO Cindy Baier invites resident Jan Jordan to speak about her late husband, resident Dr.
Stanley Cohen, and their trip to Sweden when he won the Nobel Prize in 1986.*

CEO Cindy Baier presents a crystal heart to resident Jan Jordan for sharing her story with Brookdale associates.

CEO Cindy Baier listens as resident Carolyn Modisher reads from her book,
Where Can I Find a Dinosaur?

CEO Cindy Baier visits with Carolyn Modisher and Gertrude Caldwell at Brookdale Green Hills Cumberland (Tennessee).

In April 2020, residents of Brookdale Galleria (Texas) hung 500 hearts in the windows and around the community; it was their way of showing the city of Houston that the community has a "whole lot of heart"; Blanche was one of many residents and associates who helped with this beautiful project that brought the community closer together.

CEO Cindy Baier wishes a happy 100th birthday to Carolyn Modisher.

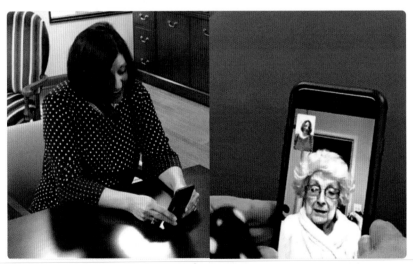

CEO Cindy Baier communicates with Annie Wilson—a resident at Brookdale Carriage Club Providence (North Carolina)—via FaceTime on her 109th birthday in 2019; when Annie was born, telephones were a novelty.

Brookdale Brookhurst (California) features a charming courtyard where residents can mingle absent COVID-19 restrictions.

Brookdale Bayshore (Florida) offers spectacular views of the ocean from its high-rise apartments.

Brookdale Hoffman Estates (Illinois) features beautiful, serene grounds.

CEO Cindy Baier works beside Margarita Fortune,
a housekeeper at Brookdale Wilsonville (Oregon),
as part of a community learning visit in 2018.

CEO Cindy Baier meets with its National Advisory Council (NAC)
of residents (including Ken Garretson, seated, and Dr. Marylouise
"Weezie" Fennell, left) in 2019.

Members of the NAC met virtually during the pandemic.

Associates at Brookdale Gallatin (Tennessee) pose in support of caregiver appreciation.

*Associates and residents raise money for the Walk to
End Alzheimer's® during the 2020 pandemic.*

*CEO Cindy Baier creates handwritten notes to thank associates
for extraordinary service.*

CEO Cindy Baier meets with (from left) Cindy Kent, Mary Sue Patchett, and Anna-Gene O'Neal, members of the executive leadership team, prior to the pandemic.

Merit Ofoegbu, a medication technician at Brookdale The Heights (Texas), uses her fist to "crush" COVID-19 against a chalk mural created for residents by a fellow associate.

CEO Cindy Baier visits the team at Brookdale New Bern (North Carolina).

Getting ready for a socially distanced Mardi Gras party.

Residents Roy and Delores get married in masks at Brookdale Richmond (Indiana).

CEO Cindy Baier visits with a resident at Brookdale Hawthorn Lakes (Illinois) in 2021.

CEO Cindy Baier visits with Lew Wallace, a resident of Brookdale Belle Meade (Tennessee), in 2021.

CEO Cindy Baier visits with resident Gertrude Caldwell.

CEO Cindy Baier visits with an associate.

CEO Cindy Baier listens to a resident, Dr. Annette Gregory, play the piano at Brookdale Tullahoma (Tennessee) in 2018; Dr. Annette was a second-generation resident of Brookdale Tullahoma (her mom had been the very first resident of that community).

CEO Cindy Baier visits Brookdale Vernon Hills (Illinois) for a ribbon cutting in 2021.

Brookdale Lisle (Illinois) offers a charming library to its residents.

Brookdale communities throughout the country are equipped with fitness centers for residents, like the one at Brookdale Carriage Club Providence (North Carolina).

Brookdale South Bay (Rhode Island) features a dazzling koi pond near the front entry.

Brookdale Geary Street (Oregon) features lush landscaping.

*Brookdale Grand Prairie (Oregon) features a state-of-the-art sauna
for residents absent COVID-19 restrictions.*

Brookdale North Naples (Florida) has a front entry featuring a fountain and palm trees.

HERO HIGHLIGHTS FROM DENISE WARREN

Joined Brookdale Senior Living Board of Directors August 2018; served as executive vice president and chief operating officer of WakeMed Health & Hospitals from October 2015 through December 2020

IT TAKES A VILLAGE!

In early 2020, my team saw frightening news reports and alarming video footage revealing a deadly virus in Wuhan, a city in China. In addition to being a board member for Brookdale, I was the chief operating officer for a major regional health system, and I was responsible for helping to identify potential health crises and making quick judgment calls on the likelihood that a particular crisis would impact healthcare operations in our facility. While Wuhan was certainly concerning, it was nearly eight thousand miles away.

When the virus arrived in Seattle, we knew it would be only a matter of time before the virus reached WakeMed in North Carolina. That time came sooner than expected when we realized that one of our most senior nursing clinicians had just spent five days in Seattle. Recall, Seattle was one of the first COVID-19 hotspots in the United States. She was sent home to quarantine for two weeks (she was fine, thank goodness!), and executive leadership immediately invoked an "Incident Command" structure to prepare for possible exposures.

Incident Command is a standardized command structure that is responsible for the command, control, and coordination of an emergency response to a particular incident. Incident Command illuminated the reality that the whole is more than the sum of its parts by creating teams from across the organization to tackle very specific problems. These teams were composed of associates varied in multi-disciplinary skills (clinical and administrative); department assignments (staffing resources, accounting, Kaizan Performance Improvement Office, nurses, physicians, etc.); and hierarchy (from wage earners to C-suite executives). By aggregating these various groups, each with a singular focus or task, we were able to leverage the diversity of experience, thought, and ideas that were needed in order to prepare for and tackle the COVID-19 challenges to come. We were determined to make lemonade out of the COVID-19 lemons we were handed.

The challenges faced by Brookdale were similar to what our Incident Command teams faced. For instance, Brookdale and WakeMed both had to manage the shortage of N95 masks. The cost of masks was significantly higher than pre-pandemic—in some cases exponentially higher—and many masks being sold during this period were counterfeit or did not provide the level of safety needed by our clinicians. As with Brookdale, safety was a critical component of caring for COVID-19 patients. To that end, we formed a multi-disciplinary task force to come up with a solution specifically for this problem.

Demonstrating the same approach to diversity as Brookdale, these WakeMed team members included engineers from the Kaizan Performance Improvement

Office, nurses from various clinical areas of the hospital, staff from Housekeeping, and a manager for the Endoscopy Department. This group experimented with multiple project ideas and prototypes—initially taking an iPhone° case, softening its plastic by placing it in hot water, then reshaping the case to create a secure fit around the nose and mouth as a makeshift mask. After multiple iterations, the team ordered a 3D printer to custom fit plastic parts. While effective, these housings proved to be uncomfortable for our clinicians, so the team went back to the drawing board.

The next idea was to find a way to clean the remaining original N95 masks we had on hand. Once again, the issue was tackled by the same diverse team. One member posed that, since we use UV robots to clean endoscopy suites and operating rooms, we might be able to use the same robots to clean masks. Yet we still had the issue of keeping clean masks separate from dirty masks. How would we return a clean mask to its original user?

After much trial and error, the team designed a protocol whereby each person placed a nametag on their dirty mask and placed the mask in a small brown paper bag. On the outside, they wrote their name and unit number. The masks were collected by Housekeeping several times per day. Housekeeping delivered the masks to the Endoscopy Department, where the staff verified that the name on the mask matched the name on the outside of the bag. Brown bags were then tossed, and the masks were hung safely by clothes pins on a rolling clothes rack (purchased at Walmart) with multiple rows of string. The team exited the room while a UV cleaning robot "cleaned" the room. After approximately five minutes, the team reentered the room and rotated the clothes rack, again exiting the room while the robot cleaned the reverse side. After another five minutes, the team removed the clean masks, placed them in a white bag, wrote the person's name and unit number on the outside of the bag, and returned the bags to their proper unit.

We achieved success!

The masks were comfortable, clean, and safe for the staff to use again. This protocol was so successful, in fact, that we began cleaning masks for nearby firehouses and EMS units.

This particular Incident Command subteam tackled a critical issue by leveraging the knowledge, experience, and creative ideas of a diverse team of leaders and associates at different levels of hierarchy and with different educational specialties, levels of knowledge, and work experience. As with Brookdale, I was pleased to see the powerful critical thinking that was possible when combined with multi-disciplinary teams that leverage diversity of thought.

One of the hallmarks of infection prevention is the ability to quickly identify symptomatic individuals. Rapid identification of infected individuals and isolation of those individuals, along with contact tracing to determine others potentially exposed, help reduce the spread of infection.

Under normal circumstances, this is a relatively straightforward, clinical process. However, scientists determined that COVID-19 was transmissible even by asymptomatic individuals. That meant *anyone* entering *any* Brookdale community represented a potential risk to our residents, patients, and associates.

For communities located in metropolitan areas where associates relied heavily on public transportation to commute to work, this required an even more considered response.

HERO HIGHLIGHTS FROM ERIKA KEEGAN

Joined Brookdale Senior Living August 2013; currently executive director, Brookdale Lake Shore Drive (Illinois)

ALL ABOARD THE (SH)ELTER (I)N (P)LACE!

In early March 2020, the odds seemed stacked against the Brookdale Lake Shore Drive community in Chicago. When the pandemic hit, we were a community of over three hundred residents and two hundred associates living and working in close proximity together in a large urban city. We were especially concerned about the safety of our associates—and the potential effect that the associates would have on our residents—since they had to rely so heavily on public transportation options to commute to work and back.

We saw similar cities, like New York City, struggle to navigate this challenging time, and it became clear to us that swift and innovative action would be needed in order to keep our beloved community safe.

The idea of "the SHIP" was born out of a leadership meeting. For several years, a group of about twenty-five Brookdale Lake Shore community leaders that included directors, coordinators, and schedulers had gathered with the goal of building trust and cross-departmental collaboration across our community. At the group's creation, we had no idea that these weekly meetings would serve as a foundation for our team as we faced our most daunting challenge yet.

When the pandemic hit, we conducted an in-depth survey of the daily challenges our associates were now facing, which included the reality of a majority of our associates traveling to and from work on public transportation; the necessity of grocery shopping without options to receive delivery services; and the complications of many associates' multi-generational households (which meant our associates were often exposed to young children, other adults with their own commutes, and immunocompromised loved ones, all within one home). Our associates did not have the choice to shelter in place as the CDC recommended, and they did not have the financial freedom to change jobs in order to minimize exposure to loved ones at home.

At one of our early leadership meetings during the pandemic, someone quietly spoke up and said, "If we could only set sail and bubble ourselves off from the world for a little bit." This simple fantasy planted a seed:

we thought if we could just buy ourselves some time, the world could learn more about this invisible threat, and we could gain advantage. This led us to move a number of our associates into Brookdale Lake Shore Drive for three weeks' time.

Located right off of Lake Michigan, each of our apartments has spectacular—some almost panoramic—views of the lake (see photo gallery). A favorite resident of ours lovingly called life at our community "one big cruise," waking up to lake views, dining in style in one of our four restaurants, and attending live entertainment and performances with friends.

It wasn't long before the notion of the SHIP became a rallying point for our mission. The goal was to shelter in place (SHIP): we gathered a cohort of associates to live and work together while the leadership spent time acquiring PPE, gaining access to testing resources, and learning more about how the disease spread along with treatment options. It's hard to fathom now, but at the time we moved in, the CDC had recommended not to wear masks. The notion of the SHIP became a pivotal decision during the early weeks of the pandemic: It limited exposure for our associates who would otherwise be traveling to and from work and interacting with others in their homes. And it limited exposure for our residents to the outside world.

As a community, the things that were once our strengths—special relationships that formed through face-to-face interactions; personalized care and support; resident gatherings, both small and large, to dine, celebrate, learn, and grow together—each of these became a threat overnight to our individual and collective health and safety.

Furthermore, our differentiated teams—which ordinarily relied on the expertise of specialized associates to care for residents in specialized ways—became a risk factor for us. During ordinary times, one resident may see anywhere between ten and fifty associates in a single day: one housekeeper, three caregivers, two nurses, a building engineer, two to three room service attendants, a programs associate, a concierge or security associate, and others as they engaged in extracurricular events and dining activities.

With the safety of our residents and associates at the forefront of our minds, we designed a clinical model in which floors three through thirty-seven became "the SHIP" and housed community members who were able to leave their homes for an extended period and shelter in place within the community. The basement level and floors one and two became "the Pier" and were supported by associates who were not able to live at the community for this duration. These associates performed the critical roles needed to bridge those sheltering in place safely from the outside world: cooking meals, disinfecting supplies, operating elevators, troubleshooting mechanical spaces, sending supplies to the SHIP, and more.

Those associates responsible for staffing the SHIP developed a universal worker model to further limit risk of exposure. Each associate was assigned to one or two floors of residents that became their "neighborhood" for those three weeks. They provided clinical services, meal delivery, housekeeping services, and light maintenance, and they checked on their well-being. They also engaged our residents with entertainment options and meaningful activities, teaching residents how to use a virtual meeting platform to connect with outside family members and neighbors.

As an unexpected benefit, deep bonds formed between associates and residents who began to learn so much more about what they shared in common. One resident and associate discovered that they shared a love of poetry and began writing poems back and forth to each other; this became a community engagement as poems from associates and fellow residents were delivered along with their morning breakfast bags. Notably, our associates also learned new skills during this time as they were stretched beyond their normal areas of expertise. This enabled many associates to grow in confidence as they expanded their career skills.

Maintaining high morale was key for our associates. On our first night aboard the SHIP, we gathered and shared why each of us had volunteered to take on this unusual challenge and we discussed the values we each held dear. As we learned more about each other and about the people we cared for in our lives outside of work, this built a foundation for our time together.

The teams composing the SHIP and the Pier met separately on a daily basis in order to check-in, learn a new skill or train others, recognize contributions from the day prior, and shake off the intensity by doing a silly dance or sharing funny stories that happened along the way. Family members of residents and associates from the outside world sent notes of encouragement and special treats as gifts for our associates. At 7:00 p.m., each "neighborhood" lit up with cheers and songs for our associates—the truly essential workers of the pandemic during this trial.

Daily communication was an important part of the SHIP's success: we sent a daily email to all associates and residents (and their loved ones) with updated information about safety measures we were taking, the status of health within the community, and importantly, messages of hope and community connection.

Twice daily, we screened our associates and residents for symptoms. Around day ten, we breathed a big sigh of relief because this crazy idea was working: our community of about five hundred people sheltering in place together was showing no symptoms and was, by all measures available, free from the virus.

We soon learned that access to testing would be available to the community within two to three weeks, so our associates felt confident that help was on its way as we deboarded and returned to our loved ones.

We did not yet realize the true endurance that would be necessary over the long term, but we had a clear sense from the get-go that this would be an epic battle—a marathon, not a sprint. We surpassed the first milestone together, which brought our community to the point where we had tools in the fight: by the end of our time in the SHIP, we had procured adequate PPE, access to testing, clinical and treatment options, and more knowledge about nature of the virus and its transmission. The success of this trial provided us with critical feedback as we tackled the many challenges to come. It united residents, associates, and loved ones in our response to bumps in the road ahead.

Brookdale associates were already proficient in screening for the flu or a fever in order to help prevent infection from spreading, but screening asymptomatic individuals introduced an entirely new level of complexity.

We watched carefully as our communities were closed to visitors in certain states by health authorities. After consultation with the board, I made an executive decision to close all communities to visitors (including loved ones and prospects) on March 11, 2020, in order to help reduce the risk of transmission to our residents and associates.

Shortly after the scientific community confirmed that people who were asymptomatic could be carriers, we took even more aggressive actions to help protect our residents and associates.[9] We launched an initiative to perform baseline resident and associate testing in every one of our seven-hundred-plus communities across forty-plus states. This baseline data became the standard by which we further evaluated and enhanced our protocols.

---

9   Hongjun Zhao et al., "COVID-19: Asymptomatic Carrier Transmission Is an Underestimated Problem," *Epidemiology & Infection* 148, no. 116 (June 11, 2020), https://doi.org/10.1017/S0950268820001235.

Once I made the decision to conduct baseline testing, our Procurement and Clinical teams worked to establish processes and guidelines. Early on, the only available tests were polymerase chain reaction (PCR) tests. This type of test involved getting a nasal swab from a resident or associate and sending it off to the lab to be analyzed. PCR tests were conducted in independent laboratories, so we enlisted testing companies, including on-site staff from the labs or local departments of health to perform the nasal swab and to prepare the specimen to be sent to the lab. The results could take anywhere from a day to a week or more to receive.

Baseline testing was only one part of our testing protocol. By April 2021, we had cumulatively completed over 350,000 tests, and our capabilities only continue to expand.

The Clinical team and ERC also had to address the special needs of our memory care residents and patients as part of our enhanced infection control protocols. Those with dementia frequently find social distancing challenging and may not remember to wear masks. Our corporate Clinical team includes experts in infection control who quickly identified a nontoxic, hypoallergenic, lotion-like skin protectant for hands and faces, which our procurement team sourced for immediate use in our memory care units. By applying this skin protectant to residents' hands and faces, we were able to create a barrier that would help prevent contaminated hands from causing infections.

Containing the Spread

As the pandemic progressed and some residents tested positive for COVID-19, we needed to help contain the spread as much as possible. Individuals who tested positive for COVID-19 were immediately isolated.

> **People Will Follow a Leader Who Shows Commitment to the Mission.**

Clinical leaders Karen Peck and Wendy McKenna were instrumental in assuring that Brookdale adapted quickly to an evolving environment with new information being disseminated almost daily. They kept their focus on working to maintain high levels of care for those they served. For residents, this meant either isolating in individual apartments or moving all COVID-19-positive residents to special resident care areas. Innovation was needed so we could continue to deliver on our mission of enriching the lives of those we serve with compassion, respect, excellence, and integrity in the face of the pandemic.

Because our communities are unique in their floor plans, creative solutions were developed for special resident care areas. Lisa Giles, district director of Clinical Services, was one of the remarkable, innovative leaders who traveled around the country to assess individual community needs, communicating what she'd learned elsewhere and working directly alongside the associates of a given community to make adjustments.

In Chicago, we rented the floor of a nearby hotel, which we designated for COVID-19-positive, asymptomatic, independent living residents from nearby Brookdale communities. For a period of time, Robyn Moore, the district director of Clinical Services, moved into the hotel along with the residents to better support them. This was a custom response based on this particular market's need and the availability of appropriate space close by.

HERO HIGHLIGHTS FROM ROBYN MOORE, RN

Joined Brookdale Senior Living June 2014; currently district director of Clinical Services for Chicago; winner of the Partnership Cornerstone Award for extraordinary actions during COVID-19

WELCOME TO HOTEL BROOKDALE!

For a period of time starting in May of 2020, Brookdale developed an innovative strategy to care for the residents of our twelve Chicago-area communities who were asymptomatic but tested positive for the COVID-19 virus during our community-wide baseline testing.

We called it Hotel Brookdale!

We knew that isolating residents who tested positive would be necessary, and we also knew that we needed a modified plan for doing so. With the support of District Director of Operations Diahn Harrison and Vice President of Administration Roger Thiele, we prepared to transfer them to dedicated accommodations specifically designed for asymptomatic COVID-19-positive residents at a local hotel.

We worked closely with the executive directors of our local communities to communicate the plan to residents and loved ones before we started testing, so they would be aware of the plan to transfer COVID-19-positive residents if they were asymptomatic. Director of Resident Program Engagement Andrea Henry led the plan for activities and sent games and iPads' for residents to stay active. Communities provided transportation, including one bus that remained at the hotel.

Regional Maintenance Technician Frank Nudo, Diahn, and I were so pleased to work with the hotel managers, who provided us with our own floor, a dedicated elevator, and a conference room, where we set up our command center and a "clean" donning area for associates. The hotel also had a centrally located kitchen, which enabled us to provide gourmet meals to our residents, who are accustomed to a high-quality of food at Brookdale. We designed the floor to follow a specific flow, including a "dirty" room at the far end of the floor where the staff could doff dirty PPE and immediately exit via the stairs.

I contacted the Illinois Department of Public Health and spoke to their head of Infection Control, who recommended that we speak to the fire department to review our plan before residents arrived. The fire chief and his assistant toured the space, and together we outlined a strategy for emergency personnel in the event we needed to transport a resident to a local emergency room. The fire chief was so impressed with our vision, plan, and setup that he asked me to consult with other organizations considering the same setup. *I had the good fortune to meet with other leaders of organizations facing similar challenges, and this developed into a community partnership that benefited us all.*

As we scheduled the mass-testing program with the communities, I moved into the hotel on the evening of May 18, 2020. We received our first four residents the next day. Over the next four weeks, we successfully isolated nineteen residents from nine of our communities. We were able to keep them occupied and happy: engaging in daily walks and activities, enjoying a makeshift "dining room" experience, and participating in virtual visits with family and friends.

Brookdale home health nurses and therapists provided specialized care to residents with care needs at the hotel. Throughout the isolation period, three residents became symptomatic and required hospitalization, but all residents successfully recovered and returned to their homes in our Brookdale communities.

This successful strategy was made possible through partnerships—within Brookdale and throughout the local community. We had a clear vision, dedicated leaders, and an impeccable plan. With the support of our Brookdale corporate leadership team and communities, as well as private and public entities all working together, we provided a truly exceptional, unique program of infection control for our residents.

In other areas, we decided to create special resident care areas within the communities. Under the leadership of Senior Vice President of Asset Management David Hammonds and Senior Director of Asset Management Steven Paquette (who was later promoted to vice president), the asset management group developed the design and functionality. This involved constructing temporary walls when needed; evaluating airflow and making upgrades where feasible; and in some situations, introducing ionization into our central HVAC system and enhancing the filtration of our central HVAC systems. We installed a device that emits positive- and negative-charged ions into the air. The ions capture particles through a process called agglomeration to make those particles larger and therefore easier to seize in the filtration of the HVAC system. Ionization also helps deactivate virus particles, so it wages a two-part battle against virus particles in the air. Resident care areas would also include donning and doffing areas for associates in an effort to help maintain infection control.

Preparing for the Vaccine

Leaders Work at All Levels of an Organization.

The reality of the pandemic was that residents and associates would be coming in and out of our communities. We could not feasibly seal our doors and never leave. It was unavoidable that our residents and patients would have to leave the community to visit medical specialists and other facilities.

What we learned was this: when there was widespread transmission of COVID-19 in the metropolitan areas where we operated, there was always a chance COVID-19 would enter our communities simply by virtue of how transmissible it was—and moreover, by the fact that people who did not know they were infected could transmit the virus.

Our belief was that the best way to help curtail the transmission of COVID-19 was through the help of the vaccine. Because then, even if somebody was exposed to the virus, they would be less likely to become infected. And if they did become infected, the vaccine worked tremendously well in preventing severe disease that resulted in hospitalizations.

We could not have been more proud and grateful that our efforts to gain prioritization for our residents and associates were successful. Yet prioritization was just the first step. It took effective coordination to provide access to the vaccine for our residents in every community as quickly as possible. In just under four months, we had offered vaccines to residents and associates in every single community.

There Are Many Ways to Accomplish a Goal.

This was the result of a massive, multi-level campaign from our clinical, corporate, field, and community teams. Brookdale had selected CVS Health° to deliver vaccines to our residents and associates under the federal government's Pharmacy Partnership for Long-Term Care Program. Our program called for CVS Health° to schedule thousands of vaccine clinics and notify Brookdale when each clinic would be held. Our goal was to get our clinics scheduled as quickly as possible, so we were constantly advocating with CVS Health° to accelerate our clinics. We implored them to let us know when there were any last-minute cancellations at other companies' communities so that we could have our residents vaccinated as quickly as possible.

To help make our vaccination clinics successful, we had to educate residents, families, and associates about the benefits of getting vaccinated; manage scheduling in a timely and efficient manner; present updated information about the vaccine as we obtained consents for vaccination from residents or the designated family member of a memory care resident; upload the rosters for the clinics; organize the clinics; and observe the residents after they were vaccinated.

The process wasn't simple, but our vaccine clinics were executed effectively because our associates and team leaders worked hard to create a culture of vaccine acceptance and facilitate the shots in a very small window of time. We understood that vaccines were critically important to help protect our residents and associates.

Andre Wallace stood out as one of our superstars at Brookdale Woodward Estates (Maryland). He took the initiative to lead the way in keeping spirits high, especially when vaccines became available. Andre committed to his role as a cheerleader for our residents, going on to dress up as a boxer to "knock out" COVID-19 during his community's vaccination clinic (see photo gallery). It was amazing to witness such leadership and a genuine caring spirit!

HERO HIGHLIGHTS FROM ANDRE WALLACE

Joined Brookdale Senior Living March 2017; currently maintenance manager, Brookdale Woodward Estates; winner of the Jackie Clegg Courage Cornerstone Award for extraordinary actions during COVID-19

GETTING READY TO KNOCK COVID-19 OUT!

From the first day that a new resident arrives, I make a point of letting them and their family members know that we understand transitions can be challenging. Our goal is to provide them with the same level of care as if they were our own loved ones—because in fact, they are!

As the leader in charge of maintenance for the community, I have learned that it's the little things that show how much we care: Taking the extra steps to make sure a resident's room is comfortable or checking to make sure the television and phone work properly. Even more importantly, we like to anticipate and solve problems before they become an issue. This type of attention to detail and care builds trust and enables us to foster loving relationships with our residents.

This foundation of trust became so important when we had to close the doors of our community to limit COVID-19 from spreading. I was determined to help our residents and my fellow associates in any way I could, helping to uplift people's spirits—including residents who became ill with COVID-19. I was part of a small team that frequently danced, sang songs, played music, and engaged in meaningful conversations with the residents. It was such a unique opportunity to learn even more about them. We talked about where they went to college, what they did after graduating, and other parts of their lives that don't always come up in ordinary times.

We made it through many months of heightened awareness and working to maintain a positive atmosphere until—at last!—vaccines became available. Brookdale Woodward Estates rallied around our vaccination clinics to encourage participation and lift spirits, turning them into positive, encouraging events when they opened.

Our executive director, Joey Estrella, came up with the idea of a sports theme for our first clinic: "We're gonna knock COVID-19 out!" We set up a boxing ring with music blaring, and I was right on board with it! Though I've never boxed, I played football in college, and I couldn't wait to get into the ring at our community. My son helped me create a boxer's costume for the clinic, and with a pretend right jab here and a left hook there, I kept the mood light for our residents and associates as they became vaccinated. I worked the room and connected with anyone who looked frightened or hesitant, and I encouraged them with comments like, "Are you ready? We're gonna be fighters!" and "Are you ready to knock this thing out?" I was able to engage folks because I had already developed their trust, and they knew I was on their side—working for their benefit. *All the efforts we had made under ordinary circumstances paid off during this extraordinary time.*

The calm positivity and expert guidance we received from corporate leadership informed our approach at the community level. We achieved a high level of vaccinations among both residents and associates, and that made an enormously positive impact on the mood of the community. All of these experiences made me a better leader myself. It was a true team effort made possible by the open hearts of our wonderful residents!

I remember another particular moment when our community associates demonstrated how quickly they could respond to an opportunity to help protect our residents. On January 14, 2021, I received a call from CVS Health* about a clinic that would be available within two days' time, which meant our residents and associates would not have to wait longer to get vaccinated. Our Brookdale Clinton

(Mississippi) associates would need to accelerate gathering all resident consent forms and uploading them to the CVS Health* system in order to take advantage of this watershed moment. I immediately said yes, knowing that our team would do everything possible to make the clinic happen, and sure enough—they did!

Within about four hours after being notified of the accelerated date, our local team had secured the necessary resident consent forms and prepared to host the clinic. The residents actually cheered and clapped when the earlier date for the clinic was announced.

In each community, we hosted at least three clinics so that all residents and associates would have the opportunity to receive and complete both shots of either the Pfizer or Moderna COVID-19 vaccine. Under the federal government's Pharmacy Partnership for Long-Term Care Program, each individual state would choose whether the Pfizer or Moderna COVID-19 vaccine would be administered. (Johnson & Johnson vaccines were not part of this program.)

The vaccine had been our primary hope for a return to normalcy, and when it arrived, it was indeed a game changer. We believed that the vaccine would be highly effective, but it was even more effective than we ever imagined. It was only one of many tools in our arsenal, but it was by far the most powerful tool!

We facilitated the administration of 120,000 shots from December 2020 to April 2021. By April, 93 percent of our residents were vaccinated. As a result, we saw a 97 percent reduction in the number of residents who tested positive for COVID-19 over this period. It really was the light at the end of the tunnel. After several more months, we learned that protection from the vaccine apparently decreases over time, which led us to host booster clinics as well.

Without a doubt, though, the vaccine greatly reduced transmission of the virus. We had such a dramatic drop in cases in a short period of time. This led to an increase in morale across our communities, because it enabled residents and patients to see their loved ones again. The chance to hug family members and hold grandchildren again after so much uncertainty was a day many will always remember. The vaccines brought our communities closer to pre-pandemic normal than they had been during the prior year.

It was a wonderful triumph. On behalf of the corporate leadership team and board, we were all deeply grateful for the opportunity to play such an important role in taking steps to help protect our residents and associates—and so proud of the associates who made it happen.

Attitude Is Everything

Looking back at the start of the pandemic, the attitude of the country was primarily fueled by fear. Americans were not used to sheltering in place at home. Likewise, the residents and patients at Brookdale were not accustomed to having limitations placed on the social activities and choices that define the senior living lifestyle. As caregivers to the people who were among the most vulnerable to the virus because of age and chronic conditions, we knew that the widespread fear coming from the outside world would enter our communities if we didn't shift the tone—and fast.

When a resident or patient moves into a Brookdale community, they are entrusting us with care for some or all aspects of their daily living. We provide them up to three meals a day and offer snacks as well. We provide fitness classes, activities, and engagement. We purposely design our communities for seniors, and their health and well-being is our top priority.

Within weeks of the pandemic hitting the US, and for a period of time, our residents were separated from the people they care about most. They were not able to see their children or grandchildren in person. They were unable to visit with friends, even if they lived in the same town, because no one knew whether it was safe at the time.

On top of that, under normal circumstances, the senior living lifestyle is brimming with activity: before the pandemic, we regularly invited performers, artists, and hobbyists to visit our residents and patients in order to engage, entertain, and breathe life into our communities. For a period of time, these social engagements were no longer an option. Our usual exercise groups and activities also had to shift as we sheltered in place and imposed social distancing guidelines. Some of our residents began to feel concerned: How would they maintain peak physical condition so they could keep their immune systems strong and healthy? Many of our usual forms of activity and engagement came to an abrupt halt when we closed our doors to outside visitors and asked residents to shelter in place.

Calm Is Contagious—Stay Positive.

Meanwhile, in order to serve our residents, our associates *have* to leave their homes and enter our communities. They come and go, which creates additional, unavoidable risk. Many residents didn't want to leave the premises to go to their usual doctor or dentist appointments, because they were afraid. Some of our residents' tolerance for risk was rapidly approaching zero—anything above that induced fear.

Given all of the variables and changes happening at once, we needed to calm the collective nerves in our communities. We had to create a sense of normalcy and reorient our residents within the communities, along with their loved ones, in a way that soothed their worries and combatted their feelings of loss and isolation.

Calm is contagious, and we knew it had to start with our Brookdale associates. As we developed new guidelines and protocols for interacting with our residents and patients, we emphasized the increased importance of maintaining a calm and reassuring tone. Our community leaders recognized and responded to this "tone from the top," and our associates followed suit, focusing on fostering positive interactions along the way.

For example, Rosita Taylor, the Health and Wellness director at Brookdale West Boynton Beach, was an extraordinary nurse who brought compassion and care to the next level. Rosita has an innate ability to bring a sense of calm to any situation, even through chaos. Upon hearing the first notice that COVID-19 had arrived in the US, Rosita served her community around the clock for over two weeks to help protect the health and well-being not only of the residents but also her fellow associates.

On most Thursdays, you would find Rosita staffing a themed cart, bringing goodies and snacks throughout her community—in a costume, no less! On Fridays, you would find her in the beauty salon washing hair, going the extra mile to make sure our residents felt loved and beautiful.

Rosita's story is the story of so many of our associates. It didn't take much to convince Rosita and our other associates to adopt a positive attitude. Her dedication and courage is the very essence of her being. She is a team player, an asset to her fellow managers and associates, and a generous spirit with a servant's heart. Rosita's attitude exemplifies the "Everyday Hero" ideal and embodies all four cornerstones of passion, courage, partnership, and trust and the Brookdale mission of enriching the lives of those we serve with compassion, respect, excellence, and integrity.

Attitude is everything, especially during a crisis. We knew that we could not control what happened around us, but we could focus on our own actions, attitudes, and reactions to these events. Focusing on gratitude became the rallying cry for our associates at every level in Brookdale. This built an attitude of resilience that enabled us to lead from the highest level through the pandemic.

To this end, at the suggestion of our Chief Marketing Officer David Cygan, our Marketing team launched a "share your gratitude" campaign on a dedicated webpage,[10] and they encouraged associates, residents, patients, and their loved ones to express thanks for all the joys and blessings they were witnessing and experiencing on a daily basis—honoring the idea that "heroes work here." Associates could see the positive impact their work had on others; residents and patients and their loved ones were uplifted and inspired. Senior Director of Web Marketing Michael McCamish (who was later promoted to vice president of Web Marketing and Technology) and his team were instrumental in leveraging our marketing technology and website to provide up-to-date COVID-19 information to the over six hundred thousand monthly visitors to the website.

Our attitude of gratitude became the circle of life that continually filled our spirits and kept Brookdale thriving through otherwise tumultuous times. The actual stories and words of encouragement became a source of inspiration for corporate team members who were not on the front lines every day but could read the stories—reinforcing the "why" of what we do!

---

10   https://www.brookdale.com/en/thanks.html.

Lessons Learned

Our efforts could be compared to a duck gliding across a lake. On the surface, the duck seems to be drifting gently through the water. When you look below the surface, however, the duck is paddling forward with energy and intent.

At all levels of the organization, our associates were making an extraordinary impact by doing as much as they could to help our residents, patients, and each other.

Given that COVID-19 was the largest public healthcare crisis in our lifetimes, the clinical team took the lead, but it didn't end there. At every opportunity, our associates went the extra mile—coming up with innovative solutions, forming alliances with outside organizations, and maintaining a positive attitude throughout.

The senior leadership team, with the oversight of the board, developed the vision and set the stage for success, and our associates on the ground were the heroes of the pandemic as they executed on that foundation beautifully.

PART II

FAILURE IS NOT AN OPTION

CHAPTER 5

Teamwork to Make the Dream Work

Attracting, Engaging, Developing, and
Retaining the Best Associates

U p until now, I've shared how Brookdale recognized the threat of the COVID-19 pandemic early, created the leadership structure to manage through the crisis, bolstered our cash liquidity to weather the storm, and improved our infection prevention and control. These actions set us up for a successful path forward. Throughout the pandemic, we maintained focus on our North Star: the health and well-being of our residents, patients, and associates.

Now, there's value in further detailing how the critical decisions we made resulted in rapid organizational changes and expert coordination among our associates across communities, agencies, and clinics in more than forty states. With our North Star guiding us, we were able to transform our business model virtually overnight.

At its core, Brookdale is a mission-driven organization: our associates maintain a strong emotional connection to our residents and patients and to each other. Traditionally, our associates, residents, and their loved ones form relationships like an extended family. The bonds between our residents and associates strengthened as we made the decision to limit access to our communities, including for family members and other loved ones. At this point, our associates leaned into an even more important role in supporting our residents and their emotional needs.

To foster this strong bond and our culture of caring, we had to continue our strategy of attracting, engaging, developing, and retaining the best associates. Within Brookdale, we have a saying that goes back to one of our founders, Dr. Thomas Frist Sr.: "Good people beget good people." We had to leverage the specialized skill sets of every member of the Brookdale team, and we wanted to honor their unique contributions and sacrifices.

This is the essence of teamwork.

Uniting Around Our Mission

Every member of the Brookdale team had a special responsibility and an important role in executing on our plan to address the COVID-19 pandemic. We assigned the work required to accomplish our plan according to the specialized roles of our team leaders and associates, and then we delegated decision-making powers to local leaders where appropriate. Team members, regardless of their position in the hierarchy, remained focused on executing their parts of the plan and trusted that other parts of the plan would be handled appropriately. We encouraged everyone to speak up when they needed help. Our expectation was that we would help each other when needed. After all, that's what teams do! Teams also lend a helping hand to each other, and as described, we have plenty of people who raised their hands to offer help in areas outside their roles.

The role of the senior leadership team was to set the strategy, to remove as many barriers as we could, to provide resources for accomplishing the work, to evaluate execution from a high-level view across the organization, and to make adjustments as necessary in order to achieve our goals. The importance of teamwork to the execution of our goals cannot be overstated. Within Brookdale, it's common to hear, "Teamwork makes the dream work."

Build a Team That You Can Trust.

It's also important to note that teams can accomplish what individuals working alone can't. There's strength in numbers, and that power grows exponentially when people unite around a mission.

Think of the mission as a rope and associates as the individual strands of it. When a strand of fiber is pulled tight, it may break. When tens of thousands of strands are woven together into a rope, the rope can bear a much heavier weight without breaking. We wanted and needed our associates to pull together to overcome the obstacles that the pandemic created—for the benefit of our residents and patients and for each other. We needed to help take care of each other.

Brookdale is the largest senior living operator in the nation, with tens of thousands of residents and associates. The complexity of thinking through all the critical issues at play was so intricate that it would be virtually impossible for a single individual to process it all at once. Thinking of each team member as a strand in the woven rope that was our mission made it more manageable. We distributed the work and trusted that everyone would deliver on what mattered most, verifying tasks through quality checks at multiple levels of the organization. Team members regularly surpassed our expectations!

But first we had to aggressively boost our recruiting efforts, hiring tens of thousands of new associates during 2020 alone. We revised our hiring practices to incorporate virtual interviews by way of video conferencing, and we specifically recruited candidates from other companies laying off or furloughing their employees—connecting with hotels and airlines to create an immediate funnel of potential associates who likely had transferrable skills that could apply to senior living. We had to staff entirely new roles, including room service attendants and health screeners, in addition to filling positions that opened up as the result of associates choosing to remove themselves from the workforce for personal reasons. We also made an ardent effort to encourage our former associates who left in good standing to return to work at Brookdale through targeted rehire campaigns.

Even as we focused on attracting new associates to our Brookdale family, we needed to engage, develop, and retain our existing associates. Our teams needed to work harder than ever before, and the stakes were the highest imaginable—literally life and death. Needless to say, it was a stressful time. So we focused on supporting our leaders and associates. We used our "Servant Leader" newsletter for supervisors to provide tools to help prepare our leaders for the challenges they were facing. We used virtual meetings with our community and field leadership and a dedicated intranet section to provide them with necessary information, tools, and techniques. One session included an exercise on deep breathing to demonstrate how as few as ten deep breaths can help a person relax and provide a sense of calm. Deep breathing is an incredible technique for lowering your heart rate, blood pressure, and the amount of the stress hormone cortisol (the body's internal alarm system) that is circulating in your blood.

Cindy Kent, then executive vice president and president of Senior Living (see photo gallery), leveraged her professional network to invite a five-star military general to lead a small working group through how the military manages during war. She also shared the concept of a Corporate Athlete®[11] to help our leaders understand that their ability to lead depends on physical, mental, spiritual, and emotional well-being.

We wanted our associates to focus on self-care and, as the airlines always advise, to put their own oxygen masks on first. This isn't easy for caregivers, whether professional or unpaid family members. It's common for individuals who are providing care to a loved one at home to neglect their own health while doing so. While Brookdale's caregivers aren't necessarily taking care of their own family members, we have a culture of caring, and our associates often form bonds with our residents that can be as strong as the bonds between family members. So we wanted to provide our leaders with tools to understand how important it was to build a focus on self-care, even if it was in five-minute increments! Several executive directors noted that they had used the deep-breathing exercise in their daily meetings and that it was helpful for our community leaders.

At the same time, it's important to remember that we were on the front lines of a global pandemic, and the demands on our associates had never been greater. We knew that residents, patients, fellow associates, and loved ones were counting on us. Together, the

---

11   Corporate Athlete is a registered mark of Johnson & Johnson Health and Wellness Solutions, Inc.

corporate, field, and community teams worked hard to respond to the unique needs of our local communities. This included understanding what barriers our leaders had and trying to remove them, at times making temporary accommodations.

In some cases, we surprised community associates with bags of groceries and household supplies (such as toilet paper—remember when *that* became a priceless commodity!) that were necessary and either difficult to find or hard for associates to acquire. When gas lines in a particular area of the country were incredibly long after a hurricane, we sent a fuel truck to our impacted communities to fill associate cars with gas so they could get to and from work. Our teams were creative in supporting our associates!

The pandemic created tremendous need. Many leaders were provided with development opportunities to participate in cross-functional task forces; others were given stretch assignments. The company Executive Coaching Connections (led by Kathy Green) donated coaching to more than sixty of our executive directors to provide additional support during the pandemic. We focused on helping as much as we could.

Nevertheless, we all experienced our own peaks and valleys during COVID-19. People were enduring challenges at work that made the days very long, and every individual's unique challenges at home only added to the pressure. Our associates were working as hard as they could to meet their families' or their own basic needs. Associates with school-aged children had to immediately figure out new childcare options when schools closed without much notice. Over 70 percent of our associates are women, and many are single parents. As the daughter of a single mom, I understood that struggle intimately.

Managing Personal Challenges

Many of our associates encountered personal and family challenges that arose over the course of time when states enacted a shutdown, and these problems became far more difficult to solve in the midst of society shutting down and hospitals reaching capacity. For me, I had to live up to my responsibilities to the residents, patients, associates, and shareholders of Brookdale while also trying to help save my sister's life.

In 2019, my sister Lisa got very sick; her liver was failing, and she was told that her condition was terminal. After this diagnosis, we had been frantically searching for a way to save her life. Given the severity of my sister's condition during the early stages of the pandemic, I knew that there might be a time when I would not be as present as I ordinarily am as the lead decision maker for Brookdale. I needed help from my Brookdale family.

Because our team is woven so tightly together—and with such a focus around our mission—I knew that I could ask for the help I needed and that we would find a way to stay focused on our North Star of the health and well-being of our residents, patients, and associates while I looked for ways to help my sister. In particular, Anna-Gene O'Neal, a registered nurse who led our home health and hospice agencies, provided me with tremendous emotional support and good advice.

Thanks to the support and connections provided by colleagues with whom I had developed professional relationships, Lisa received a life-saving liver transplant during the early days of the pandemic. I was able to stay intensely focused on my responsibilities at Brookdale while she focused on a full recovery.

PERSONAL PERSPECTIVE FROM CINDY BAIER

Joined Brookdale Senior Living December 2015; currently president, chief executive officer, and board member

MANAGING A PERSONAL CRISIS DURING A GLOBAL PANDEMIC

My family was very small growing up. My parents were both only children, and after my parents divorced, my dad's life didn't include us. In fact, my entire family (my mom, my sister, my mom's parents, and me) could fit around a small table. Losing my grandparents in 1987 was hard, and it was devastating when my mom passed twenty years later. My sister, Lisa, and I have remained extremely close after so much loss. We are the last of my family of origin; our parents and grandparents are all gone, so it was especially important for me to do whatever I could to help.

Just before the start of the pandemic, Lisa became very sick from end-stage liver disease, and her doctors told us that her condition was terminal. This was something I could not accept—there had to be a way to save her! I was torn between fighting to save her life and making the most of our time together. If I had to lose her, I wanted to give her as many experiences as I could in the time that she had left (like taking her to Maui for Christmas, where she could go deep sea fishing).

So when COVID-19 hit, I felt like I was fighting battles on every front imaginable. All of a sudden, I was fighting for our residents, patients, associates, and for Brookdale; at the same time, I was fighting to help save one of the most important people in my life.

Through my work at Brookdale, I had met many brilliant healthcare leaders, including Dr. Wright Pinson, who started Vanderbilt University Medical Center's (VUMC's) liver transplant program. He was my first call when Lisa fell critically ill, and he helped me understand that she was possibly eligible to qualify for a life-saving liver transplant. He patiently explained the process for Lisa to be evaluated and graciously answered the seemingly endless litany of questions we had. We were in a race against time, and the odds were against us.

The bottom line was that if Lisa could make it through the evaluation process successfully, she would be placed on the transplant waiting list. We had hope! The list would routinely change, prioritizing the sickest people. If she made it to the top of the list when there was a suitable match, she would receive a transplant—that is, if she lived long enough.

By the time my sister secured a spot on the transplant list more than six months later, she had become very, very sick; as a result, she was near the top of the list. The question was whether a liver would become available before she ran out of time. My sister had some very close calls while she completed the screening process and prepared for the transplant: her liver wasn't working properly, and this created a lot of complications that required her to be in and out of the hospital as her condition worsened and her doctors worked to stabilize her condition. Drs. Wright Pinson, Seth Karp, and Roman Perri, along with the team at VUMC, were simply amazing. They gave my sister incredible care and helped us understand what we needed to do during each step of the process. We stayed focused on the goal: a successful liver transplant for my sister. We had to succeed!

On April 5, 2020, VUMC called Lisa with the wonderful news they had found a donor. She needed to come to the hospital to go through the preoperative procedures while they flew the liver to VUMC and completed tests to ensure it was suitable for her. It was exciting and scary at the same time. My sister was incredibly brave; I know that she was scared, but she tried really hard not to show it. When they wheeled Lisa off to prepare her for her transplant operation, I had to leave her alone in the hospital because of COVID-19 restrictions. It was the hardest part of the day.

Lisa's surgery was successful, and she went through the initial stages of recovery completely by herself, relying on the support of the VUMC team. Lisa always makes friends easily, and she quickly became a favorite patient of most of the nurses. She did what was asked without complaint and was released from the hospital within just a few days of her surgery. Lisa's husband, Mitch, proved to be a tremendous help as she recovered. I was delighted that Lisa had the care that she needed.

Most importantly, Lisa is now happy, healthy, and thriving. My sister's strength, courage, fighting spirit, and positive attitude inspire me—she is simply amazing! She must have been in tremendous pain, and yet she never complained. She did what she needed to do to get healthy again. I will always be grateful for the amazing people at VUMC who saved her life!

Looking back, I know how incredibly lucky I am to have joined Brookdale. Without Brookdale, I wouldn't have made so many connections with healthcare leaders like Dr. Wright Pinson. If Dr. Pinson hadn't reached out to get to know me, I wouldn't have asked him for help when my sister received her devastating news. *One breakfast meeting between Dr. Pinson and me changed everything. It was the start of a professional relationship that helped save my sister's life. Relationships matter!*

Every time I see Dr. Pinson, I thank him for saving my sister's life, and I remind him that I am committed to helping VUMC save more lives. Until recently, I didn't fully understand the importance of academic medical centers and the resources they require to perform research with the power to improve healthcare. Their work translates into discoveries that help save lives.

The lesson: If it matters enough, you find a way. When failure isn't an option, it is not a question of whether you will succeed; the question is how. Pivot every time you hit a roadblock, or find a way around the roadblock, and commit to finding solutions that produce your desired outcome.

At every level in the organization, individual team members drew strength from being able to reach out to each other and share fears and troubles. There were a lot of tears, some unhealthy coping mechanisms like eating too much or too little, and many, many sleepless nights. Throughout the pandemic, people throughout the world were overwhelmed by the emotions and stress of the pandemic. At Brookdale, we supported our associates by giving them a space to process all of these feelings—providing a shoulder to cry on and a helping hand—that's the true strength of an organization.

Returning to the analogy of the emergency response effort as a conductor and orchestra for a moment, if you think of each team member as a musician within an orchestra, the mission becomes the symphony. The conductor (embodied by the senior leadership team and Emergency Response Center) directs the orchestra, composed of corporate, field, and local contributors. At various points during the symphony, the brass (for instance, clinical and resident services) plays louder than the rest of the orchestra; at other times, woodwinds (suppliers and technicians) or strings (sales and marketing associates) take over, and the brass takes a moment to steady the intensity before the next crescendo. Meanwhile, the percussion (community leadership) section is maintaining the beat in alignment with the conductors.

As one section stands out, another stands back in complement to them, and each member of a section knows how their special notes contribute to the whole. All the while, the audience (residents and their loved ones) are entrusting the orchestra to make beautiful music. They find comfort in the harmony of the many moving parts, which keeps the focus on the health and well-being of all.

Doubling Donations to Assist Associates Affected by COVID-19

> ## Help Provide Associates What They Need to Be Successful.

In an effort to strengthen the fibers of our team, we had to ensure that members of the orchestra were supported. The pandemic created unprecedented challenges for our associates, so we needed to increase our support to them.

The Associate Compassion Fund (ACF) is a nonprofit organization Brookdale established more than a decade ago to support associates during times of need. Team members at every level, corporate or otherwise, can contribute to this charitable fund for associates who temporarily need a helping hand. When an associate cannot afford to travel to a family member's funeral or needs assistance with the cost of the funeral itself, or perhaps has lost their car or incurred some damage to their house as a result of a natural disaster—they can apply to the fund and, if approved, receive either cash or paid time off or some combination of both. The ACF has been an important part of our efforts to give back to our associates, and with the modifications we made during the pandemic, it became a lifeline for many.

When COVID-19 hit, we were especially concerned about the impact on our associates. In recognition of this fact, we changed the criteria so that if an associate experienced an impact from COVID-19, we could provide additional resources. My personal goal was to make sure every associate who needed help and qualified received it.

I asked the executive leadership team and board of directors to join me in supporting our associates however they could. Every ELT member and the vast majority of our board members contributed. Many other associates across the organization did the same.

Donations to the fund more than doubled in size, enabling the ACF to donate PTO to associates who had to pause work or stay home for a variety of reasons. As the pandemic continued, and our associates continued to need help, Brookdale leaders made additional donations to support those in need. The fund also helped associates who were dealing with other temporary, troubling financial circumstances beyond their control. During the pandemic, associates who had used all their PTO could become eligible to apply for support from the fund, depending on their individual circumstances, because of adjustments we made in the guidelines.

HERO HIGHLIGHTS FROM THERESA COCHRAN

Joined Brookdale Senior Living June 2017; currently senior director of Human Resources

CHANGING OUR CHARITY'S GUIDELINES TO SUPPORT OUR ASSOCIATES

One of the most rewarding parts of my job is overseeing Brookdale's Associate Compassion Fund (ACF). Each month, our committee comes together to review applications for assistance from associates who are experiencing temporary financial troubles. We usually review problems related to a weather disaster, house fire, or the death of a loved one. *The work this committee does is extremely meaningful, because we are helping members of our Brookdale family in their time of need.*

These meetings are not without tears as we determine what help can be provided.

The COVID-19 pandemic brought the needs of our associates to a whole new level. We quickly realized that some community associates would need additional emergency financial assistance, based on the need to self-isolate or quarantine for fourteen days when they were exposed to or contracted COVID-19. Our COVID-19 policy required them to remain out of our communities in order to help protect our residents and other associates, and many of these associates had already exhausted their paid time off, which meant they would potentially have no income for a period of time. We needed to take decisive action.

We were able to modify the ACF's guidelines in the face of the pandemic to allow for associates who found themselves in this position to apply for assistance. We also made a change that allowed any associate to donate unused PTO to the fund to provide additional assistance to those directly impacted by having to self-isolate or quarantine.

I was thrilled to see the results of these changes. In 2020 alone—thanks to generous PTO donations from Cindy Baier, the executive team, and other leaders and associates— we were able to provide almost $400,000 in funds to over six hundred associates who had been affected by COVID-19. This good work continued throughout 2021. We were happy to see the number of associates applying for assistance decrease as vaccination rates increased and the country moved past the Delta variant surge.

The small team that handled COVID-19-related requests met weekly, and they started each meeting by reading out loud the thank-you notes we received. What an experience! In the middle of a busy day in corporate America, we were so thrilled to hear from our community associates—whether a medication technician or a dining services associate or others—telling us that the support they received made all the difference in the world to them. *It put things in perspective and reminded us that we were continuing to do meaningful work supporting our associates!*

Brookdale's culture is built on people helping people. The ACF is such an important part of our team efforts, and because of COVID-19 and the work the ACF did to support associates, there is a heightened awareness within our organization of the need for this type of assistance. I hope that sharing our story celebrates our associates and recognizes their incredible contributions. For this reason, all net profits from this book will be donated to the ACF in honor of our everyday heroes. If our North Star is the health and well-being of our residents and associates, then the ACF is the treasure chest reserved especially for our associates who need help as they navigate the journey.

Increasing Recognition through Awards

During the pandemic, the corporate leadership team recognized that our team members were working as hard as they humanly could. The higher a leader's position, the greater the responsibility they had to help others, but nobody had any more or any less important a contribution. The entire leadership team sought to keep all team members motivated at a time when the world was filled with fear and uncertainty. We needed to foster a sense of community and connection, and we needed to show team members at every level that we noticed and appreciated their efforts.

> A Little Recognition Goes a Long Way.

Brookdale has a rich tradition of recognizing associates and leaders, even before the pandemic. Since 2016, Everyday Hero Awards have been made monthly at the community level and quarterly at the corporate and divisional levels. Residents are often involved in selecting community winners, and the recognition is similar to an "Employee of the Month" designation. When the pandemic started, we significantly increased the number of Everyday Heroes honored in each of our communities and at the corporate and divisional levels, recognizing that we were asking so much more from our associates. We have never asked as much from them as we did in 2020, and this was an important way to honor the sheer volume of contributions being made. Between March and June 2020, we had almost six thousand Everyday Heroes winners. In addition to their award certificate, our

Everyday Heroes received a cash award, incremental paid time off, and Brookdale merchandise.

We also wanted to honor the outstanding service and accomplishments on a higher level. One of the first new awards created after I became CEO in 2018 was the Cornerstone Award (see photo gallery): Each year, we selected a total of four recipients from the most accomplished individuals across Brookdale. They were recognized for their deep strength in one of our four cornerstone principles—passion, courage, partnership, and trust.

We created these company-wide awards for two reasons. First, the awards reinforce our culture. By establishing an award for each of the cornerstones, we could shine a light on the essence of our culture as exemplified by those who visibly demonstrated our principles. Second, naming the awards for accomplished leaders who have strengthened Brookdale's foundation and made a lasting impact on Brookdale's success over time honors them.

We named our "passion" award after Bill Sheriff. Bill was CEO of Brookdale Senior Living and its predecessor company American Retirement Corporation (ARC) from 1984 to 2013. Bill was the longest-serving company CEO, and his dedicated service was evident to all.

We named the "courage" award after the Honorable Jackie Clegg. During Jackie's fourteen years on Brookdale's board, she demonstrated principled leadership and tremendous courage.

We named the "trust" award for Jim Seward. Jim served on Brookdale's board for eleven years. During that time, he demonstrated extraordinary oversight of our financial reporting, planning, and analysis. Jim looked at issues from every angle and always focused on what was best for Brookdale. Jim built trust with his colleagues, and his prescient insights on the concerning events in China made a critical difference in the earliest days of the pandemic.

The fourth Cornerstone Award is the award for "partnership." We are reserving the naming of this award for a future time, but this award is equally important.

Creating the Cornerstone Awards was a way to interweave the cultural pillars of our company with our associates' contributions in mutual celebration. Every year, the Cornerstone Awards are important, but the intensity of 2020 made our associates' contributions so much more meaningful.

Since the Cornerstone Awards are granted to the most outstanding contributors across the entire company, there are only four of them. This recognition represents the highest honor bestowed by Brookdale.

2020 CORNERSTONE AWARD RECIPIENTS:

- *Rosita Taylor*, Health and Wellness director at Brookdale West Boynton Beach (Florida), received the Bill Sheriff Passion Cornerstone Award. In accepting this honor, Rosita said that she felt a great deal of support at Brookdale, that she never felt she was alone.

- *Andre Wallace*, Maintenance manager at Brookdale Woodward Estates (Maryland), received the Jackie Clegg Courage Cornerstone Award. Andre had a great way of defining leadership as he accepted his award:

"To be a leader, you have to be someone you want to follow!"

- *Robyn Moore*, district director of Clinical Services, received the Cornerstone Award for Partnership. Robyn talked about teamwork in accepting her award: "I am so empowered by Brookdale's culture: It gives me all the tools I need to do the best work I can. I am so thankful for all our nurses. We are such a team together, and I am so grateful we have all those people to work with and partner with."

- *Terri Bliesner*, a nurse at Brookdale Home Health in Seattle (Washington), received the Jim Seward Trust Cornerstone Award. Family was the theme of her remarks. She talked about the importance of quality and ownership in her job, noting that she treats her patients like family, and that makes decisions easier.

And then there is the Servant Heart Award, a special award we created during the COVID-19 pandemic. Traditionally, we don't provide special recognition for senior leadership team members for the extraordinary contributions that they make. We expect much from our leaders; sacrifice for the greater good is part of the duty of leadership. With privilege comes great responsibility. Even so, the pandemic required sacrifices that were previously unimaginable. So many of our leaders were working around the clock with such intensity and pouring so much of their hearts into the business in order to help protect our residents, patients, associates, and Brookdale. These individuals were making enormous sacrifices for the good of others.

I wanted to let them know how much their contributions mattered to me, and I wanted them to have a symbol of the difference their efforts made. Initially we established the award as a way of recognizing members of the ECC and other corporate leaders who led the initial response to the pandemic. Then we expanded the Servant Heart Award to include outstanding contributions made by field and community–level leadership like executive directors, Health and Wellness directors, and Sales directors whose efforts made a positive impact throughout COVID-19.

We also included a number of individuals whose sacrifice or contribution went well beyond the call of duty, recognizing:

- individuals who assisted us in accelerating our residents receiving life-saving vaccines;

- one individual who stepped up to fly his personal airplane to deliver critically needed supplies to our communities when our traditional delivery services fell behind;

- executive coaches who donated their time to support our executive directors during the pandemic;

- advisors who helped us complete a mission-critical lease restructuring;

- companies who contributed PPE and other supplies to help us fight COVID-19;

- individuals who made an extraordinary contribution to our advocacy efforts for the Provider Relief Fund to help save the industry; and

- other brave individuals who headed straight into harm's way when everyone else was evacuating—heroes who protected our Louisiana communities after we evacuated our residents and associates as Hurricane Laura ravaged Lake Charles, Louisiana, and surrounding areas, and those who stayed in these communities during the hurricane to repair damage as soon as the storm had passed so that our residents could return home as quickly as possible.

While not all of these individuals were Brookdale associates, they earned a Servant Heart Award for their extraordinary service and will always be part of our extended family.

Altogether, we awarded more than 1,700 Brookdale leaders with a Servant Heart Award. For our associates, each of these recipients received a special bonus, a letter from me, and a crystal award in the shape of a heart commemorating their service and memorializing their unique contributions as we battled the pandemic. For individuals outside of the company, we hosted a virtual award ceremony and provided them with a crystal award in the shape of a heart. This little memento had such a positive impact. We heard from many recipients that receiving this award was one of the most meaningful moments in their lives.

Recognition is critically important because it's so inspirational, both to those who receive it and to those around them who see that extraordinary effort is appreciated and rewarded. And so during 2020, I sent hundreds of handwritten thank-you notes to associates who went above and beyond the call of duty (see photo gallery). Each note was specific about the contribution that the associate had made and included a "CEO Coin" that had our cornerstones of passion, courage, partnership, and trust on one side, and our mission ("to enrich the lives of those we serve with compassion, respect, excellence, and integrity") and vision ("to be the nation's first choice in senior living") on the other.

Great Assistants Improve Leaders.

My assistant, Linda DeVault, was by my side throughout all these efforts to increase recognition and always rose to the occasion. As our senior leadership team came up with ideas, she would help make them happen. Executive calendars are notoriously challenging. Standing at the helm of the largest senior living operator during a once-in-a-century pandemic took this to a whole new level! Linda is an excellent troubleshooter and helped me stay focused on what mattered most—not the least of which were the ongoing celebrations of our team members' unique contributions. Every minute of the day was as productive as possible thanks to Linda's efforts and those of so many associates like her.

Enhancing Our Retention Efforts

As a leader, others say that I have high expectations but am fair. Fairness is important, so our leaders worked hard to evaluate decisions through the lens of fairness. We wanted team members to feel not only valued but also that they were being treated equitably. We went to great lengths to maintain and improve retention of our corporate and community-level leadership during the worst of the pandemic. Given the increased demands placed on our associates, we worked hard to balance their needs with those of our residents, patients, and shareholders. Being fair was entirely appropriate and critically necessary.

We also went to great lengths to treat our hourly associates fairly. This included redeploying workers whenever possible as jobs were paused by the pandemic, increasing recognition, and continuing to provide appropriate compensation and benefits. At the beginning of the pandemic, we realized that our clinical leaders were mission critical because this was a public health crisis of major proportions. Therefore, we made it a top priority to focus on recognizing our nurses at the height of the pandemic. During this time, we implemented a one-time bonus for our licensed nurses in recognition of the rapidly increasing market demand for skilled nurses and the critical importance of these associates to our success.

We also needed to recognize the significant impact the pandemic had for our leadership so we could compensate them fairly. Regardless of the position that someone has in the company, Brookdale makes it a point to treat them appropriately for the purposes of retaining our best workers—and because it's the right thing to do.

Early in the pandemic, we announced that we would guarantee bonuses to our leaders for a short period as we charted the path through the pandemic and established targets that recognized our new operating environment. This included both corporate and community-level leaders—but excluded Brookdale's top officers. We needed our leaders to focus on our North Star of the health and well-being of our residents, patients, and associates without worrying about the financial loss they would otherwise personally incur because of the impact of the pandemic. With the help of our visionary Finance team and a decisive effort to batten down the hatches, we knew we could follow through on this promise.

The vast majority of our associates are hourly wage earners. If you're earning an hourly wage, your compensation depends on how many hours you work and is completely independent of whether or not the company does well in a given year.

For our salaried leadership, a portion of their compensation is tied to the company's financial performance and progress on strategic initiatives—also known as incentive compensation. At the community level, most incentive compensation is a quarterly or annual bonus. Above the community level, leaders may receive bonuses or a combination of bonuses and long-term incentive compensation (such as restricted stock or restricted stock units).

The moment the pandemic became a reality for Brookdale, I knew that the financial portions of our bonus plans were unlikely to result in any payment. Almost immediately, our equity value dropped by about 80 percent, which meant that the corporate and field leaders—those whom we needed to execute our pandemic strategy—were going to lose a significant portion of their compensation through no fault of their own. Even though our associates are mission driven, they still have responsibilities to provide for themselves and their loved ones, and this was concerning to many.

We knew that we needed to take action to retain our leaders. The performance of our company relies on people serving people. We build our business one relationship at a time, and it starts from the top. We needed to help protect our people so that they could help protect our residents, patients, and ultimately, our shareholders.

For the first quarter—at a time when many other companies were furloughing workers, cutting bonuses, and reducing pay—we instead maintained pay and guaranteed bonuses. We announced internally that we would pay bonuses based on our performance for the first quarter, as compared to the budget. For the second quarter, we shared with those affected that we would fully guarantee bonuses. For the second half of the year, we established new targets that reflected our best understanding of the impact of the pandemic.

We believed that it was important to be fair to our leaders and recognized that our shareholders had seen very significant declines in our stock price as a result of the pandemic. These decisions balanced the needs of our associates and leaders with the needs of our shareholders. I believe that taking early action served us well.

Lessons Learned

As we set out to attract, engage, develop, and retain the best leaders and associates to manage the pandemic, we found innovative ways to achieve each of these goals.

First, we needed to unite around a common mission: we knew we would not withstand the pressure of the pandemic as individual threads, but we could get through this if we united around a common woven rope—our mission.

Next, we had to ensure we could attract enough people to perform the incremental work needed on a daily basis. It's fair to say that virtually everyone was impacted by the pandemic in some way. I will always be grateful! for the leaders and associates who stepped up to help others and for the critical role that our Associate Compassion Fund played in supporting our associates in need.

We also increased our engagement efforts by recognizing the outstanding contributions being made by our associates and leaders at every level of Brookdale. Lastly, we established a unique response to compensate our associates fairly for their efforts in order to improve retention as the pandemic turned into a marathon.

It's a well-known fact that heat and pressure turns ordinary carbon into a diamond. By banding together and valuing the importance of hard work, problem-solving, and each team member's responsibility to the whole, Brookdale associates at every level contributed to our mission and helped us withstand the greatest pressure ever placed on our team. Looking back, it was through these strengths we developed as a team that we shine even brighter now.

CHAPTER 6

Winning Locally

Balancing Our Central Command Response
to Empower Local Leadership

Brookdale is the largest senior living operator in the industry, and we take responsibility to help lead the entire industry by example. Throughout the pandemic, we shared our knowledge by speaking at our trade organization's operational and clinical panels.

Our industry is largely dominated by "mom-and-pop" operators who manage one to five communities. Our sheer size gave us an enormous advantage to leverage resources as well as a responsibility to do more as the industry leader. We can afford to invest resources into our clinical efforts, including research into how best to care for residents and how to help make the challenges of aging easier for seniors. Our capabilities are unmatched by any other senior living operator in the nation.

On the other hand, our size meant that we had to respond to the pandemic in over seven hundred communities every day. Brookdale's operations are complex, and we needed to be nimble. As a result, we leaned into our established strategy of winning locally, first formalized in February 2018.

At that time, Brookdale had been focused on competing nationally and centralized many decisions in our corporate offices, so our new winning-locally strategy represented a significant shift, delegating greater decision-making powers to our local communities. On certain matters, the corporate team could never respond as quickly and suitably as the local leadership, which was familiar with local market conditions and the unique preferences of our residents within individual communities.

To win locally, we had to determine what decisions needed to be centralized for consistency throughout the company and what decision-making powers could be delegated to the communities. Having simplified our operations in the years leading up to the pandemic gave us a great advantage: corporate leadership was laser focused on what we do best across the nation, deferring to local leadership whenever possible on decisions that were unique to the local market or community. The hard work of refocusing Brookdale was largely behind us and beginning to pay off.

We were hitting our stride, well positioned to win locally, when the pandemic hit.

Strengthening Our Corporate Position through Relationships

Brookdale has a broad continuum of care. Historically, we've operated many different types of communities, including one of the largest home health and hospice businesses in the nation. Residents and patients have options for independent living, assisted living, memory care, skilled nursing, private duty services, and access to home health, hospice, and outpatient therapy—in our communities and through third-party or venture partner services operating across more than forty states. This breadth and depth of services has given us an insider's perspective into the healthcare continuum unmatched by any other senior living provider.

Over the last few years, the healthcare industry has begun to transition from a pay-for-service (paying for a single visit to see a doctor) to a value-based care model (paying for a service—like a hip replacement—at a composite rate that includes all of the services necessary, regardless of complications). These changes will undoubtedly lead to improved health for individuals and community populations at a lower cost.

Senior living operators can help improve the health and well-being of our residents, because we deliver good nutrition, encourage exercise, and promote an active and engaged lifestyle, among other things. Healthy lifestyles may help reduce the cost of healthcare for those responsible for paying for it (for example, the government through Medicare). At the same time, healthy lifestyles may help reduce risk for healthcare providers (like hospitals). Innovative care options (like telehealth and hospital at home) have grown in popularity over the years in response to changing conditions in healthcare. Many of these innovative programs have been particularly helpful for seniors.

As a result, Brookdale took the initiative to pilot innovative new care models in some of our communities prior to the pandemic. We wanted to see if we could help improve our residents' lives by supporting the value-based care goals of nearby healthcare providers and hospitals. These providers are sometimes willing to take on added risk if they can better gauge the full scope of care required for a specific service (like a knee replacement), including the cost of patient support systems. As the largest senior living operator, we have the unique ability to work closely with hospital systems and serve as an additional resource when a patient is recovering from surgery, for instance. A patient can stay with Brookdale while they gain the strength and abilities to transition back to their home life, even if for only a week or two. In exchange, the hospitals are paid a set amount by payers (like insurance carriers) for that specific procedure and take responsibility for the quality of care, health outcomes, and the total cost for the episode of care.

In other words, there has been greater integration between healthcare entities and senior living in recent years, and this represents a unique opportunity. Whereas Brookdale and others within the healthcare industry used to operate more independently of one another, we started taking the very first steps to operate more interdependently in the year or two leading up to the pandemic. Given Brookdale's focus on innovation, we were able to capitalize on these accelerating changes in healthcare.

Innovative care models became a key factor in Brookdale's success in weathering the storm of the pandemic. Gaining more experience conducting telehealth appointments placed us at the forefront of our industry. Moreover, hospital-at-home options enabled doctors to conduct remote patient monitoring (through blood pressure, pulse oximeters, etc.), even when someone wasn't in a hospital bed, for example. In some cases, a patient is better off recovering from specific illnesses or surgeries at home with their loved ones, or in a senior living community with caring associates, while continuing to be monitored via technology.

Another excellent opportunity that arose through the course of the pandemic was the creation of a joint venture with HCA Healthcare—one of the nation's leading healthcare organizations—through the sale of 80 percent of our interest in Brookdale Health Care Services (BHS).

This transaction occurred in mid-2021 after many months of hard work by Executive Vice President of Corporate Development and President of Continuing Care Retirement Communities Todd Kaestner; Senior Vice President of Corporate Development Teddy Hillard; Chief Compliance Officer John Blackwood; and Senior Vice President, Chief Accounting Officer Dawn Kussow and other corporate teams; as well as Anna-Gene O'Neal and our other leaders from BHS. It was an opportunity to capitalize on the changing healthcare trends while continuing to provide our residents with access to high-quality services. It was also a way to provide additional liquidity for Brookdale, a continuing need after what we'd spent combating COVID-19. This transaction didn't change the services we offered; it transitioned ownership of the vertical from a subsidiary operation to a partnership while our residents maintained access to quality services. For our shareholders, it provided the opportunity for our retained 20 percent interest to grow more quickly.

Strengthening the corporate position of a company by leveraging assets is a major step for helping to ensure success down the line—a win-win for all. We may be only in the early stages of the changes underway in healthcare, but our corporate strategy has given us an advantage far beyond other senior living providers.

Differentiating Services for Success

Many of Brookdale's corporate functions act as "Centers of Excellence." These departments provide oversight, functional expertise, and best practices for our community leaders, helping to elevate offerings for residents. The Centers of Excellence regularly answer questions, review policies and protocols, and provide tools for community use.

> ## Accentuate What Differentiates Your Brand.

There are three primary areas where I believe Brookdale is differentiated with best-in-class offerings: clinical expertise, memory care capabilities, and emergency response.

1. CLINICAL EXPERTISE

Having strong clinical expertise at the corporate level elevated our ability to deliver essential supplies and to support our communities with effective infection prevention and control protocols. Our community leaders and associates have expressed how much they appreciated being part of Brookdale during the pandemic, because we were able to assist them with essential needs that would have been extremely difficult to manage without corporate support. This included the PPE that our procurement team sourced when it was largely unavailable and the protocols our corporate teams created with the most updated information available to help keep our residents safe and engaged.

HERO HIGHLIGHTS FROM KAREN PECK, RN

Joined Brookdale Senior Living October 1999; currently East Division vice president of Clinical Services

BREATHE, JUST BREATHE

My journey over these many months of the pandemic has been a roller coaster ride, to say the least. On February 28, 2020, I received a call from Kim Elliott, senior vice president of Clinical Operations (now chief nursing officer), explaining the need for a conference call to discuss COVID-19 outbreaks.

At that time, there were no communities in the East Division affected, but the situation quickly changed as COVID-19 started spreading across the United States. Suddenly I was on video conference calls fourteen hours a day, seven days a week to discuss and help prevent and manage transmission of emerging positive cases. Communities and associates were looking to me for the best direction I could possibly give them. My response: "Let's get on a call to walk through this."

Many of our associates were scared, anxious, and overwhelmed. My mantra to the teams was "Breathe, just breathe." I assured them that they were going to be okay and that we had a myriad of resources to help them through the challenges.

Fortunately, Brookdale had already created the Emergency Command Center. Every day, sometimes multiple times a day, we gathered more information about this powerful and relentless virus. Because the information changed so rapidly, it was important for me to quickly interpret the information, communicate it to our teams, and remain available for the myriad of questions that kept coming.

Because the hospital systems and skilled nursing facilities were overloaded, we eventually set up our own special resident care units in some communities to isolate the residents. Thankfully, our Procurement team worked behind the scenes to obtain equipment and PPE. Our Asset Management team worked tirelessly to help build these units with necessary barriers, entrances and exits, and systems to help control air flow, among other tasks.

Various states interpreted the CDC guidelines differently—so much so that there were multiple calls with health departments and epidemiologists so we could all agree on how to proceed. Many professionals looked to Brookdale for advice. A number of health departments complimented our isolation units and remarked that our skilled nursing facilities were better than any they had ever seen. Training, training, and more training was the norm: retraining was constant as we learned of new protocols and strains.

Throughout these challenges, my role was to inform and inspire the teams, remain upbeat, and maintain a sense of humor. After many days and many more months of staying strong, my emotional well-being was challenged: I was not sleeping, not eating correctly, not exercising, and crying more than ever. Thankfully, I learned that shedding tears and showing my vulnerability helped the teams—it validated that it's okay to cry and be scared.

As leaders, we play an important part in empowering people, providing them with tools to carry on, and giving them permission to be real and vulnerable. This virus is not gone, and as each variant comes, we learn more about how to manage it. We still need to communicate, listen, and share resources and tools as we continue retraining on our protocols.

We also need to find new ways to take better care of ourselves. The stress and exhaustion of all these months have taken their toll. We have hope in the knowledge that this virus is not going away but is likely to become less threatening over time—crucial hope for a quieter future and a return to some semblance of pre-pandemic normal.

I am happy to say I am sleeping better, eating better, and exercising a little more these days. I am making a conscious effort to spend more time with family and friends, albeit in smaller group settings.

I have never experienced anything like this pandemic. However, I'm grateful that I work for a company that provides support and resources to help us through. I am so grateful for all our associates who have worked so diligently to help keep our residents and associates safe.

This experience has taught me the vital need to communicate well and validate associates' feelings. I, for one, will continue with my mantra: "Breathe, just breathe."

Together, we will persevere.

2. MEMORY CARE

Brookdale's Alzheimer's and dementia care capabilities also differentiate us from other senior living operators. Alzheimer's disease and other dementias can be especially challenging for persons living with dementia, their loved ones, and caregivers alike. Thus dementia care communities offer an ideal environment for people living with various forms of dementia. Under the leadership of Senior Director of Dementia Care Program Juliet Holt Klinger, Brookdale has built an industry-leading program. Juliet has been a true pioneer in the dementia care space for thirty-five years. During her fifteen years at Brookdale, she has focused on programmatic standards that uphold person-centered care principles such as consistent assignment of care partners and putting the residents before the task.

With us, residents experience apartment-style living that feels like home, surrounded by their friends and nurturing associates. Our dementia care program features a person-centered approach that's designed to help residents feel a sense of belonging and purpose while also preserving their sense of self. We accomplish this through a commitment to consistent care assignments, relying on the same associates to assist an individual resident whenever possible. Our secure dementia care environments have been specifically designed to support the losses experienced with dementia. Residents are able to participate in our daily path of engagement, which encourages them to build on current skills through evidence-based programming. Brookdale's team of divisional dementia care managers provides an extra layer of support and expertise to each specialized community.

As part of our focus on dementia care, Brookdale has consistently supported a leading organization seeking a cure for Alzheimer's disease. During 2020, in the midst of serving and supporting tens of thousands of residents, patients, and associates during the pandemic, we maintained our commitment. With the efforts of our associates, residents, and vendors, we raised almost $1.2 million for the Alzheimer's Association's Walk to End Alzheimer's[12] (see photo gallery). That amount is slightly higher than what was raised in each of the previous two years, which is a noteworthy feat considering this was done in the midst of a global pandemic! Including this contribution, Brookdale has raised more than $19 million since 2008 to support the care, support, and research efforts of the Alzheimer's Association, and we are focusing on raising *more!*

3. EMERGENCY RESPONSE

The third area where Brookdale differentiates itself (based upon our national scale) is in our emergency response to natural disasters such as wildfires and hurricanes. It would be hard to overstate the complexity of operating a senior living community during such a natural disaster.

Because of its size and scale, Brookdale has developed policies and procedures and an infrastructure that can respond rapidly to emergencies faced in any given year. Brookdale maintains industry-leading disaster planning in large part due to significant corporate and regional management support. Brookdale has the expertise, processes, and scale to shelter in place as a first choice, and this allows us to provide a level of comfort for our residents during a very stressful time. In the rare instances when evacuation is required, we use carefully tailored plans and extensive resources to temporarily relocate residents as safely as possible, often to another Brookdale community. Resources such as company-owned portable generators, strong vendor relations covering multiple aspects of a variety of potential disasters, and a cross-functional group of corporate and regional leaders who can quickly

---

12   The Walk to End Alzheimer's is owned by the Alzheimer's Disease and Related Disorders Association, Inc.

make decisions to support the teams directly serving our residents make Brookdale an industry leader in disaster response.

We're routinely scanning for potential natural disaster threats to our residents, and when a situation arises, we follow the lead of local authorities as we discern whether it is safer for our residents to shelter in place or evacuate. When evacuation becomes necessary, our associates transfer residents and their pets to a new location and provide a continued high level of service but in a different setting. During evacuations, our associates frequently leave their own loved ones behind to travel with our residents and their pets as they work to help provide appropriate nutrition, hydration, and medication assistance in addition to engaging activities, personal care, and suitable lodging.

Given that many residents require walkers or wheelchairs, the logistics of transporting residents can be complicated. Many residents need assistance boarding buses (either our community buses or buses that Brookdale charters to support evacuation). In addition, our community associates usually transport the residents' durable medical equipment in a separate box truck that follows the resident buses. In most cases, we evacuate to another Brookdale community, but when this option is not available, we may rent part of a hotel to house our residents, their pets, and our associates, all the while striving to provide the level of service that our residents are accustomed to experiencing.

During ordinary times, managing the threat of hurricanes, wildfires, and other natural disasters is a challenging ordeal, as one might imagine; navigating these threats while helping to keep residents and associates safe during the COVID-19 pandemic would have been unimaginable—had we not already had such substantial experience in handling other types of crises.

Executive Vice President of Community Operations Kevin Bowman, who during the pandemic served as our West Division vice president, has provided great leadership for the division during a number of natural disaster situations. He, along with Division Vice Presidents Laura Fischer and Ben Ricci (both of whom were promoted to these roles during the pandemic) and Vice Presidents of Administration Yvonne McLaughlin and Roger Thiele, help maintain the focus of our field and community teams on the health and well-being of our residents and associates during a crisis.

For example, it was no small feat evacuating a community that was already sheltering in place during the Scotts Valley, California, wildfires in August 2020. And in a separate event in February 2021, the Texas severe winter storm Uri brought a unique challenge that we hadn't previously experienced. An extended period of extreme cold shut the electric grid down, and precipitation made the roads too icy for most people to travel. Thankfully, our communities were able to shelter in place with the help of generators and emergency supplies of food, water, and medicine.

Even so, as the deep freeze continued, we needed to obtain additional food, water, and medicine, but our suppliers were not able to deliver as usual due to the treacherous conditions. Our residents were depending on us, so we needed to find a solution. Leaders throughout Brookdale joined together in the search for creative solutions. Zade Watts, the executive director of Brookdale Champions in Houston (Texas), contacted a group of Jeep enthusiasts within the local area. Members of this club helped deliver much-needed supplies, and the board was impressed by the resourcefulness of our teams in coordinating the response to help keep our residents safe and warm during a crisis that shut down most businesses for about five days. Between our Emergency Response Center communicating with our field and community teams and our local leadership working with our associates to deliver exceptional care, this was a true example of winning locally that made all the difference for our residents. The board couldn't have been more proud!

Corporate Guardrails and Community Decision Rights

A key to winning locally was empowering our community leaders with greater autonomy within bounds, while also providing them with access to the capabilities that differentiated us nationally. When combined with our local points of difference, this would allow our teams to win locally by providing them with a compelling offering that allowed us to demonstrate why their local Brookdale community was different and better than its competitors.

> ## Have Clear Decision Rights.

Think of this in terms of guardrails: Our corporate infrastructure sets broad parameters in order to create consistently high standards across the company. Corporate, for instance, is responsible for determining which consistent, clinical quality measures are to be implemented company wide, along with other important matters of compliance, like person-centered care for our memory care facilities. From there, each community has flexibility within those bounds to build custom experiences—tailoring their pricing and sales options (within pre-established guidelines), unique and special dining experiences, creative marketing campaigns using tools provided by our national marketing experts, and community events and activities—based on the unique culture and needs of the residents.

The net result for local leaders is that they're able to attain creative discretion, differentiated service offerings, and better crisis management tools when facing events that may impact their communities. For Brookdale residents, the result is a higher-quality, smoother, and more delightful experience overall—an effect that could never be achieved solely from a top-down corporate edict or from a local community operating in isolation.

Our hierarchical structure operates as a traditional field management structure where communities are supported by district leadership, districts get assistance from regional leadership, and on up the chain to me. Our field management organization is complemented by our Centers of Excellence (like Clinical, a vertical within the corporate leadership team), which provide our communities with thought leadership and best practices.

Creating guardrails allows enough flexibility for communities to win locally while maintaining effective and appropriate controls.

Pivoting Sales and Marketing

One of the most significant decisions that we had to make during the pandemic was whether and when to close our communities to visitors—and that included closing them to prospective residents. This was of enormous consequence, because we traditionally need to attract about half of our population size in volume annually in order to maintain our occupancy. Our local leaders worked hard to come up with creative approaches that would lessen a potentially devastating impact to Brookdale's bottom line—and enable community introductions, virtual or otherwise, to interested parties.

> ## Focus Intently on Your Customers—without Them, You Have No Business.

Our local Sales leaders stepped up to the task and met prospects on the porches of their communities—socially distanced and masked, naturally!—or set up tents in the parking lot to hold socially distanced visits with interested residents and their loved ones. Senior Vice President of Sales Rick Wigginton and our Sales team continued to innovate by hosting virtual visits and sending personalized video messages to help build a connection between Brookdale and our prospects. Amazingly, thousands of residents decided to move into our communities without even being able to fully tour, and we slowly gained momentum in rebuilding our occupancy. By March 2021, we were able to report occupancy improvements, starting a multiple-month trend of increasing our resident census.

HERO HIGHLIGHTS FROM RICK WIGGINTON

Joined Brookdale Senior Living May 2019; currently senior vice president of Sales

SALES AS A GATEWAY TO SERVE

A typical sales process looks something like this: build rapport and discover needs, offer a solution to address those needs, address any objections, and close. In senior

---

housing sales, however, the buying decision involves a much greater emotional weight.

The initial inquirer is usually an adult child starting the search on behalf of their parent. It's emotional and hyperpersonal. Often there has been a loss that drives the need to explore a senior living community. Maybe one parent has died, leaving the other alone; Dad's cognitive abilities are declining; Mom's failing eyesight means she can no longer drive; there's some household task that's getting harder. The emotions can be heavy.

Many times, the older person doesn't know that the kids have started exploring a move for them. So once you've been able to help the child appreciate that moving to a Brookdale community can help Dad live better, you've still got to convince Dad, who has no intention of leaving his current house. The daughter tours; the other siblings tour; Dad tours. A great deal of engagement is necessary to get this important decision right.

Brookdale Sales team members are known for their excellent customer service skills. Many of our associates see their role as a calling to help loved ones solve the challenges of aging. On a typical visit, we sit with a prospect, side by side on a couch or at a table with a cup of coffee, and talk intimately with an adult daughter, for instance, about the loss of her mom and the need for a higher level of support for her dad. This type of in-person sharing gives people a true sense of hope.

As the prospect tours the community, meets staff and fellow residents, and starts to understand the next steps, they quickly warm up to the idea that life really can be better lived as a resident in a thriving community. Experiencing the community in person—hearing laughter, tasting the food, and asking the staffers important questions—has always been considered essential to the Sales team as we meet potential customers. Moving into a community usually requires selling a home, so naturally new residents want to visit and meet other people who live there before they move in. We had no idea that none of this would be possible for a time.

The COVID-19 pandemic dramatically and abruptly stopped almost all in-person visits virtually overnight. The brusquely presented challenge to solve became, *How do you help people connect and "feel all the feels" that are so important in such an emotional decision when you can't meet in person?*

With necessity being the mother of invention, we quickly reinvented our means of engagement. In some markets, we were able to meet on the front porch of a community with social distancing and "tour" by looking through windows. In others, we were able to enter the community with prospects but had to head directly to a designated area away from current residents. And in many markets, for a long while, video was the extent of being able to "see" each other. It was significantly better than having a telephone conversation, but for many seniors, for their adult children, and even for our sales professionals, learning how to use video on a mobile device or computer was a unique challenge.

Through trial and error, we developed ways to leverage technology in order to create experiences that enabled searching prospects to get a sense of community. Rather than engaging only with the Sales associate, we trained other associates and resident volunteers to speak with prospects on mobile devices, helping to answer questions and offer words of encouragement along the way. It was so much more important than walking through the building with an iPhone˚ showing real estate on a screen.

One of our assets as a team is a common understanding that sales is our gateway to serve.

As a result of this caring approach, Brookdale communities were able to welcome thousands of new neighbors even during the most challenging months of the pandemic. Not being able to tour in person was hard for our prospects. It was hard for our teams as well. But as the song goes, people who need people are the luckiest people in the world.

By keeping our focus on people front and center, we were able to adapt, pivot, and repivot over and over to serve our mission.

Our communities did an extraordinary job supporting the Sales teams. Our Sales professionals quickly learned new skills in technology, and residents helped us find creative ways to engage, since they had an interest in strong occupancy for maintaining vibrant communities.

Our executive directors and department leaders and staff knew that the challenges of aging didn't press

> pause for people out in the world during the pandemic.
> The needs were real, and we knew we could help—and
> we did. We made life better for a lot of families during a
> tumultuous time.

Likewise, our local Sales teams developed innovative approaches to work around the halting of in-person marketing events that are ordinarily executed. These events help make Brookdale more familiar to potential residents, their loved ones, and also to third-party referral sources, such as healthcare professionals who are traditionally called on to make patient referrals to our communities.

Community Sales professionals work within corporate marketing guidelines to ensure that they highlight the best their community has to offer. For example, photography is important to showcase the quality of life residents can experience. Operating with clear branding guidelines, community leaders are able to showcase real community events and activities as they occur, which in turn helps prospects see themselves being able to enjoy community life among friends. This helps our local Sales professionals make a strong connection with interested prospective residents and exposes them to the culture of a community.

Throughout the pandemic, our Marketing teams developed campaigns to demonstrate a given community's focus on the health and well-being of our residents—for instance, through hydration, nutrition, fitness classes, and mental health. We also pivoted our monthly, in-person, continuing education program for clinical professionals. This program is specifically for clinical professionals who provide patient healthcare in the local markets, and we usually host the program in our communities as a way for these clinical professionals to get to know us. Because of the pandemic, we shifted to virtual sessions and added topics about COVID-19. We received great interest from this change from healthcare professionals, increasing attendance to these virtual events to record levels in 2020. Sales professionals from local communities in turn built deeper relationships with more healthcare professionals, illustrating how Brookdale can deliver a higher quality of life to patients they support.

During COVID-19, our Marketing teams shifted to more engaging videos to capture life in the communities in an effort to focus on virtual presentations and engagement.

> ## Empower People as Close to the Customer as You Can.

Our corporate Marketing team took a thoughtful approach to monitor that our messaging fit the tone of the broader public sentiment. Even when our communities were closed to visitors, our senior living advisors from our centralized Connection Center answered questions from thousands of prospects who completed web forms or called for information. Our local teams customized the tools created by the corporate Marketing teams to connect within their local market. They also built relationships with prospects who sought additional information about the community. We knew that associates at our communities were selfless in caring for our residents. So we felt it was appropriate to thank our associates and ask others to thank our everyday heroes as well through campaigns. This authentic content highlighted our brand by recognizing the genuine gratitude others had for our associates and residents during a global pandemic. While corporate Marketing leaders could provide updated information on COVID-19 and educational content to attract prospects, local Marketing leaders focused on sharing gratitude for the lifestyle and support for residents that was occurring within the walls of a given community.

HERO HIGHLIGHTS FROM DAVID CYGAN

Joined Brookdale Senior Living August 2014; currently chief marketing officer

ENGAGEMENT WITH PROSPECTS AND HEALTHCARE PROFESSIONALS

Throughout the pandemic, we had to adjust all aspects of how we support our communities, including the development and execution of marketing programs. When we locked down our communities to outside visitors, we knew traditional methods of hosting on-site events and meetings outside of the community were not going to work. While interest in senior housing remained strong among those using the internet to research our industry and Brookdale, we had to rethink how to engage prospects and healthcare professionals at the community level.

We knew that COVID-19 was going to change how we could conduct tours at our communities, so we assembled a cross-functional team to address the technology, systems, processes, and knowledge that would be required to shift to a virtual environment. We leveraged our digital advertising and social media channels across our communities to promote virtual tours as our Sales team focused on conducting virtual events and seminars. All the while, we knew we still had to make prospects feel welcome and motivated to take the next step in their journey, which was selecting the right community and apartment home.

We surveyed prospects and medical professionals to gauge their perceptions of COVID-19 and the impact on our industry. Not surprisingly, there was high anxiety and concern around health and well-being. We needed to understand how our audiences perceived our response to the pandemic as well as expectations for further engagement. For both audiences, being transparent and providing relevant, up-to-date information about our response to the pandemic was imperative.

We leveraged our marketing technology platform to connect with prospects and healthcare professionals. Brookdale.com became our go-to destination to share information about our response to COVID-19, as did each of our community's Facebook pages and other social media platforms.

Healthcare professionals and prospects alike wanted to understand as much as they could about COVID-19, as well as safety protocols in place at our communities. We were able to provide the information that customers wanted—fast—and our hard work paid off. Through our ongoing pulse surveys, Brookdale was noted as having the most effective response to the pandemic compared to other large operators participating in the survey. What's more, Facebook recognized Brookdale as an exemplary social media leader for our COVID-19 response.

As we know, the entire healthcare system was under enormous pressure due to the pandemic. We had to continuously provide care for our residents and accept new residents when allowed by state and local regulations. With healthcare professionals serving as the eyes and ears for their patients' well-being, maintaining relationships with them was critical. Our Sales and Marketing teams leveraged technology to conduct virtual sales calls and host webinars. We were able to institute processes to appropriately transition new residents into our communities. By continually capturing the voice of the customer, this allowed us to be responsive to an ever-changing environment, making us stronger as a company.

Resilience is defined as the capacity to recover quickly from difficulties, toughness, and the ability to spring back into shape.

In times of crisis, leaders and their leadership skills are put to the test. In challenging times, do you fight, flee, or freeze? Confronting the challenges presented by the pandemic head on and running through scenarios helped me break down our strategy into smaller actions.

At the start of the pandemic, the Marketing leadership met daily. I've been blessed to have an incredibly talented and tenured leadership team that continually found ways to innovate and solve problems quickly.

Leading our digital, direct response, social media, and creative teams is Vice President of Marketing Shelly Riera.

She was critical in developing messaging strategy and establishing an around-the-clock team who remained on standby to develop communications and messaging. Senior Director of Marketing and the Connection Center David Lovely (who was later promoted to vice president) did what many thought to be impossible by leading the effort to transition our entire Connection Center's operations to a work-from-home environment within thirty days. We didn't miss a beat with performance, and the new model continues.

Responsible for our marketing systems and website, Senior Director of Web Marketing Michael McCamish (later promoted to vice president of Web Marketing and Technology) and his team were able to launch new webpages and content overnight, all the while monitoring performance and engagement.

Senior Director of Marketing Operations Karrie Yager was instrumental in reinventing processes to ensure real-time integration across all of our marketing channels. Senior Director of Digital and Direct Response Matt Melander led our efforts to ensure our entire digital platform supported our new COVID-19 messaging and associate recognition campaigns. Senior Director of Social Media and Brand Kristin Puckett launched our external pulse surveys to capture prospective resident and healthcare professional sentiment regarding our industry-leading response to COVID-19.

As a leadership team, we focused on three core phases—crisis management, stabilization, and recovery—which

> allowed for greater transparency, highlighted our progress, and kept us moving forward. We redesigned work processes to match each phase and kept focused on supporting our frontline teams.
>
> The ability to demonstrate a calm demeanor, clearly outline the challenges ahead, and share a vision with my team helped us navigate through unchartered territory. I'm proud of the work our team accomplished: we are proof that the seemingly impossible is in fact ... possible.

During the sudden shift that led to closing our doors to visitors, local leaders stayed focused on our resident satisfaction. Before the pandemic, we had improved our Net Promoter Score—a measure of customer satisfaction—by more than 20 percent compared to our previous survey just two years prior.

Truly, it's difficult to imagine a more challenging operating environment than managing a senior living community during a pandemic, particularly one that was closed to visits from loved ones. After all, those visits are such an important part of satisfaction for most residents. So we were over the moon when, in November 2020, Brookdale ranked highest in the J.D. Power's 2020 U.S. Senior Living Satisfaction Study. This was a survey of resident/family member/friend's satisfaction with senior living communities, and Brookdale ranked #1/ Highest in Customer Satisfaction (in a tie with another company) among Assisted Living/Memory Care communities. Brookdale was ranked #1 in these four factors: Community Staff, Resident Activities, Resident Apartment/Living Unit, and Community Buildings and Grounds. It was quite a stellar accomplishment!

Lessons Learned

For two years before COVID-19 became a threat to our communities, Brookdale had established a specific goal of transferring more decision-making to local communities, where appropriate, as part of a broader strategy on winning locally. The corporate team had spent a lot of time on restructuring our leases and optimizing our portfolio. These efforts provided us with greater financial flexibility. At the same time, we streamlined our portfolio and concentrated more decisions in the hands of local leaders.

As the pandemic progressed, it was vital to make decisions in the best place possible. Some decisions needed to be made at corporate and executed consistently across the company, and others were best handled by our local leaders. We analyzed our decision rights carefully.

The corporate team focused on establishing itself as a hub for gathering resources for distribution within our communities, as well as sharpening our tools and defining and updating our company-wide protocols. The local teams focused on decisions that were related to local regulations, unique market conditions, or specific preferences of a community's residents.

Because we had already made significant progress implementing our vision to win locally in the prior years, our field operations were more efficient. Our local leaders benefited from the deep functional expertise in our Centers of Excellence and adapted protocols as they saw fit within specified guardrails to respond to the needs of their individual communities. We were able to move quickly while benefiting from strong procedures and oversight.

CHAPTER 7

Cultivating Community Engagement

Fostering Meaningful Support through Creative Connections

n pre-pandemic times, Brookdale pursued four avenues of engagement: large groups, small groups or clubs, individual pursuits, and external programming partners. Although our residents found value in each of these approaches, the two most common forms of engagement involved large groups and external partners (such as musicians, artists, and speakers) who would visit our communities and engage with our residents.

The residents also enjoyed opportunities to travel outside of the community, whether that meant something as simple as taking a day trip to local shops or as elaborate as taking a cruise together.

Obviously, in the wake of COVID-19, social distancing precluded large group activities from taking place in the same way that they did before the pandemic, and this required the corporate, field, and local community teams to reimagine our approach to engagement.

Brookdale's engagement associates leaned into our creative avenues of engagement—individual (in-room) pursuits and small groups or clubs.

Practically overnight, we had to balance helping protect our residents and associates with the need to deliver essential daily services that promoted not only health but also well-being. Community engagement activities and events directly impact all six key elements of Optimum Life*—emotional, physical, social, spiritual, intellectual, and purposeful. We needed to work quickly to find alternative methods for maintaining the foundation of the senior living lifestyle.

Our local everyday heroes innovated quickly while navigating four different waves that impacted resident engagement: the initial wave, the in-room wave, the technology wave, and the public wave.

The Initial Wave

> ### Time Is Short—Make Every Day Count!

We knew things would not be the same once we closed our doors to outside visitors. The global pandemic forced us to reassess our approach to providing engagement that impacted residents across the nation. Within days, we saw a new normal kick in. Mitigation strategies recommended by the CDC and state and local authorities were put into place, including social distancing and limited face-to-face interactions.

Social distancing guidelines expected us to maintain a space of six feet between individuals and limited the number of people that could come into contact with each other. No more than ten individuals were allowed to convene in one space at a time. The new recommendations halted large group gatherings, which included nearly all programs and outings on the monthly calendar. In some instances, state and local governments implemented more restrictive requirements, which we incorporated as well.

Immediately our local heroes stepped in and rose to the occasion, and we began to see pictures and hear stories of creative solutions being put into place. Our programming associates seemed intuitively to know just what to do as their talents and skills were put to the test.

Hallways allowed for social distancing, so these spaces were quickly used for daily exercise and happy hours. Several communities organized a "drive-in" movie shared experience for those living in the same hallway. Residents sat in comfortable chairs pulled from their apartments and placed in their doorways. From there they could watch movie screenings at the end of the hallway with their neighbors. Like the hallway exercise programs and happy hours, these events created a sense of togetherness to help combat any unwanted feelings of loneliness.

As the infection control protocols and restrictions continued week after week, the families and loved ones of our residents were greatly missing their usual in-person visits, so window visits became a creative solution (see photo gallery). Communities would dedicate a space on the first floor with a large glass door or window for visits. They would bring in comfortable chairs and, where practical, provide phones so residents could both see and talk to their loved ones.

Some communities created window tic-tac-toe games so that residents could play games with their grandchildren. On one side of the window or another, one person would draw the tic-tac-toe boxes on the window. Each would take a turn marking *X*'s and *O*'s with a dry-erase marker on either side of the glass, engaging with smiles and laughter.

Others used the window to create a shared dining experience, with the resident on the inside and the family on the outside. For residents living on the first floor, many loved ones painted the windows of their loved ones. Our residents were so relieved and excited to see their loved ones!

Window visits were a unique way of encouraging and raising the spirits both of our residents and their loved ones on the other side of the glass. We relied on these types of visits to celebrate birthdays and anniversaries or just send greetings, and they happened in any weather, rain or shine. Windows were used for loved ones to stay connected visually, and this also became a way for those in the public to express goodwill. We were surprised again and again with imaginative, creative ways for our residents to engage.

Our creative programming associates leveraged their long-standing contacts within the greater community while also engaging with some newcomers wishing to spread goodwill. Windows were a way for anyone willing to come and visit. This included local church groups singing hymns, farmers walking their livestock around, local musicians playing instruments, loved ones with dogs showing their pets, and folk singers with guitars entertaining our communities with solos or duets. Many of these moments came about as a result of our associates leveraging their community contacts with daycares, schools, churches, or local attractions, in addition to a flood of incoming offers.

In other communities, we converted our parking lots into makeshift amphitheaters. The performers set up outside, and residents listened to the concert through an open window in their apartment or from socially distanced seating outside.

As time pressed on, communities found an even more creative way to celebrate holidays and major milestones through parades (see photo gallery). Family members and friends grabbed their keys, balloons, and signs to celebrate. Parades conveyed a powerful message to our residents: "We care!" Just as parades had been carried out to celebrate high school or college homecomings, the parades that supported our communities demonstrated the love we all had for our residents and reinforced the collective sense that we were all in this together.

Even members of the greater community—groups like rotary clubs and veteran motorcycle clubs—came together to bring smiles and support. In some instances, local police officers went out of their way to accommodate these rallies by shutting down the surrounding streets as long lines of vehicles passed by our communities. We saw hundreds of parades popping up in celebration of the 2020 spring and summer holidays, including Mother's Day, Father's Day, Memorial Day, and the Fourth of July. Our residents were quoted in news stories across the country, saying, "This lifted our spirits" and "They love us."

The In-Room Wave

> Seniors Benefit from a Life Well Lived.

Health and safety protocols limiting resident activities and accessibility within communities started in mid-March. The in-room wave made everyone stop for a moment, pause to reflect, and consider how to best manage this new normal. It's undeniable that in-room isolation can have a toll on one's mental health at any age, but we saw hope emerging in our residents, which seemed to indicate the kind of resilience that results from a life well lived. Our engagement associates were spending significantly more one-on-one time with each resident to develop deeper relationships, and together, our residents and associates began exploring new pursuits and long-forgotten interests. As ideas came up, an associate would take the necessary steps to provide the tools, supplies, or resources needed to pursue these interests.

A story out of New York tells us about how a resident rekindled her love of sketching. She began hosting FaceTime° calls with her grandchildren to use them as models for her sketches, all while maintaining social distancing in the comfort and convenience of her apartment. Another resident discovered a new passion for painting after attending a wine and watercolor class by way of video conference, and she's been painting ever since! Other residents endeavored to check off items on their bucket lists as they learned to play an instrument, spoke a new language, or tried their hand at poetry.

Several years ago, Brookdale launched a "Celebrate Aging Film Festival" to help combat ageism. Residents and associates would work together to create a short film to be entered into a national competition. Our very own "Academy" would select the best films to be screened at a national celebration hosted from the Franklin Theater in Franklin, Tennessee, near our corporate headquarters. Brookdale would host a trip for the residents and associates who were finalists to fly in for the screening, which would be attended by individuals from around the country who came together for this black-tie event.

In 2020, we realized it wasn't safe to hold this annual competition in the midst of the pandemic. We needed a different creative outlet for our residents, so we decided to launch the First Annual National Poetry Challenge! This gave our engagement associates an opportunity to celebrate and acknowledge the creative expressions of our residents. It was a timely and wonderful way to facilitate emotional expression through the written word. To process, understand, and then communicate one's feelings through writing was powerful and therapeutic for those who participated.

Early on in the pandemic, one associate and resident in Chicago started writing poems back and forth. Community leaders used this opportunity to ask other residents to submit their poems, which were then printed and attached to the breakfast bags that were shared with all residents in the mornings.

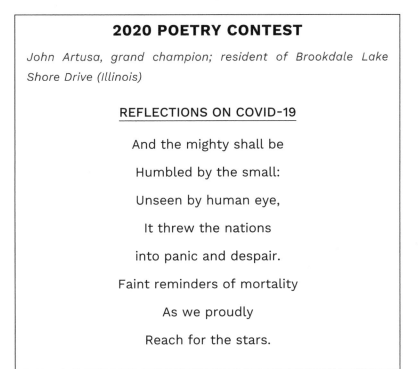

2020 POETRY CONTEST

John Artusa, grand champion; resident of Brookdale Lake Shore Drive (Illinois)

REFLECTIONS ON COVID-19

And the mighty shall be

Humbled by the small:

Unseen by human eye,

It threw the nations

into panic and despair.

Faint reminders of mortality

As we proudly

Reach for the stars.

We also had to think differently in order to transform our in-room dining service into an uplifting experience with social elements. Faced with an otherwise bleak scenario, our dining teams embraced meal delivery as a great opportunity to interact with residents. Some of our dining associates contributed their personal talents and skills to design themed food carts (see photo gallery), and socially distanced happy hours remained an anticipated favorite for our residents whenever possible. At various communities, dining associates played the piano or guitar as meals were being delivered. Every opportunity to engage was a chance to make residents feel special and to provide much-needed opportunities for socialization.

HERO HIGHLIGHTS FROM MARJAN KODRIC

Joined Brookdale Senior Living August 1997; currently vice president of Dining Services

OFFER GUIDANCE, SHARE BEST PRACTICES—AND THEN GET OUT OF THE WAY!

We view our dining services as more than simply providing nutritious meals in a clean and inviting environment; the dining room experience at Brookdale has always been an experiential and fundamentally social concept.

When the COVID-19 pandemic hit, we had to close our dining rooms (due to large-capacity space restrictions) and pivot to in-room dining. While we were accustomed to providing room service as an option for residents who requested to dine within their apartments, this option was only rarely requested. *Prior to the pandemic, virtually all of our residents preferred socializing in our dining rooms during mealtime. Transitioning to provide room service to every resident—for up to three meals a day, every day—was an unprecedented challenge.*

One of the earliest best practices we observed in our communities came from Brookdale Glen Ellyn. Illinois had just implemented a shelter-in-place order, and the dining room at the community was closed. The Glen Ellyn team was the first to use this as an opportunity to transform their meal delivery into a themed food truck concept. The dining team created a menu centered on a specific cuisine and decorated the food transportation carts to match, replete with dining associates dressed in attire to complement the theme. They even played music during the meal deliveries, whether that meant blasting CDs on the carts with speakers or encouraging talented associates to play the guitar or piano alongside the carts to add to the overall experience.

On Fridays, when the community had traditionally hosted a happy hour for the residents (which typically included light appetizers and both mock and regular cocktails), they found a way to continue the tradition during the pandemic, transforming happy hour into a made-to-order beverage and cocktail party on wheels—including delightful appetizers, themed carts, and lively music.

After sharing Glen Ellyn's best practices with other communities, the floodgates opened up, and we received several emails and photos from other communities who took inspiration from their lead and implemented their own creative approaches. Communities were creating a wide range of food truck concepts, including New York deli (made-to-order sandwiches), spa day (granola and fresh squeezed juice), ice cream trucks for dessert, and international cuisines (Italian cuisine, Asian cuisine, etc.). *Our themed carts and food truck concepts gave our associates the opportunity to interact with our socially distanced residents and offer a welcome dose of good cheer as we rolled out the new, in-room dining routine.*

We witnessed the emergence of another best practice when dining associates from various communities wrote personal handwritten notes to residents and included them on the food trays as a gesture, along with a special dessert or snack—meant to uplift their spirits and add a personal touch. The notes read, "Have a great day, and please enjoy this extra treat!" This enabled us to make a personal connection with our residents even without face-to-face contact.

From the corporate side, it was our job to provide helpful guidance and support as our local leaders managed the abrupt transition away from communal dining. However, it was truly our dining associates on the community level that made all the difference as we reimagined the in-room dining routine as a socially distanced yet energizing and heartfelt experience.

When we reached out to one of the communities to express our thanks for all their hard work and dedication developing these best practices, the feedback from one of our associates truly captivated our mission to lead with a servant's heart: "I'm so thankful I have a job that I both enjoy and see as my vocation."

I recently celebrated my twenty-four-year service anniversary with Brookdale. Over the years, I have learned not to be surprised when teams rise to the challenge in the face of dire situations: *If you hire people for their*

> *passion, the next best step is to ensure they have the proper tools and support—and then get out of the way!*

Throughout this intense period of in-room isolation, it was important to our corporate, field, and community leaders to provide as many resources as we could to support our engagement associates and residents. As engagement leaders spent more individual time with each resident, relationships deepened, and our associates submitted feedback to local, field, and corporate leaders. They reported a need for additional tools to engage each resident in a personal and meaningful way.

One of the ideas that came out of these discussions was the idea for the Engagement Room Service door hanger (see photo gallery). Improving on the idea of the room service door hanger from a hotel stay, we created a door hanger that encouraged residents to request in-room items to support their individual interests.

We also created a weekly paper newsletter known as "Your Well-Being Memo." Each memo offered a variety of ideas, including a diagram of an exercise to keep moving, an inspirational quote, and a brain game (where they might be asked to match items, make words from a group of letters, complete a crossword puzzle, or word find—these games came from our "Flex Your Brain" concept, which is a part of our "Brookdale Brain Fit" signature program).

One of the challenges our residents faced during this time was the inability to participate in our daily exercise classes. Our daily exercise program, called Brookdale B-Fit, is an associate- or resident-led exercise class that is usually offered "live" daily.

Infection control protocols implemented with the arrival of COVID-19 no longer allowed us to offer live classes. To adapt, we created the B-Fit Mini Workouts—paper memos that provided visual cues and daily tips to encourage moving throughout the day. They were created by the Resident and Family Engagement corporate team in support of the "live" classes being postponed; they helped to keep a visual cue available to remind and encourage ongoing movement. We knew well the importance of daily exercise, especially during the in-room wave when residents were in their apartments for much of the day.

Where possible, many communities held exercise programs in the hallways. Interested residents positioned themselves outside the doorway of their apartments, which maintained social distancing and allowed them the ability to participate in their daily B-Fit exercise program. Finding creative ways to engage in daily exercise, even given the infection control protocols, provided a dose of oxygen to the muscles and a boost to the spirit!

Giving Back Is Powerful.

The pandemic further highlighted the many ways our residents served as sources of inspiration. Considering all that was happening in the world, many residents took the initiative to focus on the power of giving back. As various needs arose in the news or on social media, a number of our residents felt compelled to contribute something meaningful to the greater community—both within Brookdale and beyond. They asked, "What can we do?" Our associates were inspired to see residents sewing cloth masks for donation, giving their time, and doing what they could to contribute. Residents and community associates also continued the annual fundraising we host annually for the Alzheimer's Association. Other residents dressed up as Santa and Mrs. Claus and hosted virtual visits with children before Christmas.

PERSONAL PERSPECTIVE FROM CINDY BAIER

Joined Brookdale Senior Living December 2015; currently president, chief executive officer, and board member

RESIDENTS SHARE THE WISDOM FROM A LIFE WELL LIVED

One of the most treasured aspects of working within the senior living industry is the opportunity to get to know the amazing residents who call Brookdale home. *Our residents are truly extraordinary human beings—with rich lives and good hearts and wonderful legacies they've created.*

Dr. Edgar Arthur Reed, MD, JD, (Dr. Ed) was a resident in Brookdale Green Hills Cumberland (Tennessee) with whom I had the good fortune to make a personal connection. I enjoyed meeting Dr. Ed in the community and running into him as he participated in our annual company-wide event called the Celebrate Aging Film Festival (mentioned above). Dr. Ed kindly shared special anecdotes with me about life in the community and stories about his family, and we enjoyed discussing current events and observations on the wider world. At the end of his life, Dr. Ed made an effort to ensure I knew when he was transferred into hospice, and I had the opportunity to visit him there. When I entered his room, I was so touched to see a framed picture that he and I had taken together at the Celebrate Aging Film Festival (see photo gallery), right alongside pictures of his family and a handful of personal items he kept with

---

him in his final days. The photo showed Dr. Ed teasing me—and me giving it right back to him! The photographer had captured a moment that meant a lot to both of us, and my heart was warmed to find out we held mutual admiration for one another.

Jan Jordan is another resident with whom I instantly connected. Jan is a resident of Brookdale Belle Meade (Tennessee). Jan and her late husband, Stanley Cohen, lived with us for several years, and Jan continues to be an important part of the community because she is highly engaged with both the residents and associates. Jan makes it a point to help other residents feel welcome and get involved in life in the community. When we met, Jan shared with me some helpful observations about her time at Brookdale and mentioned that she had a cat she wanted me to meet. As I entered her apartment, I noticed photos of Jan and Stanley's trip to receive the Nobel Prize, and I was so intrigued to learn more. Jan mentioned that she was giving a presentation on their trip in her community. I asked Jan if she would also talk to our corporate and field associates about her life with Stanley (who had won the Nobel Prize in Physiology or Medicine in 1986) and their trip to receive the prize. She readily agreed. In July 2021, Jan captivated everyone who listened to her story (see photo gallery). We were able to celebrate Stanley's life with Jan, and we learned a lot about the fascinating achievements of Stanley Cohen and enjoyed reliving some of the happiest moments of their life together. Although Jan lost Stanley in February 2020, just prior to the pandemic significantly impacting the

United States, their love will live on forever. Importantly, Stanley's contributions have made the world a better place, and we were so proud to have him as part of our Brookdale family.

Carolyn Modisher is another resident, also from Brookdale Green Hills Cumberland, with whom I had an immediate connection. One day, I visited the community to have lunch with a handful of residents who agreed to share with me stories about their experiences during the pandemic, and Carolyn was one of the kind residents who volunteered to participate in the meeting. She talked about her family and how they shaped her experience within the community. She revealed to me that she had written a book for her daughter when her daughter was young, which she titled *Where Can I Find a Dinosaur?* During my community visits, I would read parts of the book out loud to her, or vice versa (see photo gallery). Carolyn is a very talented writer, and I felt so honored that she shared her book with me. I talked about Carolyn's book with her daughter, and I was able to see just how much it meant to both of them. Her book featured a crocheted dinosaur on one of the pages, and I wanted to find one to give Carolyn at her hundredth birthday party. Neither Linda DeVault nor I could find exactly what I was looking for, so we chose a small green plush dinosaur and felt it would be a meaningful gift. I was happy to see the joy that it brought Carolyn. It was so wonderful to be able to celebrate her hundredth birthday with Carolyn and her family and friends in October 2021. She beamed as she danced, told stories, and spent time with the people that she loved.

The Technology Wave

People Need Other People.

Within a matter of weeks, the use of technology surged as residents sought out creative methods of staying connected, informed, and entertained. Technology purchases surged for all ages. Worldwide tablet shipments in the second quarter of 2020 were over 37.5 million, including an estimated 14.3 million iPads° shipped by Apple°.[13] Our seniors were part of this trend, leaning into the use of iPads°, Chromebooks°, and tablets to soften feelings of loneliness by connecting with loved ones.

Our Brookdale engagement associates were well prepared on this front. In 2016, we had launched iPads° company-wide at all Brookdale communities in an effort to foster engagement. Skype and FaceTime° were already being used regularly prior to the pandemic, so when Zoom°[14] became one of the de facto leaders of the technology push during COVID-19, our associates were able to immediately harness the power of this relatively new video conferencing platform.

---

13 "Apple Shipped an Estimated 14.3 Million iPads Worldwide in Q2 2020 amid Surging Tablet Market," *MacRumors*, published August 3, 2020, https://www.macrumors.com/2020/08/03/apple-shipped-14-3-million-ipads-q2-2020/#:~:text=Apple%20shipped%20an%20estimated%2014.3%20million%20iPads%20in,the%2011.9%20million%20sold%20in%20the%20year-ago%20quarter. Apple, iPad, iPhone, and FaceTime are registered trademarks of Apple, Inc.

14 Zoom is a trademark of Zoom Video Communications Inc.

Along with Skype and FaceTime*, residents quickly adapted to Zoom* to connect with social groups, family meetups, and individual meetings. Community associates set up video conferencing stations and assisted in coordinating schedules to help connect residents with loved ones. Family video chats provided loved ones with the ability not only to hear each other but to see each other in real time. This had a powerful impact on reducing anxiety and stress all around. Zoom* enabled loved ones to be on a single screen together all at the same time—in some cases, it was the first time a resident might have seen certain family members in years.

Residents began using the platform to connect with friends for happy hours, participate in exercise classes, and attend the graduations and weddings of children and grandchildren. We witnessed loved ones cooking and sharing meals together simply by leveraging technology. These virtual, face-to-face interactions enabled a large number of our residents to stay connected—and even grow closer to loved ones—during the most difficult of times.

Technology also opened the door for our seniors to engage with the wider world from the comfort of their homes. Museums from around the world (like the Uffizi Gallery in Italy) had closed their doors due to the pandemic yet found ways to connect with the public via virtual tours on their websites. The general public of all ages engaged with YouTube to share special talents, like singing or playing instruments, and our residents enjoyed watching whole families singing together; father-daughter duos and singer-songwriters created videos of themselves playing instruments and singing. There was an outpouring of goodwill from the general public that provided entertainment and smiles during the difficult months, and none of this was lost on our residents.

Additionally, the San Diego Zoo and Georgia Aquarium introduced live webcams to watch their animals from anywhere across the nation. Iconic theaters (like the Lincoln Center in New York) began streaming recorded symphonies and opera performances. A wealth of virtual arts and culture became available for human consumption, and our residents were eager to experience an amazing array of virtual visits during this unprecedented time in history.

We leveraged the use of technology to provide engagement between our residents and their loved ones and to take advantage of the inpouring of virtual programming opportunities provided by the general public. Most of our residents used their phones and tablets to engage with virtual programming, based on their interests. For those without their own device, we used our in-house iPads® to make these opportunities available when the interest was there. Our role was to ensure our residents knew about and had access to the types of virtual programs they enjoyed.

Again, this is where our everyday engagement heroes stepped up: they sought out every virtual opportunity they could find and shared them with the Brookdale community when residents discovered new favorites.

HERO HIGHLIGHTS FROM CHARLES RICHARDSON

Joined Brookdale Senior Living May 1997; currently senior director of Resident and Family Engagement

NURTURING FRIENDSHIPS THROUGH "CLUB" CULTURE

From day one of the pandemic, the engagement associates at Brookdale stood strong. We had to ask a tough question: What was the appropriate response in the midst of uncertainty, not knowing what the future would hold? First we had to face the reality head on that our long-standing avenues of engagement were no longer possible. As the necessity for social distancing became clear, we were determined to find new ways of engaging with residents without relying on our usual calendar of group-based activities. Our engagement associates considered their options carefully, knowing they would have to proceed without outside volunteers, entertainers, or company vehicles for community outings.

Our associates started by encouraging the safest avenues of engagement, including individual, in-room pursuits and small clubs. Hallway programs, window events, community parades, and technology communications soon evolved and became vital activities for lifting spirits all around. Next, our engagement associates spent more time developing deeper connections and meaningful relationships with each resident.

As a result, Brookdale shifted our focus to nurturing powerful friendships and emphasized programming that supported this goal—namely through the development of a "club" culture. We have seen all types of clubs focused on such activities as walking, painting, gardening, and knitting; some of our resident favorites include coffee clubs, card clubs, and movie clubs. Clubs empower residents to lead their own creative programming—on their terms and at various times throughout the week, including in the evenings or on weekends. This places the resident, their friends, and their club ideas in the driver's seat, relying on our engagement associates to schedule, cohost, or gather supplies and resources in support of these pursuits.

We have learned so much—looking back at the storm of COVID-19—and I think it's fair to say we have identified a silver lining in our engagement efforts: we realized the "one-size-fits-all" calendar of large group programs may not be our ideal long-term strategy. *We will always value and support the socialization of large group opportunities, but sometimes a meaningful and engaged life is best found in a smaller, more intimate club setting.* We will never underestimate the power of a one-on-one connection and the friendship that results from more meaningful connections. We now appreciate more than ever that resident friendships are key, and these friendships are now the primary driver for our programs, events, and new opportunities.

Rather than asking residents to reflect on what they "liked to do," we have started asking the more aspirational question of what residents "would like to do next" as they engage within our communities. *This opens new doors and keeps the focus toward what's next!*

Learning Is Critical to Innovation.

In response to our engagement associates' efforts, we began hosting company-wide support calls weekly. Leveraging our hundreds of communities at Brookdale, we gathered best practices, new ideas, and fresh approaches from across the country, prompting the creation of a new publication for our associates titled *Engagement Weekly* (later retitled *Engagement Monthly*). It was an excellent way to compile all ideas in a central location and to spotlight specific community successes, and it reminded our associates and residents that we were all in this together!

The Public Wave

As the infection control restrictions continued and weeks turned into months, the fourth wave of community engagement was initiated by the public. News reports shared stories about the impact of social isolation and the increased possibility of depression for all ages—and particularly for older adults.[15] Upon hearing the sad reality, many individuals within the general public were inspired to take action. From coast to coast, our associates shared anecdotes of good Samaritans reaching out because they wanted to do more for those within senior living communities. Many individuals and groups contacted either our corporate office or our community leaders directly with innovative ideas to help assure our residents that they were being held in high regard—and loved!—by the public.

Students from local schools created phone-a-friend programs and routinely sent requests—both to our corporate office and our local communities. Universities contacted our communities in order to connect students who were isolated in their dorms with senior living residents as a means of fostering intergenerational relationships. Representatives from the University of South Carolina reached out

---

15   Liz Seegert, "Social Isolation, Loneliness Negatively Affect Health for Seniors," Association of Health Care Journalists, published March 16, 2017, https://healthjournalism.org/blog/2017/03/social-isolation-loneliness-negatively-affect-health-for-seniors/.

to our corporate engagement team, for instance, and we offered the opportunity to our communities as an opt-in program. Several residents signed up and were paired up with dorm-bound students. The purpose was not necessarily for residents to serve as mentors but to foster connection between humans in the same situation of having to isolate—just from different generations! A number of relationships developed and delivered heart-centered connections lasting well into the pandemic.

Move Quickly and Be Agile.

Additionally, volunteers contacted our communities daily, offering to send letters, host video chats, or make phone calls. Parents mailed drawings from their children to our communities, promoting a message of joy and cheer.

Our engagement associates also leveraged Facebook to request pen pal connections. As a result of the generous outreach of so many volunteers, pen pal programs for our seniors flourished. In one case, a community received hundreds of responses within just a few days. It was awe inspiring to witness such an outpouring of goodwill and heartening to affirm the value so many people placed on seniors in society.

Lessons Learned

We witnessed the herculean efforts of our engagement associates at Brookdale during this critically challenging time. They navigated wave after wave of changes from the moment we started social distancing to the time we had to close our doors to the public. Our engagement associates demonstrated sharp intuition and creativity at every turn.

These innovative approaches to engagement deeply impacted our residents and their loved ones (in ways that may never be fully understood!) when we were asked to do the unthinkable: cease in-person visits. The solutions our associates developed—and the lessons we learned from their efforts to address an immediately vexing situation—will undoubtedly live on in our communities and in the minds and memories of our residents.

Our associates are inspirational leaders who exemplified one of the most important lessons we learned from the pandemic: "Be ready to change everything!"

We have a saying at Brookdale: "Focus on what matters most." The pandemic required us to do just that. As we stripped away many of the activities that filled our daily lives, we were able to focus intently on the most important elements of life. After we had taken care of psychological and safety needs (the fundamentals in Maslow's hierarchy of needs), we could focus on love and belonging, as well as needs for esteem and self-actualization.

CHAPTER 8

Removing Barriers to Success

Ensuring Financial Stability through Urgent Lease Restructuring

n Chapter 3 (Securing Resources for Financial Flexibility), I discussed Brookdale's need to secure cash liquidity—fast. This chapter reviews one of the methods we used to help ensure liquidity continued. It wasn't enough to refinance our debts; new financial actions were needed to better manage our leases. Although we made great progress in securing resources at the start of the pandemic, restructuring our largest lease (which covered the leases for a number of our communities) helped ensure we could maintain appropriate and adequate liquidity in the medium to long term.

In our industry, it is common for leases to have financial covenants. These are tests that are designed to protect the landlord from financial harm. Separately, credit agreements often have covenants that require the borrower or debtor (Brookdale) to be in compliance with all financial covenants (including lease covenants). In other words, if you violate a covenant in a lease, a cross-default chain reaction could start across your capital structure—meaning debts could become "current," or due at once.

Addressing the initial cross-defaulting domino—a lease covenant violation—is why lease restructuring was so critical early in the pandemic. If we had a covenant that was at risk, our capital structure was at risk, which would put our liquidity at risk.

As discussed previously in Chapter 3, the number one pitfall to avoid when running a business is to never, ever run out of cash.

Lease Restructuring to Ensure Stability

To remove this capital structure risk, we quickly moved to restructure our largest lease within the first few months of the pandemic. If we didn't achieve the lease restructuring quickly, the financial consequences were potentially severe.

> ### Look for Win-Win Transactions.

Negotiations were extremely difficult. We had to negotiate aggressively, and we ultimately found a win-win solution that suited our landlord's needs along with our own. But this required around-the-clock efforts that proved to be highly strenuous in the short term. It's fair to say that we approached our financial issues with the same intensity that we placed on our response to help protect our residents, patients, and associates—because the consequences for failing to do so were potentially severe.

There are harsh realities when running a business, and the necessity of maintaining financial stability is one of them. Given the scope of uncertainty in the world at the start of the pandemic, it was impossible to predict all the consequences if we were unable to meet our lease covenants for any reason.

The only way we could help protect our residents, patients, associates, and ultimately our shareholders was if we took steps to protect Brookdale, thereby helping to maintain the necessary cash liquidity to pay for our response to the COVID-19 pandemic.

HERO HIGHLIGHTS FROM CHAD WHITE

Joined Brookdale Senior Living March 2007; currently executive vice president and general counsel

BALANCING SHORT-TERM FLEXIBILITY AND LONG-TERM OPTIONS

In times of uncertainty or rapid change, maintaining flexibility is key. There is no doubt that the COVID-19 pandemic generated a tremendous amount of change over a short period of time. In the early days of the pandemic, companies in many different industries were also experiencing an uncertain financial future, and senior living companies were particularly impacted, given the demographics of our customer base.

Within our industry, many operators (including Brookdale) lease a number of their communities from third-party landlords, typically in a master-lease structure where multiple communities are leased in one lease agreement. In exchange for paying rent amounts that almost always

---

escalate on an annual basis, an operator receives the benefit of the economics of running its business. This means that senior living operators enjoy the benefit of receiving revenue from new and existing residents as they maintain responsibility for covering all operating expenses (including labor costs, taxes, insurance, and capital expenditures), and they also retain any remaining cash flow after paying rent to the landlords (typically large corporate institutions, such as public real estate investment trusts—REITs).

Prior to COVID-19, many of these leases were already either close to breakeven or in fact underwater for many operators; in other words, the operator was losing money after operating expenses and rent were satisfied. This would have happened as the leases may have been entered into many years prior, and rent escalations had outrun the growth in the operator's net operating income. The pandemic only exacerbated this situation as revenues from customers dropped significantly and expenses increased rapidly (including increased labor costs and costs for PPE and other COVID-19-related expenses).

Shortly following the start of the pandemic, Cindy Baier charged the senior management team (including the members of the Management Investment Committee) to review our lease portfolio to determine whether we could make improvements to the terms of our various leases or otherwise limit our potential financial exposure in the face of the existing uncertain environment. One of the leases we quickly identified was our thirty-five-property master lease with LTC Properties.

Historically, the LTC lease had been a well-performing lease that produced positive cash flow. The existing term of the lease was scheduled to expire at the end of 2020, and we were faced with the decision of whether or not to renew the lease for another ten-year renewal term—a decision we needed to make in short order just a few months into the pandemic. However, it was not clear how much or how long the performance of this lease might be impacted by COVID-19, given the uncertainty in the environment. *Throughout our discussions, it became clear that we needed to obtain greater short-term flexibility within the lease without losing the ability to maintain the lease over the longer term.*

The team quickly went to work on potential solutions. Over the course of a couple of months, we were ultimately able to negotiate and execute a win-win transaction that realized both parties' objectives. For Brookdale, we managed to achieve important flexibility that allowed us to exit the lease (or renegotiate terms) if the pandemic negatively impacted performance for an extended length of time (so that we wouldn't be forced to bear negative cash flow over an extended period); meanwhile, we held the option to retain the lease for the longer term if the lease maintained (or quickly returned) to its historical level of performance. We achieved this agreement by breaking up the ten-year renewal term structure into separate one-, four-, and five-year optional renewal terms. We also were able to improve other terms of the lease that ended up providing us with greater corporate transactional flexibility and the ability to receive landlord funding for capital improvement projects at the leased communities intended to help further drive improved performance. In addition, in recognition of the rent cost pressures and uncertainties caused by the pandemic, LTC subsequently proactively provided Brookdale with an abatement of six months of rent escalation.

Through collaboration, a focus on finding solutions that work for both parties, and a renewed commitment to our partnership cornerstone, we were able to achieve a positive outcome that protected Brookdale's interests in the midst of substantial uncertainty.

Scenario Planning to Achieve Flexibility

> **Do Scenario Planning: Act Strategically, but Move Quickly.**

Our efforts started with scenario planning. We worked through multiple scenarios as we considered how various levels of revenue loss and incremental costs would impact our capital structure and liquidity. We needed to review every single lease and loan agreement with a fine-toothed comb in order to manage all conceivable circumstances that could cause a potential default.

Once we had a grasp of possible scenarios that could lead to a potential default and the possible consequences, we negotiated agreements that would give us the flexibility to navigate through the crisis.

Brookdale has long had an incredibly talented team of leaders that focus on corporate development and serve on our Management Investment Committee (MIC). This includes Executive Vice President of Corporate Development and President of Continuing Care Retirement Communities Todd Kaestner, Executive Vice President and General Counsel Chad White, Executive Vice President and Chief Financial Officer Steve Swain, Executive Vice President of Finance and Treasurer George Hicks, Senior Vice President of Corporate Development Teddy Hillard, and Senior Vice President of Corporate Development and Strategic Initiatives Chris Maingot.

Approach Problems from Multiple Angles.

This group provides valuable insights. If our community associates are the limbs of the company that connect to our residents, this core group represents the tree trunk. They each have sharp skills and creative instincts, the keen ability to approach problems from all angles, and the courage to engage in intense debates as we evaluate the benefits and challenges of a particular course of action. Collectively they also have over a century of experience in our industry. Our MIC worked masterfully to identify the issues that we needed to address.

George Hicks, Steve Swain, and Teddy Hillard took the lead on our loan agreements. Meanwhile, Senior Vice President and Chief Accounting Officer Dawn Kussow and Senior Vice President of Tax Joanne Leskowicz provided support on the financial reporting and tax impacts of all of the potential solutions. We focused on the cash flow of the leases as well as covenant risk. For a single, near-term lease maturity, we were able to negotiate a one-year renewal that would allow us to assess the impact of COVID-19 on the portfolio and then retain the option to renew for a longer term if warranted. On other leases, we negotiated covenant flexibility.

> ## Don't Let Fear Paralyze You.

As a result of intense scenario planning, we set out to restructure our largest lease. Given the importance of this negotiation, I personally led the effort with significant support from Todd Kaestner, Chad White, Steve Swain, Teddy Hillard, Dawn Kussow, and Chris Maingot, along with a team of outside advisors. Joseph "Joe" Coco (of Skadden, Arps, Slate, Meagher & Flom LLP) and several other key advisors were absolutely incredible during this process. We talked at all hours, speaking early in the morning and continuing on the deal in the late hours of the night, seven days a week. The entire negotiation process lasted a few months, which felt like one long, never-ending day. At the time, I questioned whether I had the stamina to keep going, but I knew that it was critically important to Brookdale, so I fought through the exhaustion. Others did as well.

Strategic Negotiations to Reach a Final Agreement

> ## Triage so That You Can Focus on What Is Most Important First.

The strategy behind our negotiations was critically important. I spent a great deal of time discussing alternatives with Guy Sansone (nonexecutive chairman of our board of directors) and Lee Wielansky (chairman of our investment committee). Both Guy and Lee provided perspectives about how our counterparty might view various potential deal points. We also discussed how investors could view both sides of the deal. Their respective insights were invaluable!

Our entire board stayed involved in the full gamut of negotiations involved, conducting in-depth discussions of our strategy and overseeing final approval of the transaction. We all knew the pivotal nature of reaching an agreement, and we needed everyone's help to accomplish it.

HERO HIGHLIGHTS FROM TODD KAESTNER

Joined Brookdale Senior Living September 1984; currently executive vice president of corporate development and president of Continuing Care Retirement Communities

CONFIDENCE OF UNDERSTANDING INCREASES ODDS OF SUCCESS

Present-day Brookdale was created through a series of transactions in 2005 and 2006 involving three predecessor companies, each of which had a different area of focus. Predecessor entity Brookdale was a Chicago-based company that operated within high- and mid-rise urban and dense suburban markets with product types that emphasized independent living and hospitality.

Alterra was a Milwaukee-based company that had developed a large number of standalone, wood-frame (i.e., single-level) assisted living buildings and often colocated, standalone wood-frame memory care buildings. Alterra mostly pursued secondary and tertiary cities and less dense suburbs for development.

American Retirement Corporation (ARC) was a Nashville-based senior living company that owned and operated entry-fee continuing care retirement communities as well as rental-based continuing care retirement communities—both of which typically featured independent living, assisted living, and skilled nursing components and memory care in some cases. ARC had also developed and operated a number of freestanding assisted living and memory care buildings. Further, ARC started and operated a home health and hospice business.

Following the merger of these companies and retaining one predecessors' name, Brookdale continued to grow primarily through acquisitions. It was through this series of transactions and subsequent mergers and acquisitions that Brookdale inherited the large Ventas master lease.

The Ventas lease had been extended multiple times, and lease payments had grown to significantly exceed the operating cash flows from the leased properties, leaving Brookdale with exorbitant negative cash flow from the master-lease properties. With the arrival of the COVID-19 pandemic, the negative cash flow position was exacerbated, heightening our need to resolve the situation.

Prior to opening discussions with our landlord, it was imperative that we comprehensively understood our interests and objectives, along with our counterparty's interests and objectives. We were careful to assemble an expert team of advisors to enable significant prenegotiation focus in order to identify multiple alternative paths and options for a lease restructuring transaction. As a precondition to choosing a particular set of goals, our combined team of external advisors and internal members sought to ensure that our perspectives were well founded, nuances were considered, and we believed that we fully understood our landlord's position.

These negotiations occurred against the backdrop of the COVID-19 pandemic, with all of its associated uncertainties, and this created a strong sense of urgency for both parties. Neither Brookdale nor Ventas could define the other party's worst-case pandemic scenario, which increased the pressure for achieving a workable lease restructuring. We needed to create a significant financial safety margin to help protect our residents, associates, and shareholders.

Once confident in fleshing out the interests and objectives of both parties, we were able to be creative in structuring an outcome acceptable to both parties. Certainly it isn't possible to know in advance what elements and items are most highly valued by the counterparty during negotiations.

In the end, we traded certain assets plus a cash payment for debt and lease obligation relief, issued warrants for common equity, allowed the landlord to provide additional debt financing, reduced future rent by $500 million over the ensuing five years, avoided a further lease extension, and eliminated a number of material consent rights and financial covenants. Importantly, the final agreement removed all financial covenants from the lease and deleted certain provisions that could become effective in the event of a change-of-control transaction.

The uncertainty created by the COVID-19 pandemic significantly aided us in reaching agreement, as it increased our sense of urgency.

When Winston Churchill said, "When your best isn't good enough, you have to do what is required," he spoke to the recognition of the possibility of winning and the commitment to perform at levels beyond what the team believed they were capable of achieving. In our case, this only came from our resolve and tenacity, based upon our confidence of understanding the positions and concerns of both parties.

After a rather protracted series of challenging and intense conversations, we were able to execute a win-win transaction that represented the largest lease restructuring in Brookdale's history by solving the largest long-term structural problem within our lease portfolio. This resulted in the preservation of liquidity, so we could proceed in managing the pandemic without having to worry about the impact of this lease.

HERO HIGHLIGHTS FROM DEBRA CAFARO

Currently chairman of the board and chief executive officer of Ventas, Inc.

INDUSTRY LEADERSHIP, UNPRECEDENTED CHALLENGES, AND CREATIVE SOLUTIONS

Ventas, Inc., an S&P 500 company, is a premier partner to leading care providers across demographically driven real estate. As one of the largest senior living owners,

Ventas has communities that are typically operated by brand name companies such as Brookdale. At the outset of the COVID-19 pandemic, relying on its diversified business model, Ventas acted quickly and proactively to successfully navigate through the unknowns of the pandemic and keep its enterprise strong and stable for all its stakeholders. Ventas prioritized the health and safety of its employees and the residents and employees in its senior living communities, 121 of which were leased to and operated by Brookdale.

Ventas understood its role as a stabilizing force within the senior living sector during a time of extreme financial, operating, and clinical stress. It took seriously its responsibilities to the industry, its business partners and operators like Brookdale, and the residents and employees in its communities. When Brookdale came to Ventas during the pandemic with a request for rent relief, both companies understood how much was at stake: the stability of Brookdale was critical not only for Brookdale's shareholders and all those who lived and worked in Brookdale senior living communities, but for the reputation of the senior living industry among investors and consumers generally.

As a result, Ventas committed to work with Brookdale toward an agreement that would both protect Brookdale's present and future while also benefiting Ventas's stakeholders. The path to the narrow area of overlap among both companies' sometimes competing goals was tricky at best and impossible at worst; the difficulty was compounded by the fact that the enormity of the pandemic made future outcomes both unpredictable and widely dispersed.

Working closely with its counterparts at Brookdale, Ventas used its experience in analyzing complex situations, its multidisciplinary management team, and its innovative problem-solving approach to reach a mutually beneficial new agreement that was balanced, thoughtful, and accounted for a wide range of potential outcomes. The negotiations were tough. Both sides were relentless yet constructive. They could get over hurdles because both companies had been intentional in building trust over many years and across various levels of each organization—up to and including the CEOs—which proved to be a vital linchpin for reaching the ultimate win-win outcome.

The final transaction, which had many components, gave Brookdale significant near-term financial relief, financial stability, and liquidity, so it could focus on taking care of seniors and employees during the pandemic. It also provided Ventas with discounted up-front consideration to mitigate rent shortfalls and created alignment between the companies by giving Ventas the opportunity to share in Brookdale's future success.

This stands as an example of Ventas living its values while at the same time advocating for its stakeholders and finding creative ways that it and its partners—and more importantly, the senior residents and associates in Brookdale-Ventas senior living communities—could thrive in the future.

Lessons Learned

We learned so many leadership lessons from our experience. We were successful because we triaged our situation and solved our most urgent, mission-critical issues first. We dedicated ample resources to addressing the problem and solicited advice from peers with relevant knowledge—building a team with a creative problem-solving mindset, the willingness to work incredibly hard, and the necessary expertise to negotiate a proper solution.

We operated with a sense of urgency that matched the importance of the issue and committed to finding a win-win transaction in the end. Lastly, we kept all critical stakeholders involved throughout the decision-making process.

I am forever indebted to the people who helped us solve this crucial problem for the sacrifices they made to ensure our success. Thankfully, our leaders were willing to go the extra mile to solve a most difficult problem under an otherwise virtually impossible time frame.

Success on a high-visibility project instills confidence. Associates are more confident—in themselves and their teammates—and management is more confident in associates and the team. Tapping this high-trust muscle in the future will decrease execution risk and naturally lead to more opportunities for associates.

Our success reinforced the importance of teamwork and taught us that what may seem impossible is actually possible!

CHAPTER 9

A Culture of Caring

Honoring Feedback and Recognizing
Heart-Centered Contributions

The culture of an organization is its lifeblood. It provides our team members with helpful cues on how to act and what they should prioritize, no matter what's going on in the external environment. Brookdale has developed a culture of caring, because our mission is focused first and foremost on people supporting people.

There's always a balance between mission and margin, and when the pandemic hit, it was clear that, at least for the short term, the pandemic would dramatically impact our margin. However, because our culture hinges on people taking care of people, it was possible to align the organization with our North Star: the health and well-being of our residents, patients, and associates. If there was ever a time when a choice wasn't clear and someone needed to make a decision, they would know what to do based on the culture. To reinforce our expectations, we highlighted desired actions through our culture moments.

At the corporate level, we made an effort to share distinct culture moments at various meetings throughout the company, because they emphasized the fact that so many of us were feeling the same way. A culture moment might be a letter from a resident highlighting extraordinary support that they had received, or a story told by an associate who described the efforts of another Brookdale team member helping a resident live a better life. Sharing culture moments made life better, especially while everybody was under stress, because our culture was the first place we went when we needed to center ourselves and remember why we do what we do and what impact our actions have.

What we stand for at the end of the day—pandemic or not—is critically important.

The Birth of Community Learning Visits

When I first became Brookdale's CEO, I reached out to Bill Sheriff (Brookdale's longest-serving CEO, leading from 1984 to 2013) to see if he would serve as a mentor for me. After much discussion, Bill agreed. One of the most poignant experiences we had was spending time together talking with residents and associates during a community visit with Bill. I learned so much from talking to residents and associates during this visit that I decided that our senior leadership team would benefit from working side by side with our associates in the communities. If the entire senior leadership team could spread out across the country for a week to work within the communities, we could learn a lot that would accelerate our turnaround strategy. This is how our community learning visits began.

John Artusa

Resident of Brookdale

Bahar Azhdari

*Senior Director and Associate
General Counsel, Brookdale*

Dr. Jordan Asher

*Brookdale Board Member; Chief
Physician Executive; and Executive
Vice President, Sentara Healthcare*

Dave Baier

*Husband and Advisor to
Chief Executive Officer*

Dr. Jeff Balser
President, Chief Executive Officer,
and Dean, Vanderbilt University
Medical Center

Marc Bromley
Brookdale Board Member;
Advisory Board Member, Nancy
Creek Capital Management, LLC

Frank Bumstead
Brookdale Board Member;
Principal Shareholder, Flood,
Bumstead, McCready &
McCarthy, Inc.

Debra Cafaro
Chairman of the Board and Chief
Executive Officer, Ventas, Inc.

Theresa Cochran
Senior Director of Human
Resources, Brookdale

Julie Davis
Consultant and Former Vice
President of Communications,
Brookdale

Dr. Marylouise "Weezie" Fennell
Resident of Brookdale;
Chair, Brookdale's National
Advisory Council

Vicki Freed
Brookdale Board Member; Senior
Vice President of Sales, Trade
Support, and Service, Royal
Caribbean International

Angela Haley
*Vice President of Clinical
Operations, Brookdale*

Dan Huffines
*Vice President, Associate General
Council, and Assistant Secretary,
Brookdale*

Hayley Hovious
*President, Nashville Health
Care Council*

Rita Johnson-Mills
*Brookdale Board Member;
Founder and Chief Executive
Officer, RJM Enterprises*

Erika Keegan
Executive Director, Brookdale
Lake Shore Drive

Marjan Kodric
Vice President of Dining Services,
Brookdale

Robyn Moore
District Director of Clinical
Services, Brookdale Chicago

Anna-Gene O'Neal
President of Hospice Service Line,
HCA Healthcare

Mary Sue Patchett
Former Executive Vice President of
Community and Field Operations
and Commander of Emergency
Command Center, Brookdale

Karen Peck
Vice President of Clinical Services,
Brookdale East Division

Ron Raben
Resident of Brookdale; Member,
Brookdale's National Advisory
Council

Charles Richardson
Senior Director of Resident and
Family Engagement, Brookdale

Guy Sansone
Nonexecutive Chairman of the
Board, Brookdale; Cofounder,
Chairman, and Chief Executive
Officer, H2 Health

Jim Seward
Brookdale Board Member

Andre Wallace
Maintenance Manager, Brookdale
Woodward Estates

Denise Warren
Brookdale Board Member; Former
Executive Vice President and Chief
Operating Officer, WakeMed
Health & Hospitals

Kathy White

Executive Director, Brookdale
Wilsonville

Lee Wielansky

Brookdale Board Member;
Chairman and Chief Executive
Officer, Opportunistic Equities

Janie Wood

Resident of Brookdale

Cindy Baier
President and Chief Executive Officer

Kevin Bowman
*Executive Vice President of
Community Operations*

David Cygan
Chief Marketing Officer

Kim Elliott
*Senior Vice President and
Chief Nursing Officer*

Laura Fischer
West Division Vice President
of Operations

David Hammonds
Senior Vice President of
Asset Management

George Hicks
Executive Vice President of
Finance, Treasurer

Teddy Hillard
Senior Vice President of
Corporate Development

Tara Jones
Chief Information Officer

Todd Kaestner
Executive Vice President of
Corporate Development,
President of CCRCs

Dawn Kussow
Senior Vice President and
Chief Accounting Officer

Joanne Leskowicz
Senior Vice President of Tax

Kathy MacDonald
Senior Vice President of
Investor Relations

Chris Maingot
Senior Vice President of Corporate
Development and Strategic Initiatives

Mary Kay O'Dea
Senior Vice President of
Shared Services

Jaclyn Pritchett
Senior Vice President of
Human Resources

Ben Ricci
*East Division Vice President
of Operations*

Steven Swain
*Executive Vice President and
Chief Financial Officer*

Sara Terry
*Senior Vice President of Resident
and Family Engagement*

Chad White
Executive Vice President of
General Counsel and Secretary

Rick Wigginton
Senior Vice President of Sales

It was incredible to work shoulder to shoulder with our community associates and directly serve our residents. This allowed us to connect with our mission and hear directly from our residents about their experiences. We did everything from cleaning rooms to cooking and serving meals, discussing dining and other issues with our residents, and participating in visits with prospects, shadowing our executive directors to better understand "a day in the life." If you combined the experience of all of our leaders who participated, we covered almost every role and all of the critical activities and processes that happen in our communities.

We listened carefully to our associates to understand how we could better enhance our processes and improve their work experience, and we engaged deeply with our residents to discern what was working well and what areas we could improve.

> ## People Closest to the Customer Have a Huge Impact on Success.

Our community learning visits provided incredibly valuable firsthand experience to our senior leadership team and energized all of us in the years following. Those in our corporate offices rarely have the benefit of working directly in the communities with our residents and associates, but they got to see the direct impact we have on their lives. Through this experience, we all got a closer look at who our residents are as people and what is most important to them.

Because of the importance of our community associates, we follow the guideline, "If you aren't serving a resident, serve someone who is." In other words, if you aren't directly serving a resident on the front lines, help serve our associates who are serving our customers.

The community learning visits allowed leaders to see firsthand the direct effect our associates have on residents' lives.

These community learning visits reinforced to us the importance of Brookdale's mission as we debriefed our experience and identified opportunities to improve our services. It afforded us a unique opportunity to assess our culture. At the end of the day, you have to see a company's culture where it lives to fully appreciate its power.

For us, our culture is most visible within the communities and in the relationships between our residents and associates. Armed with the unique perspectives we gained from these community learning visits and years of shaping our mission-centered culture leading up to the pandemic, our senior leadership team was so much better equipped to support the culture when it mattered most.

PERSONAL PERSPECTIVE FROM CINDY BAIER

Joined Brookdale Senior Living December 2015; currently president, chief executive officer, and board member

CULTIVATING UNDERSTANDING THROUGH COMMUNITY LEARNING VISITS

Early in my tenure as the CEO, before any inkling of the pandemic to come, I decided that our senior leadership team needed to conduct community learning visits.

What better way to understand the challenges that a housekeeper faces than by cleaning rooms side by side? I felt lucky to work alongside housekeeper Margarita Fortune during my first week of community learning visits at Brookdale Wilsonville (Oregon) as she taught me about the work she had done for twenty years (see photo gallery). Residents expressed how much they enjoyed visiting with Margarita as she cleaned their rooms—they felt it was like getting a visit from a family member!

What better experience is there to learn about feeding our residents than by working in the kitchen? Working as food servers gave our senior leadership team an invaluable perspective on the importance of knowing each resident, not only by name but knowing what they each like to eat and drink and more about their interests. You can't deliver service with a smile unless you can help make the residents genuinely happy!

Shadowing our associates on the ground level also gave us a chance to hear directly from our residents. For me, the insights I gleaned from these experiences created an important foundation as I studied our community operations. My fellow executives expressed a similar feeling: we learned so much through these efforts, and they energized us as we established our approach to the pandemic, because they connected us even more closely to our mission.

When the pandemic hit, we were able to leverage our unique experiences from these community learning visits to inform our strategy and help us lead through the crisis. Given my prior experience as a cook, combined with these experiences working in Brookdale's kitchens and dining rooms, I understood what was required to prepare and serve meals, and I quickly understood the challenges of moving meals from our dining rooms to resident rooms. Many of our executives instantly recognized the obstacles that we would need to overcome in order to succeed. My key takeaway: it's important for leaders to have firsthand experience with as many parts of the business as possible.

Creating the National Resident Advisory Council

Even after the success of our community learning visits, I contemplated other ways our senior leadership team could participate in opportunities for regular, direct interaction with our residents. Brookdale is a business of people taking care of people, so it was critically important to make sure that we remained focused on our residents' perspectives.

Many communities have resident councils, so I proposed the creation of a national resident advisory council (NAC), which was formalized in 2019. We asked a longtime resident of one of our Florida communities to serve as the founding chairman. Ken Garretson was already deeply engaged with his community and had an existing relationship with Brookdale's senior leadership team, because he had been involved with the resident advisory council for our Entry Fee Continuing Care Retirement Communities business. Ken loved traveling to other Brookdale communities and talking with residents. He would often visit our corporate office in Nashville to share this feedback (on a no-name basis) to help Brookdale improve its operations. Because of these visits, I had built a strong relationship with Ken. He was a natural choice to initially lead the NAC.

Prior to the pandemic, NAC members from around the nation traveled to Nashville annually to meet with our leadership team over the course of a few days and participated in other meetings via conference call. When the pandemic hit, traveling wasn't practical, so we transitioned our NAC meetings to be held virtually. It was fortunate that we already had the NAC in place prior to the pandemic, because it provided the corporate leadership team with an incredibly valuable forum for understanding how our response to COVID-19 was affecting our residents. We were grateful to hear their perceptions on what was working well and suggestions for improvement.

> ## Listen More Than You Talk.

Our residents who served on the NAC offered a number of excellent insights. As the pandemic continued, we increased the frequency of our meetings between the NAC and our senior corporate leaders. I think Brookdale is a better organization because of actions we have taken in response to NAC feedback. For example, at their suggestion, we communicated directly with residents to reinforce their understanding of Brookdale's financial strength to allay any fears that would have come without having information. Also, their feedback helped shape the rollout of a new telecommunications package to residents. Additionally, we have formed an NAC subcommittee on resident technology to continue our understanding and improvements.

One of the greatest joys of working in the senior living industry is the opportunity to serve the incredible people who join our communities as residents. Seniors are filled with wisdom and deserve to be honored, supported, and encouraged to share their life's lessons and passions. The more that we can hear their perspectives, the better! Many of our residents lived through the eradication of smallpox, for instance. This experience helped them understand quickly how vaccination could help control COVID-19.

We knew that we needed to gather as much feedback as possible from our residents in order to gauge the effectiveness of our response. One specific survey of residents and their loved ones received almost ten thousand responses, and this helped us assess our response to the COVID-19 pandemic and the execution of our operating strategies to support and engage the residents within our communities—and helped us develop further ways to support engagement within our communities.

Aligning with Our Mission

Another thing that I admire about the senior living industry is that it is filled with people who want to help others. While we have robust competition for prospects, companies within our industry are often eager to assist one another during natural disasters and other emergencies in order to help promote the safety and well-being of the seniors we all serve.

It is an understatement to say that obtaining PPE during the COVID-19 pandemic was extremely difficult in the early stages of the pandemic.[16] Brookdale was well positioned, because we had the size and scale to create entirely new supply chains to help source PPE and other supplies needed for our residents, patients, and associates. Many of our smaller competitors struggled to source supplies they needed, particularly N95 masks.

Early in the pandemic, a competitor called. They had a community with a COVID-19-positive resident, but they didn't have the appropriate PPE. Could we help? they wondered. We had sourced enough PPE for our immediate needs, albeit at a substantial premium.

---

16 "Shortage of Personal Protective Equipment Endangering Health Workers Worldwide," World Health Organization, published March 3, 2020, https://www.who.int/news/item/03-03-2020-shortage-of-personal-protective-equipment-endangering-health-workers-worldwide.

Nevertheless, we quickly agreed to ship them enough N95 masks to meet their immediate needs. Helping a competitor when we had the means to do so was consistent with helping save as many lives as we could.

When the world was in crisis and the way forward wasn't always clear, our North Star helped us find our path. Our culture of caring helped us to resolve not only what was immediately important for Brookdale and our residents and associates, but also for the common good.

HERO HIGHLIGHTS FROM KATHY WHITE

Joined Brookdale Senior Living November 2015; currently executive director, Brookdale Wilsonville

RESIDENTS CAN LIVE ANYWHERE—BUT THEY CHOOSE BROOKDALE!

My personal journey in this industry started in 1999 when I joined a senior living management company as an accounting manager for another company. Not having prior senior living experience, I enjoyed the ongoing and amazing education I received in my eleven years there. I learned everything I could about this industry well beyond accounting.

I sincerely believe that this experience—including that particular company's massive growth from 40 communities to 285 communities in nine years, as well as an extremely difficult court-ordered closure in 2010—

---

unknowingly prepared me for the next chapter of my professional career in senior living.

During my last two years with that company (leading up to its closure), I succeeded in keeping my team focused on our task of serving the communities and their residents—and most importantly, supporting each other through very dark and stressful times (including eventual layoffs for all involved).

When that company closed in December 2010, I had no doubt my next chapter would be as an executive director of a community where I could truly touch the lives of our seniors and their loved ones and lead a team of associates from a much more personal and hands-on level. I served in other communities before being led to Brookdale.

I joined Brookdale Wilsonville as the executive director in November of 2015. I was familiar with the community and was honored and excited to make Wilsonville, Oregon, my new community home. The community had a positive reputation within the Wilsonville area. Known for high occupancy and great care and service, I was looking forward to keeping those standards.

However, I soon learned that there were many challenges within the community. Rather than trying to point fingers, I looked around and said to the team, "The challenge is on. Let's build occupancy and do everything we can for our residents!"

Within one year, we filled the community to 100 percent occupancy! We had developed a team of professional and dedicated leaders who all stood out for their collective and individual talents. I was lucky to surround myself with smart and gifted teammates.

We held our 100 percent occupancy status for forty-one months straight—up until the summer of 2020 and COVID-19, when a few residents left to be closer to their loved ones. But I was so pleased that most felt the safest right here in the community. While we could not do in-person tours of our community, residents bravely moved into their new homes, sight unseen. *In spite of having to tackle two brief bouts of COVID-19 that year, our residents' loved ones trusted us and applauded the team's efforts to remain vigilant and compliant in the fight against an invisible enemy.*

My personal mission has been to maintain the standards we set for helping to safeguard the community and enhancing our residents' quality of life—even during COVID-19. I have high expectations for my team and myself, and I push for excellence in service and kindness in our relationship to others.

We never forget that our residents can go anywhere to live, but they choose us! During orientation with new associates, I try to reinforce this message by reminding them, "If not us, then who?"

Never did I dream my journey in senior living would involve both a pandemic and the toughest labor market in our lifetimes. The COVID-19 pandemic brought many different kinds of challenges, including a seismic change in the labor market as workers reevaluated their priorities

> or had to deal with new issues related to childcare. But even with these unfathomable challenges, I have such a deep appreciation for those who have fought with me and continue to fight! My team inspires and amazes me each and every day.
>
> For me, being a leader during this time was so rewarding, because I had a great team with me as we faced the battles and celebrated our successes together.

Brookdale has always been mission driven, and an important part of our business is serving individuals with dementia and Alzheimer's disease. We want to make the challenges of aging easier and would love to help find a cure! Keeping in line with this priority, we host a major fundraising campaign for the Alzheimer's Association every year. Our senior leadership team is incredibly proud of the fact that we were able to raise almost $1.2 million for the Alzheimer's Association's work during 2020, when many charity efforts around the world stalled. This was slightly more than had been raised in each of the two previous years. Normally our fundraising efforts involve in-person events, but we were able to pivot these events to a virtual setting with amazing success. Our leaders were so proud of the impact of our efforts. To date, we have now raised over $19 million for the Alzheimer's Association.

Continuing to make contributions to the higher good is ingrained in our culture of caring.

We were also focused on providing additional financial support to our associates during such trying times. As the CEO, I deemed it important to lead the way to help support the associates that needed it most. I asked that my contributions—all of which funneled directly to our associates through the Associate Compassion Fund (ACF)—be dedicated to our hourly associates wherever possible. I was so grateful that our entire executive leadership team and virtually all of our board members made significant contributions as well.

Additionally, we provided a great deal of information and helpful resources to our associates through our Brookdale intranet. From updated guidelines on resident testing (including dementia care considerations) to vaccine education and talking points, applications for the ACF, and personal testimonials, videos, and helpful links related to emotional health and well-being, our intranet served as a central hub and virtual treasure trove of resources for our associates. Our Human Resources team, which met and anticipated the needs of our associates, took a heart-centered approach to supporting associates through the most difficult trials of their professional lives.

HERO HIGHLIGHTS FROM
JACLYN PRITCHETT

Joined Brookdale Senior Living October 2016; currently senior vice president of Human Resources and member of Brookdale's Emergency Response Center

OFFERING THE BEST VERSION OF OURSELVES

When you have teams of servant leaders and a culture of caring, it feels natural to take care of everyone else before yourself. It's who we are and what we do. As parents, it's only natural to put our children first. *Likewise, our nurses put our residents first; our leaders put their teams first.*

However, a balance is needed to ensure we are offering the best version of ourselves.

With over fifteen years of human resources and psychology experience and a master of arts degree in industrial-organizational psychology, I knew as a leader what to do and the science behind it when the pandemic hit. Yet I was not doing it myself, and I felt like a hypocrite. Several division presidents, field leaders, and I created presentations for Brookdale's Corporate Athlete® program, and I discussed psychological challenges our associates were likely facing: things like imposter syndrome, compassion fatigue, burnout, Zoom® fatigue, and more. Associates quickly reached out to confirm that our findings had validated their experiences.

One associate shared, "It was so therapeutic to have what I've been going through shared as the collective feeling. [It] helps me put things into perspective and feel more supported.... [W]hat we're going through is shared." Another said, "I felt like I was the only one feeling that.... [I]t was good to see our leadership's human side."

Associates wondered, How did I know what they were going through, enabling me to speak so directly to them? The answer was simple: it was what I felt myself. There were times I questioned, Why me? Surely there's someone more capable, I thought.

I am just a normal person. I was burned out and exhausted after working seven days a week, twelve- to sixteen-plus hours a day while working as a leader on the ERC, leader of my teams, and personally experiencing what most households did in 2020: my two-year-old daughter pulled out of daycare, my seven-year-old son going to virtual school, my husband supporting our family so I could dedicate my focus on work, and my family quarantining within our home, uncertain what the future looked like.

Over time, I've learned that I have two diverse sides that make up who I am. The artistic/dreamer/hope side and the achiever/competitive/driver side. In stress, I tend to lean more toward the achiever side, focusing on what needs to be done and by when and how to execute with excellence.

I have to pause to remind myself of the hope side. Throughout the pandemic, hope was easy to lose. No matter how dark, it is important to search for the glimmers of goodness. I had to step away, even if only for a minute, to balance who I was as a leader, teammate, wife, and mother. I integrated the things that gave me energy into my experience. For example, I love gardening and photography, so I would pause for five minutes to sit in my garden with a cup of tea while focusing on the ordinary yet extraordinary beauty in the details within nature while praying or meditating. Those brief moments would help balance me and give me energy to persevere, filling me with hope so I could then provide hope to others.

Relying on teams and trusting others is crucial during a crisis. At the same time, it is just as important to trust in yourself. *To bring calm to the chaos of crisis, it is necessary first to calm yourself.*

The Interplay of Culture and Vision

One of the things that really concerned me during the pandemic was how we would maintain our culture through the hardest times. The key to sustaining a culture of caring is to tie it to a vision of the future. At Brookdale, our vision is "to be the nation's first choice in senior living." I want to create a company that will last forever, because the work we do is so important. Our culture needed to inform our daily decisions so that we could work toward a bright future.

A leader aims to create a vision for their organization that everyone can believe in and stand by. You want your associates to both see the possibilities of your vision and make sacrifices to help achieve it. The interplay of vision and culture is critical to Brookdale, because we want to provide our unique style of caring, heart-centered services to seniors for generations to come. The work we do is that important!

As we considered how to cultivate a servant's heart on a daily basis, we also wanted to create a more lasting incentive for our associates through merit-based awards and enhanced recognition for their everyday efforts over time.

> **Showing Appreciation Is One of the Most Important Things You Can Do.**

COVID-19 required a lot out of our leaders and associates at every level, so we immediately expanded our Everyday Heroes program to recognize more of our associates who went above and beyond the call of duty to serve our residents. Winning associates received a cash award and paid time off, as well as Brookdale merchandise. Between March and June 2020, we had almost six thousand Everyday Heroes winners.

We also created a new award called the Servant Heart Award. This award was fitting for the times, because COVID-19 revealed so many associates who personally sacrificed additional time, energy, and talents in support of our residents and associates, as well as Brookdale. The winners truly demonstrated their "heart" for the business and service of senior living.

HERO HIGHLIGHTS FROM VICKI FREED

Joined Brookdale Senior Living Board of Directors October 2019; currently senior vice president of Sales, Trade Support, and Service, Royal Caribbean International

STANDING OUT IN A WORLD FULL OF O'S

Nobody is too old for an alphabet lesson—at least not one like this. When it comes to being an extraordinary leader, you don't have to be CEO or even manage a team. You just have to inspire people to make a difference in how they feel. It goes beyond doing your job well. *Leadership means adding a special touch that's uniquely you.* That's where the alphabet comes in—specifically the letters O and Q and how they represent successful people.

Just like the shape, an O is someone who is well rounded. They're knowledgeable in their field, and they practice great customer service. Most professionals are O's, and there's absolutely nothing wrong with being one. O's are great. You'd expect everyone on a successful team to be an O. But that's the point. If you're surrounded by colleagues

---

who are all very talented people, how do leaders stand out from the pack? The answer is going from an *O* to a *Q*.

Q's are different. Like the letter, they possess an extra hook that differentiates them: they make a special mark on the people they come across. When an *O* becomes a *Q*, they're not just part of the pack of talent—they're leading it.

When you leverage that special something that makes you a *Q*, you're doing more than standing out—you're enhancing your personal brand. Even working for a company that has its own brand and image, you as a professional have one too. But keep this in mind: your brand is only half what you intend to create—the other half is the perception and emotion that others have about you.

Think about how you would describe yourself and your brand, and then take that list of your personal attributes and ask your trusted friends and advisors to confirm those qualities. Do you see yourself the same way that others see you? You can't directly change a perception, because it isn't yours. But you can influence it. And that's where your *Q* mark comes in.

You might be thinking, "This sounds great! Tell me what I can do to become a *Q*." But the truth is, nobody can tell you what to do. There's no cookie-cutter method. And that would defeat the whole point of being a *Q*—it wouldn't be unique to you if anyone could do it. But I can give you some of the qualities that can set *Q*'s apart.

I call them SUMS: (S)imple, (U)nexpected, (M)emorable, (S)ignature.

1. *Simple: do something simple, so you can do it consistently.*

2. *Unexpected: make people stop and say, "Wow."*

3. *Memorable: make it memorable by making it personal.*

4. *Signature: develop your signature mark; only you do it!*

Here's an example of a Q leader: One of the Q's I've met delights me every morning, turning the ordinarily mundane experience of buying a cup of coffee into something special. At my local Starbucks®,[17] one barista in particular adds a little personality to each sale that caffeine just can't match. She opens each transaction with, "Can I pour you a cup of happiness today?" It makes me smile every time! A greeting like that is so simple but makes an otherwise ordinary routine stand out—and demonstrates real leadership.

When it comes to finding your own hook, perhaps it's something you're already doing but maybe not regularly. Or it could be something you are doing regularly but need to make more special and personal. If you need to start from scratch, begin by listening: *when you listen to those you're serving, you can pick up on some amazing cues— pun intended!*

Your Q mark will not only make you extraordinary in your job, but it will also make a difference with every resident in your care. It will connect you in a wonderful way. That is the real takeaway here—connection.

I challenge you to answer this: "What's that one little mark that can make me a Q?" Everyone can have one.

---

17   Starbucks is owned by Starbucks Coffee Company.

> And once you find it, watch how quickly you leave your mark on others.

Lead by Example

There is no question COVID-19 challenged our leaders at all levels. One of my core beliefs is "Never ask someone to do something you would not do yourself." Our team worked incredibly hard through the pandemic, and I was determined to invest every ounce of my energy into helping our leaders, associates, and Brookdale succeed. There was no doubt this decision would have a high personal cost, but I genuinely believe that leadership is a privilege that comes with great responsibility. If you want to be a leader, make sure you're prepared for the responsibility it entails.

> ## People Want to Be Part of Something Bigger Than Themselves.

People naturally look for leaders to follow so they can be part of something much bigger than themselves. It is a leader's responsibility to set the example, clearly communicate the vision, and help create a culture that people want to be part of. Moreover, leaders must lead with integrity.

Prior to the pandemic, I made it a point to write hundreds of handwritten notes a year, thanking people for what they've done. It's always been an important part of my responsibility, and it became more critical during COVID-19 because team members at every level of the organization were doing incredible things. The notes included a Brookdale "CEO Coin" printed with our mission and vision, along with our cornerstones. This coin was intended as recognition for outstanding work and was also a reminder of our focus on enriching the lives of those we serve with compassion, respect, excellence, and integrity and of our vision to be the nation's first choice in senior living. I felt this coin helped connect us through our shared values.

For those who have made sacrifices above and beyond the call of duty, it means so much to be personally recognized and honored.

Lessons Learned

The quality of the people on your team can mean the difference between success and failure. People don't realize how much they can accomplish until they are truly tested.

Brookdale leaders accomplished many seemingly impossible tasks by reaching deep within themselves for strength; by banding together, we beat the odds. We were able to overcome so many obstacles because we knew what was at stake—the health and well-being of our residents, patients, and associates and the financial stability of Brookdale.

It's natural for humans to seek to become a part of something much greater than themselves. That's why there is a need for leaders to set the vision and create a culture that attracts the right talent and ensures that a company is aligned with a higher purpose.

The culture of an organization is constantly changing. Taking time to reinforce the behaviors that are important is critical to maintaining it. People are happiest in a culture where they can be themselves, so be careful to ensure that the people that you hire share the values of the company.

If teamwork means tying the threads of the rope around a central mission, then culture is the inner code that rests inside the hearts of each of the associates on your team. Take the necessary steps to create a culture with meaning, and make an effort to applaud the individuals who best exemplify it.

People who are willing to work hard, believe in a company's mission, and work well together can accomplish virtually anything!

This is the foundation of all execution.

PART III

LEADERSHIP TAKEAWAYS

CHAPTER 10

Nurturing Diversity

*Reaching Peak Performance with the Inclusion
of Diverse Voices and Perspectives*

A s the leader of the largest senior living operator in one of the most diverse nations in the world, I have always personally valued diversity and found it important when building high-performing teams. From the time I started as CEO at Brookdale, I've made a concerted effort to deliver on my commitment to promote diversity throughout our organization.

Diverse perspectives are informed by a wide range of identifying factors in life, including race, sexual orientation, ethnicity, gender, age, and religion. Diversity also springs from factors like where you grow up, where you went to college or trade school—even *whether* you went to college or a trade school!—and where you work and live; and it includes core personality traits, like how you process information, how you solve problems, and how you recover from stress. Importantly, diversity includes functional expertise, industry experience, and role specialization as well.

Advocating for Diversity with Intention

When I joined Brookdale in 2015, the executive leadership team and board of directors did not fully reflect the population we served, nor did they fully reflect our associates, and I felt strongly that we could improve our performance as a team by increasing our diversity. Research demonstrates diverse teams perform better than others. One report found that companies "in the top quartile for ethnic and racial diversity in management were 35 percent more likely to have financial returns above their industry mean, and those in the top quartile for gender diversity were 15 percent more likely to have returns above the industry mean."[18]

Further, it's been reported "[O]rganizations with at least one female board member yielded higher return on equity and higher net income growth than those that did not have any women on the board."

Harvard Business Review concludes, "[N]onhomogeneous teams are simply smarter." The results speak for themselves. But promoting diversity requires a proactive approach: change requires action.

I believe that the proper approach is to conduct a thorough review of a diverse slate of qualified candidates before hiring and ultimately to hire the best candidate for the position. With this strategy in place, I have long advocated for diverse candidates to be considered when new executives or board members are appointed. We've interviewed so many amazing people, and I feel we have always selected the best candidate. This hiring strategy has resulted in our board and leadership team achieving greater diversity over time.

---

18   David Rock and Heidi Grant, "Why Diverse Teams Are Smarter," *Harvard Business Review*, published November 4, 2016, https://hbr.org/2016/11/why-diverse-teams-are-smarter.

According to the US Department of Labor, 80 percent of healthcare decisions are made by women.[19] Within Brookdale, 70 percent of our associates and 80 percent of our residents are women. Thus, I believed it was important to consider more women for leadership and board roles.

During 2018, we transformed the demographics of the leaders who made up our board of directors, and by the end of the year, our board had achieved gender parity for the first time in its history. We had been able to add Rita Johnson-Mills, a very talented director who also brought a racially diverse perspective to the table. When we increased our board to nine members in 2020 (with the addition of Dr. Jordan Asher), we still had nearly equal gender representation.

Our intent was to find the best in class in the skill sets that we needed, and we were able to build diverse lists of both men and women; members of our board were chosen because they were the best candidates. We learned that an effective way to build inclusive lists from which to interview was to leverage our own professional networks in addition to executive search firms, rather than relying exclusively on professional recruiters. This included sourcing candidates from programs designed to develop leaders seeking their first seat on a board of directors.

Through the efforts of Kathy MacDonald, our senior vice president of Investor Relations, our focus on diversity captured the attention of the New York Stock Exchange (NYSE). In May 2020, the leaders of the NYSE invited me to join their board advisory council. The purpose of the NYSE Board Advisory Council is to identify and connect diverse board candidates to NYSE-listed companies seeking new directors. I have been so fortunate to have this opportunity to

19   Kristyna Wentz-Graff, "Women Responsible for Most Health Decisions in the Home," OHSU, published May 11, 2017, https://news.ohsu.edu/2017/05/11/women-responsible-for-most-health-decisions-in-the-home.

help place board candidates by fostering connections with companies seeking new directors.

Diverse Teams Perform Better.

Brookdale has also received recognition in this area as a Corporate Champion from the Women's Forum of New York for our commitment to board representation for women. Brookdale is a "W" Winning Company for its commitment to board diversity, as honored by the national organization called 2020 Women on Boards. We received a 2020 Corporate Citizenship Award from the Committee for Economic Development of The Conference Board, given annually to a company that demonstrates a strong commitment to corporate responsibility practices and whose leaders are actively engaged in supporting and expanding those efforts. It's also been recognized as a Gender-Balanced Board by 50/50 Women on Boards®.[20] Additionally, Brookdale was honored as a corporate inductee to the Board Walk of Fame by Cable,[21] a Nashville-based women's networking organization.

As we focused on diversity within our board, we also made similar efforts for our leadership team. My goal was to interview a diverse slate of candidates and to hire the best. At the same time, promoting from within is also important. Thus, my approach has balanced attracting talented executives from outside our industry with promoting proven leaders from within Brookdale and the senior living industry. In my opinion, identifying a diverse slate of candidates raises the bar, because it expands the list of talented individuals who are considered.

20   50/50 Women on Boards is a trademark of 50/50 Women on Boards, Inc.

21   "Brookdale Senior Living Honored for Gender Diversity on Board of Directors," Brookdale, published November 16, 2018, https://www.brookdalenews.com/brookdale-senior-living-honored-for-gender-diversity-on-board-directors.htm.

Diverse teams perform better. It happened at Brookdale.

An amazing fusion of ideas has occurred as a result of the collaboration between our veteran leaders (some with more than thirty years of senior living experience) and newcomers to our industry. Several of our recent external hires possess unique healthcare or functional expertise, and their voices have led to a burst of creativity in adapting best practices from their experiences. Executives with deep knowledge outside of senior living (like hospitality or other parts of the healthcare continuum, including hospital systems) have also added enormous value to our business.

Inviting leaders with a diverse range of perspectives to our leadership team has strengthened our leadership practices and improved our analytical tools. This would not have happened without an intentional focus on diversity. We are a business of people taking care of people, so it's of highest importance that we listen to a wide range of perspectives.

The key to increasing diversity is this: Remove as many barriers as possible. Maintain an attitude that everyone is invited to participate, and trust that the best will succeed. As the CEO, my goal has always been to build the best team in our industry. The only way to achieve this goal, in my opinion, is to ensure everyone has an equal opportunity to succeed.

PERSONAL PERSPECTIVE FROM CINDY BAIER

Joined Brookdale Senior Living December 2015; currently president, chief executive officer, and board member

GIVE PEOPLE A CHANCE!

I was in my mid-twenties when I was sent to the shipyards of Groton, Connecticut, to lead a major project—tasked to lead a group of men in their fifties and sixties at the time. During this period, it wasn't even advisable for a woman to walk alone in the shipyards.

On my first day, it was clear to me that the team wasn't interested in hearing what I had to say. What could a "young girl" know? *I was committed to proving my worth and showing them that I could help, so I focused on winning over the team, one person at a time, starting with the informal team leader.* I listened attentively to what he had to say and answered all of his questions thoroughly, demonstrating my deep knowledge of the subject matter and my passion for the project. I asked for his perspective and offered solutions where needed. Ultimately the leader of the group was convinced that I knew what I was talking about, so he decided to work closely with me, and eventually, so did the entire team.

We worked together for several months, and in the end our project generated hundreds of millions of dollars of cash. We were so proud of our work! We came from very different backgrounds, but in the course of a few months, we became a close-knit team. For many years after the project ended, I returned to Groton, Connecticut, for a team reunion, because these relationships mattered to me.

This experience taught me a great deal in the early years of my professional career. Most importantly, *I learned that many people simply need a chance to make a difference.* From this point forward, I have made it a point to help provide opportunities to anyone who wanted a chance to lead and had the right skills.

Fast forward to Brookdale: Frank Bumstead was one of the directors who interviewed me during Brookdale's CEO succession planning process. At the time, Frank knew me as the CFO who was in control of the company's finances, but he didn't know as much about my approach to building teams or my strategy for the company. I shared my vision for Brookdale. I also shared with Frank my experience in the shipyards and explained that my approach to leadership was to find the best people with the right skills and encourage them to work together. I emphasized my point with one of my husband's favorite D. Wayne Calloway quotes: *"Leaders take eagles and teach them to fly in formation."* Frank listened carefully, evaluated my ideas, and ultimately offered to discuss my strategy for Brookdale with other members of the board. It was a wonderful honor to have Frank's endorsement— someone who was so widely respected willing to advocate on my behalf and serve as a mentor.

Without Frank's help, I wouldn't be where I am today.

Even within an industry, there is diversity in focus and experience. For instance, experience within the healthcare industry varies based on the point within the healthcare continuum in which a person gains experience. Working in a hospital system is different than working for a payer or insurance carrier, and all of those are different than working in home health, hospice, or senior living.

One of the challenges of senior living is that it's constantly changing; this is also one of the greatest strengths of our industry—every challenge can be seen as an opportunity. The pandemic accelerated changes that were already underway in healthcare. This created the opportunity for us to form a joint venture with HCA Healthcare through their purchase of 80 percent of Brookdale Health Care Services—providing our company with additional liquidity in the midst of the pandemic while still enabling our residents access to quality healthcare services in their community. I believe this opportunity was realized because we had an amazing, diverse range of leaders who saw the change in the industry as an opportunity to leverage one of our important assets.

To extend the analogy of the conductor and orchestra once more, adding diverse voices to a team is the equivalent of adding new instruments to the symphony. Identifying skilled musicians who play the piccolo, oboe, or castanets may be harder to do than finding trumpet and violin players, but the sound they add to the orchestra enhances the performance.

> ## Create a Diverse Slate of Candidates and Hire the Best.

Likewise, working to identify diverse candidates to lend their voices to leadership decisions also enhances the process of decision-making—especially important when the matter impacts the health and well-being of our residents, patients, and associates.

We were already seeing steady improvements in the operation of our leadership team by virtue of the efforts made to encourage diversity in the years leading up to the pandemic, and this set us up for success as we assessed the many different groups our decisions were impacting.

As we increased diversity, our leadership team adapted quickly to the changes, opening up to the creative solutions posed by newcomers and committing to cross-functional teamwork across the many verticals within Brookdale. This included adopting new analytic frameworks and benefiting from an expanded network of contacts contributed by newcomers. This fusion of creative thinking and varying methodologies for problem-solving helped us make better decisions.

My belief that diverse teams perform better was affirmed when the pandemic hit. Having different perspectives in place well before the arrival of COVID-19 helped us move more quickly because we could assess the problem from so many different angles. As a result, I believe in diversity even more strongly today and continue to advocate for seeking diversity at all levels of Brookdale.

HERO HIGHLIGHTS FROM BAHAR AZHDARI

Joined Brookdale Senior Living February 2016; currently senior director and associate general counsel

HONORING DIVERSITY WITH A MINDSET OF ONENESS

From a young age, my parents imprinted on me the truth of the oneness of humanity. I have held fast to that belief, allowing it to shape both my professional and personal views. The COVID-19 pandemic has further reinforced them. Never before have we seen so clearly and vividly how similar we all are: within weeks, a tiny virus made its way across the globe—hitting every country, infecting citizens indiscriminately, and redefining priorities. *Working to help contain the spread required us to set aside our personal preferences and comforts to come together for the greater good. Indeed, we depended on one another for our collective sense of peace, security, and well-being.*

Because the pandemic upended both private and work life, companies also had to adapt. Some businesses did so quickly; others lagged behind. Brookdale recognized early on what was happening and made moves to address the needs of residents and associates. Our leadership team and associates worked tirelessly to implement an operational transformation and gain an advantage as we faced an evolving and unfamiliar situation that impacted seniors disproportionately.

The pandemic also disproportionately impacted people of color. As a company with a diverse workforce, we could not ignore this disparity, especially when it came to educating our associates about proper infection control for a novel virus, the importance of screening symptoms, and why quarantining when exposed was essential to mitigate spread. Concurrent with the growth of the pandemic, our nation was rocked by social unrest related to unfolding events of racial injustice. As individual discussions began, companies also wanted to reiterate their commitments to diversity, equity, and inclusion.

For Brookdale, it was an opportunity to show our associates—who were working so hard to do what needed to be done for our residents—that our values (as stated in our cornerstones of passion, courage, partnership, and trust) were truly reflected in our operations. The company's commitment to diversity was clear through the words and actions of our CEO Cindy Baier. From the time her tenure began as CEO in 2018, Cindy was vocal about the need to diversify Brookdale leadership, starting with the executive leadership team and board of directors.

By the summer of 2020, mindful that our associates were experiencing a world like no other due to the emotional toll of the pandemic and social unrest, we wanted to make sure we were preparing them for the current and future post-COVID-19 world by developing programs to assist with career advancement; we also expanded sources from which to recruit talent and created messaging and education for our associates around infection control and wellness.

Next, we enhanced our educational efforts as we followed the development and emergency use authorization of the COVID-19 vaccine. We worked to create a culture of vaccine acceptance prior to our first vaccine clinics, and we continued the effort through our decision to require associates to be vaccinated, subject to limited exceptions. This meant promoting the efficacy of the vaccines and encouraging associates to get them; at the same time, we had to acknowledge the reality and legitimacy of vaccine hesitancy for people of color due to decades of earned mistrust of the medical system as well as a historical lack of access to care and disparities in care. We created videos and educational materials, and we also invited medical experts from different backgrounds, races, and specialties to participate in "Ask the Expert" sessions focusing specifically on the COVID-19 vaccines. These efforts yielded positive results.

The pandemic reshaped priorities for many. For me, it reinforced our oneness and interconnectedness. I was pleased to have the opportunity to help Brookdale with its inclusion and diversity efforts, and I am excited to see what we continue to do as we look to the future.

Honoring Diversity of Perspective

At the beginning of the pandemic, I relied on the Brookdale board for their perspectives in establishing our emergency response. Thankfully, we had paid special attention to improving the diversity of thought, experience, and expertise, in addition to increasing racial and gender diversity across the board (literally). One of the earliest lessons we learned reinforced the powerful effects we were already experiencing from the multiplicity of voices who were advising me.

Dr. Jordan Asher was specifically invited to join the board in order to variegate the perspectives of the leaders overseeing the ship's journey. Prior to Jordan joining, our board did not include a licensed physician. I moved quickly to recommend that we add one. We interviewed a diverse slate of physicians, and Jordan was the best fit for us. We were delighted when Jordan joined our board, and his appointment came at the perfect moment. Just days after he joined the board, Jordan raised one of the first red flags in the pandemic—the stunning prediction that we might not be able to send our residents to the hospital in the event they fell ill with COVID-19—and this opened our eyes to new concerns, so we could plan accordingly.

Jordan offers a substantively different perspective—both in his clinical expertise and in his role as chief physician executive for a hospital system—than other members of the board, because of his deep understanding of the clinical issues at play for our residents. While other board members held some shared perspectives—for instance, Denise Warren had hospital system experience, but she approached it from the financial perspective of balancing mission with margin as well as an operational perspective—expanding these perspectives to include diversity of expertise helped us throughout the pandemic.

> ## You Can't Get the Best People if You Exclude Some from Consideration.

The role diversity plays is in expanding the full scope of possibilities and solutions we consider. This was a pivotal dynamic that characterized our board at the start of the pandemic, and it served us well. We were able to rely on the specific expertise that we needed.

Here's the way it played out. As I faced tough decisions—high-level, life-or-death decisions—I had to think about who would best be able to help me analyze each matter in order to make an informed decision. For issues that directly impacted the health of our residents, I knew I could rely on Jordan's perspective, because he was a physician and was charged with leading his health system's COVID-19 response. I also talked with Denise, because she understood the operations of a healthcare system. I talked with Anna-Gene O'Neal, because she was a nurse who led our home health and hospice agencies—and had special relationships within the healthcare industry by virtue of her connection to the Fellows Program at the Nashville Health Care

Council as well as her participation in the council's COVID-19 task force.

I also talked with Kim Elliott, at the time our lead senior living clinician, and Cindy Kent, who had served as the president and general manager of 3M's Infection Prevention Division before joining Brookdale. With the benefit of such a wide variety of perspectives, I felt confident in my ability to analyze an issue from multiple angles and make a well-informed decision. Having leaders with specific, relevant, and diverse expertise to rely on was critically important throughout the pandemic.

Diverse Perspectives Increase Success

Maintaining a commitment to diverse viewpoints made us keenly aware of unique challenges that affected members of the Brookdale community as these issues came to light.

No corner of America was untouched by the pandemic, and due to Brookdale's broad geographic reach, many of our associates experienced complications in their personal lives based on where they lived. For example, associates who had to rely on public transportation saw their usual routes changed or reduced to accommodate social distancing or city staffing concerns. Others experienced difficulty in completing basic tasks, like shopping for groceries due to supply-chain disruptions. Of course, people had different experiences depending on where they lived, whether on the coast, in big cities, or in small towns.

In addition, there were different cultural aspects to vaccine acceptance. Depending on factors as varied as state of residence, race, or religious beliefs, a person's willingness to accept a vaccine differed. What we found is that people wanted to hear from medical professionals, but they wanted to hear from medical professionals they trusted and who looked like them.

Our focus on diversity also shaped our leadership perspective in various ways.

First, having diverse board members was particularly helpful as we organized our vaccination efforts. People of different ages, cultural backgrounds, and religious beliefs evaluated vaccinations differently. Dr. Jordan Asher and Rita Johnson-Mills helped us think through the best approaches to enhancing our vaccine clinics, including methods of communication and our specific messaging. We needed to think about diversity as we determined which experts we could engage to answer questions our residents and associates had about COVID-19 vaccines.

Second, leaders have different definitions of quality—particularly those who have joined Brookdale's leadership team or board from different industries. Think about it this way: every organization is focused on different quality metrics. At Brookdale, one of the quality measures that we have relied on is Net Promoter Score. Not every company uses this particular metric. One of the benefits of adding individuals with diverse experience in different industries is that they helped us think about quality from many different perspectives.

Prior to joining Brookdale's board, Rita Johnson-Mills served as the president and CEO of UnitedHealthcare Community Plan of Tennessee. In this role, Rita focused on quality metrics that would help those under her care obtain better health outcomes at a lower cost. In other words, she focused on quality as a technique to help manage population health. Rita's experience helped our leadership team set company-wide standards, which sharpened our focus on quality.

HERO HIGHLIGHTS FROM
RITA JOHNSON-MILLS

Joined Brookdale Senior Living Board of Directors August 2018; currently founder and CEO of RJM Enterprises

IMPORTANCE OF QUALITY IN A PANDEMIC ENVIRONMENT

The COVID-19 pandemic highlighted a number of strengths and weaknesses in our healthcare system, many of which impact the quality of care provided in senior living communities and hospitals. It reinforced our belief that decisions should not be centered solely on the bottom line. Our core service revolves around the quality of life we provide to our residents and their ability to interact meaningfully with family, friends, and associates. The definition of quality care has taken on new meaning in a post-COVID-19 world.

One of the primary strengths we realized and celebrated was the dedication of our amazing associates. They continued to perform their jobs and show up for our residents during an unprecedented time. They deeply understood the importance of the personal care for residents living in our communities, and they increased their efforts when family members were unable to come visit inside the community.

Many companies are witnessing the high cost of these sacrifices, as first responders and caregivers have been so overworked and overstressed they are now leaving the field.

At Brookdale, we met the challenge of burnout head on. We offered competitive compensation and paid time off, and we worked hard to maintain open communication with our associates and residents. We encouraged associates to make suggestions and conducted surveys of our workforce. This allowed associates to provide input and offer suggestions for improvement. *The leadership team believes very strongly that an engaged and empowered employee base will always go the extra mile in caring for our residents.*

Due to the temporary closure of physician and dental practices, we saw many individuals put off routine care needs. Even now, as we play catch-up, we are still finding that some people are not comfortable returning to provider offices. This has led us to consider greater reliance on alternative care options, such as telehealth.

Another unanticipated benefit that occurred as a result of COVID-19 was the renewed focus on enjoying the outdoors. More than ever, our residents and associates have enjoyed opportunities to go outdoors to take in fresh air.

Additionally, with fewer people out and about, we witnessed a revival of wildlife wandering around our communities, which helped to lift the spirits of our residents. We heard reports of wild birds and friendly critters exploring the grounds of our communities more than they had prior to COVID-19, and this was a thrilling new development for our residents.

We have continued to look for additional ways to enhance the quality of life for our residents so they can thrive. We have reopened our communities to visitors. We have improved our associates' vaccination rates. We are listening to and learning from nature and insights from our associates and residents. Our residents are once again engaging in social activities, such as movie night, concerts, and educational workshops. Many residents are thrilled by our white-tablecloth dinners and the socialization that comes with them.

We are currently looking into more activities that will improve the quality of life for our residents, including educational opportunities, mindfulness classes, and even fashion shows!

In most instances, when we think about quality, we start from a clinical perspective. COVID-19 has reinforced the importance of adding quality practices for social and emotional well-being. Mental health has always been as important as physical health, and the pandemic has helped us achieve an even greater understanding in this area of well-being. *The pandemic helped us explore the many areas of improvement so we can continue to serve our residents with high levels of care.*

Again, we viewed vaccines as shots of hope, and we worked very hard as a team to make sure that our residents and associates had both streamlined access to the vaccine and the information they needed to make an informed decision. However, we understood that vaccine education was not a one-size-fits-all matter. People wanted to hear from experts who looked like them: they wanted to hear from peers and advisors they trusted. We made a concerted effort to ensure our messages were being delivered by as many different and diverse voices as possible.

We incorporated diversity into our vaccine education, and we made a special effort to connect with medical professionals who are Latinx and Black to help lead the effort to encourage vaccinations where possible. At every point, we focused on our North Star: the health and well-being of our residents, patients, and associates.

We also launched a peer-to-peer campaign to increase our vaccination rates. Associates who shared their reasons for getting vaccinated in our "Give Hope a Shot" campaigns brought with them unique perspectives based on their different cultural experiences. Across Brookdale, our leaders who were overseeing the vaccine initiative went the extra mile to provide the information that our residents and associates needed to make this critically important decision.

Where a resident remained vaccine hesitant, we spent additional time tending to their concerns from a place of compassion and a desire to understand, never coercing. Our residents come from a wide variety of backgrounds that make up their worldview, and we remained sensitive to every resident's needs while maintaining our focus on finding solutions. I firmly believe that our strong history of encouraging diverse voices enabled us to quickly achieve a high resident vaccination rate.

When the COVID-19 vaccine became available, it was initially hard for me to understand why anyone wouldn't want it, because we had experienced so much upheaval from our ordinary operations and daily living. The shots, in my estimation, were a necessary and welcome development in the course of the pandemic. I saw them as "shots of hope."

Like many professionals who enjoy a measure of privilege, I did not fully appreciate that there could be hesitancy among many within the Black community to trust the COVID-19 vaccine due to past medical experiments. I needed to learn more about the topic, and I welcomed the education so that I could better understand a perspective that differed from my own. This experience reinforced to me why seeking out opinions from individuals with different perspectives and from diverse backgrounds and races matters.

HERO HIGHLIGHTS FROM ANGELA HALEY

Joined Brookdale Senior Living August 2015; currently vice president of Clinical Operations

PROMOTING VACCINE ACCEPTANCE AMID DIVERSITY

When COVID-19 vaccines were nearing approval by the CDC and ready for distribution to our industry toward the end of 2020, we were excited and committed to a prompt and efficient rollout. Due to Brookdale's population of residents and associates and the tremendous efforts of our team, we were afforded early access before the general population. We knew that widespread adoption of vaccines across all populations was critical to containing the virus.

We led with hope that we could make a positive impact on the health and well-being of our residents, patients, and associates, and we remained firm in our belief that the newly developed COVID-19 vaccine would alter the course of the pandemic. We wanted to schedule and execute these clinics as soon as possible. Through tireless collaboration and coordination among our field and community leaders, along with the help of our pharmacy

---

partner (CVS Health') and others, we administered our first vaccine clinics in mid-December.

We realized that our speed in facilitating vaccines to our community residents and associates didn't mean that everyone would accept them. We needed a plan for enhancing communication and addressing concerns.

For months, we had been educating, training, and preparing. We hosted multiple training opportunities, held open-forum question-and-answer sessions, and readied our communities for the socially distanced vaccine clinics to come. Yet concerns among the general populace began to surface, and we noted that there was fear, mistrust, and skepticism about the vaccine. Since Brookdale is generally representative of the greater US population, concerns among some of our people began to surface as well.

We had to recognize that while everyone had been struggling throughout the pandemic, some people struggled more than others. We needed to hear from diverse voices within Brookdale: different age groups, different races, LGBTQ+ associates, pregnant and nursing women, and working parents.

As an organization, diversity, equity, and inclusion practices are critical priorities for us. With the vaccines, we had a targeted opportunity that could impact the trajectory of the pandemic and ultimately benefit our residents, associates, and their families. *We had to create a culture of vaccine acceptance, which meant we needed to stop and listen to all concerns.*

We had a rapidly changing situation with more questions than answers. We offered more and more information and sought to understand what made the biggest difference: Did it help hearing from doctors? From fellow associates who had been vaccinated? From somebody vaccinated a month ago? From residents? One sure thing Brookdale associates have in common is the love and respect they share for our residents.

We learned that although each individual might have their own perspective and opinion about the vaccine, ultimately people want to feel heard and understood and to have their questions answered.

One-on-one conversations proved to be more helpful for individuals who were vaccine hesitant, so we ramped up these opportunities. We enhanced our training in order to address the uncertainty, and we provided our printed materials in multiple languages. We created a "Vaccine Weekly" bulletin specifically catering to the community-based population that was less likely to receive the emails and online messaging we'd been developing.

We shared videos of a variety of voices at Brookdale—people voicing their "why"—all emphasizing the hope of moving beyond COVID-19. Our resident vaccine acceptance rate was initially higher than our associates, so we embarked upon a campaign called "Do It for Me" featuring a broad range of residents to appeal directly to our associates through heartfelt videos.

We created tool kits and resources to manage emotions, help ease anxiety, and encourage communication. We engaged our associates through a direct-text campaign, held town hall–style meetings, and created a marketing campaign and battle cry: "Give Hope a Shot."

Ultimately, one of the most effective ways of addressing doubt among our diverse population was through collaboration with a diverse group of medical experts. With the goal of increasing awareness, understanding, and engagement, we created an "Ask the Expert" speaker series to communicate key COVID-19 research and findings relevant to all associates. We selected experts in infectious diseases and fertility, professors of medicine, and immunologists from diverse universities and backgrounds. They spoke to a broad audience on all aspects of vaccine—safety and effectiveness as well as pregnancy, breastfeeding, and fertility—bringing together both wisdom and scientific perspectives on a difficult topic. In one case, they presented in two languages, and they all made themselves available to open and candid question-and-answer sessions afterward.

These vaccine acceptance challenges provided some of our greatest lessons during the pandemic and reinforced some of the basic approaches we were already implementing in actively helping to foster a deeper awareness and understanding of the concerns of the diverse cultures, genders, ethnicities, ages, backgrounds, and voices that make up Brookdale. I believe we are a better organization because of these experiences, and I'm so grateful I was able to take part.

Diversity Expands Understanding

At the start of the pandemic, PPE was extremely difficult to obtain.[22] Cindy Kent joined Brookdale in January 2020 as executive vice president and president of Senior Living from 3M. When I first met Cindy, I was impressed by her experience within healthcare, and I was delighted to recruit a talented and diverse woman.

Partner for Understanding.

When the pandemic hit, and the need to source more PPE was imminent, Cindy was one of the first leaders I approached for guidance and contacts who could help us procure much-needed PPE, directly from 3M if possible. Because of Cindy Kent's connections, we were able to source an incremental eighty thousand 3M N95 masks through McKesson and three million 3M surgical masks through Grainger. While we weren't successful in sourcing as many products as we needed through 3M at that time and had to look elsewhere for more, Cindy's knowledge of the products and sourcing gave us a clearer understanding of some of the obstacles we would need to overcome in order to meet our needs. We realized that our traditional supply chain was not going to be sufficient, so our Procurement Department immediately began screening hundreds of vendors from around the world to source essential PPE.

Diverse leaders also enhanced our communications efforts so we could relay information to the wider world as we sought to foster

---

22 "Shortage of Personal Protective Equipment Endangering Health Workers Worldwide," World Health Organization, published March 3, 2020, https://www.who.int/news/item/03-03-2020-shortage-of-personal-protective-equipment-endangering-health-workers-worldwide.

understanding. During the pandemic, we produced a vast array of videos to communicate with associates, residents, and the public. We used this opportunity to showcase leaders who had a wide variety of expertise, and this had the added benefit of reflecting our diverse leadership. Hearing from a diverse panel of experts undoubtedly soothed the nerves of many viewers as we shared important updates on our efforts to help prevent and fight the pandemic within our communities.

Lessons Learned

The challenge of every leader is to recognize the talents and vision of emerging leaders and then cultivate their skill sets to the fullest capacity. You can help your team members develop and grow by looking for ways to help them achieve their goals so your company continues to attract the best and brightest leaders to your industry. Sometimes this means leaders move on to the next opportunity faster than you would like, but with change comes opportunity.

Leaders have a unique opportunity and a great responsibility to show others the path to success. I am lucky enough to be in a leadership position of a world-class organization and to serve as a visible role model to others so they can see what's possible.

When I was promoted to CEO, many residents and associates reached out to tell me how thrilled they were to see a woman as CEO of Brookdale. I consider myself an ordinary person who took on an extraordinary role.

Being a CEO is a balancing act. I needed to learn new skills so I could help Brookdale succeed and to show others that even someone with a humble beginning can make a significant contribution.

Leadership is a wonderful privilege that comes with great responsibility. But access to leadership positions is the necessary first step.

This is the important takeaway in making the case for improving diversity: show people what's possible, ensure they have access to opportunities, and you will be amazed at how they rise to the occasion.

CHAPTER 11

Embracing the Senior Living Lifestyle

Leading the Industry as We Enter the New Normal

Throughout the book so far, we've discussed the core values, key principles, leadership lessons, and granular insights that the pandemic taught or reinforced for our board, leadership team, and associates as we navigated this unprecedented challenge.

Viewing our experience from an even higher level, we also learned a great deal about the importance of the senior living industry to the common good—not only as supporters and stewards of our residents' lives but also as essential connectors and aggregators between various industries that make up the broader economy. Standing at the intersection of healthcare, hospitality, and real estate, the services we provide form the foundation for a large sector of American society.

As the pandemic created the need to shelter in place, businesses in every sector of society were assessed based on the "essential" nature of their services when government agencies enforced restrictions. The senior living industry was not only essential—it was treasured. The population we serve represents some of the most beloved members of society: family matriarchs and patriarchs, accomplished professionals and academics, friends, mentors, former teachers, pastors, farmers, merchants, and military veterans.

We hold seniors dear because, as a society, we honor and respect those who came before us, and we want them to live long lives and excel in all the dimensions of an Optimum Life˙: the emotional, physical, social, spiritual, intellectual, and purposeful.

The trials endured by senior living during COVID-19 underscored the importance of the services we provide to the citizens who adopt and benefit from the senior living lifestyle.

Combatting Loneliness

Hands down, one of the greatest benefits of the senior living lifestyle is the role it plays in reducing loneliness for seniors. Loneliness can be incredibly difficult for people at any age, and for seniors, it's shown to have significant, adverse impacts on health and well-being. Seniors suffering from loneliness have a higher risk of dementia and Alzheimer's disease, as well as a higher risk of heart attack and stroke.[23] Loneliness has the impact of smoking almost a pack of cigarettes a day![24] For seniors, loneliness is not only a matter of mental health but also a serious health issue with potentially devastating consequences.

Senior living communities help residents to enjoy the rewards of a meaningful and active social lifestyle. It frees them from the burdens

---

23   "Social Isolation and Loneliness among Older Adults in the Context of COVID-19," Global Health Research and Policy, June 2020.

24   Nick Tate, "Loneliness Rivals Obesity, Smoking as Health Risk," published May 4, 2018, https://www. webmd.com/balance/news/20180504/loneliness-rivals-obesity-smoking-as-health-risk.

of homeownership and having to prepare meals for themselves or eat alone. Senior living residents can truly focus on the things that give their lives joy and purpose.

PERSONAL PERSPECTIVE FROM CINDY BAIER

Joined Brookdale Senior Living December 2015; currently president, chief executive officer, and board member

FULFILLING A SENSE OF PURPOSE

It was during one of my community learning visits at Brookdale Wilsonville (Oregon) that I met our resident Janie Wood. *Janie was so full of sparkle that I could hardly believe the story she told me.*

Janie confided that before she came to Brookdale, she had a quality of life that was difficult to endure. She never left her bed—never! Twenty-four hours a day, seven days a week, Janie was in bed. She ate in bed, relieved her bowels and bladder in bed, and received sponge baths. Janie was just existing—not living.

When Janie moved into her Brookdale community, our team was determined to change her bad days to good— and we maintained our commitment by tending to her health and well-being every day!

First, we had to work with her on the most basic goal— simply helping her get out of bed. As she made steps to engage in the ordinary activities of daily life, she took her first shower, ate at a table again, and eventually enjoyed meals in the dining room with other residents! *We helped Janie learn to walk again, which totally transformed the*

---

world as she had known it—the former world in which she had been confined and restricted in her movements. I think it's fair to say that we helped Janie regain her purpose in life.

Janie has such joy now, and we have truly fulfilled our mission of enriching her life. When I had the opportunity to meet her, Janie told me her story and cautiously warned me that she wouldn't be able to get through it without crying—but she clarified that they were tears of joy! She cried from a deep sense of gratitude, because she believed we had helped her get her life back.

That's the work we do every day in alignment with Brookdale's North Star.

We are able to build trust with our residents by listening, understanding, and partnering to solve problems. We focus on establishing genuine relationships and succeeding through partnership.

I can't imagine anything more important than the work Brookdale does on behalf of our precious residents in helping them fulfill a sense of purpose in their lives.

For family members, senior living allows the family the opportunity to leave behind the tricky business of caregiving or care coordinating so they can focus on their familial roles again as spouse, mother, father, daughter, son, or other loved one, which is really the heart of the relationship. With the help of senior living support, a daughter can receive assistance in making sure her mother is eating, taking her medication, and keeping house. She can just spend time with Mom as her daughter, and they can both be themselves and enjoy the precious time they spend together.

During the pandemic, senior living became all the more important.

When we think of the stressors that most of us went through during the shutdown, we can only imagine how the harsh effects of quarantining were multiplied for seniors living on their own. Many seniors living alone and not connected to an organized community faced the prospect of having to go to the grocery store by themselves, processing their fear of contracting the virus, and feeling vulnerable to being exposed to viruses without the support of clinical teams that supported assisted living residents and the availability of staff to help twenty-four hours a day.

> ## Senior Living Helps Manage the Challenges of Aging.

Compare this level of anxiety to the comfort many of our residents experienced from being in an environment with a wide range of protocols and resources to help keep them safe. Our residents benefited from being surrounded by many friends and from being in an environment that screened for symptoms and used testing to reduce risk. Our residents were able to be as engaged as they wanted or as sheltered as they chose to be, depending on which technologies they used and their willingness to engage in creative socially distanced activities through hallway programs with the support of our friendly associates—and window events, thanks to helpful hands on the other side of the glass.

We learned to adapt our business model in order to maintain socialization that our residents are accustomed to experiencing, and this changed the way we do business for the better even as we head into our new normal.

HERO HIGHLIGHTS FROM DR. MARYLOUISE "WEEZIE" FENNELL, RSM (SISTER OF MERCY)

Joined Brookdale Senior Living as a resident of Brookdale West Palm Beach in Florida in April 2014; currently chair of Brookdale's National Advisory Council

TREATING SENIORS WITH GENTLENESS AND RESPECT

At various times throughout the COVID-19 pandemic, I remember thinking back to earlier in my life, when the nation faced a public health crisis over polio. I'm sure everyone here at my community remembers that time in history. During several summers, we couldn't go outside. Even during school vacation, we couldn't go anywhere. We had to stay in our own yard with our own families, because polio was ravishing the cities. It was a time when people pulled together.

So as we started to understand the similar threat of this new public health risk, I was thankful to see how seriously Brookdale was taking COVID-19. Very early on in the crisis, they quickly changed how things operated within our community. At first, dining room tables were separated, and the number of people at a table was limited, and then we moved to room service for meals. Some of my fellow residents thought the initial changes were an overreaction at first, but I was personally grateful for the changes, because I knew they were intended to keep us as safe as possible from the threat of a mysterious disease.

I commend the way our Brookdale team handled the changes. They were extremely kind, even with residents who challenged them. Our associates encouraged and listened to residents and shared information with us. Gentleness was important, because residents were at different levels of understanding at the start of the pandemic as we came to realize how serious it was.

Throughout my life—which has included serving on hospital boards of directors, as a college president, and as a Sister of Mercy—I have found that organizations are most likely to succeed with four behaviors, all of which Brookdale's team exhibited: 1) respect the people, 2) be kind to the people, 3) treat people in a dignified way, and 4) be compassionate. That applies whether you are supporting an eighteen-year-old just starting college or an eighty-year-old in a senior living community.

I discovered that my experience played out consistently across Brookdale when I spoke to a friend who lives at a Brookdale community in Rhode Island, where she was going through similar changes to what we were experiencing in Florida. We received information from Brookdale in various ways, including letters, phone calls, "robo-calls," or small-town meetings. We were so pleased to see how well Brookdale always stayed on top of things.

Several times, I remember hearing new developments in the national news and finding out that Brookdale was already on top of it, letting us know how they had prepared to respond to the new information. For example, when the media started running stories about the imminent availability of a vaccine, Brookdale was quick to let us know when our community vaccination clinic would be held. We were well taken care of!

I was happy to be on Brookdale's National Advisory Council (NAC) in 2020 and to chair it in 2021. This gave me the chance to interact with the company's top leaders, including CEO Cindy Baier, and to provide understanding that helped guide Brookdale's response to COVID-19.

Usually, the NAC gives feedback about things like whether new furniture will meet the needs of seniors. But for COVID-19, Cindy made it clear that the leadership team was looking for deep insights from the resident perspective, because it would help Brookdale do everything it could to help keep residents (and associates) as safe as possible.

It gave me great confidence in Brookdale's ability to lead us through any crisis.

Differentiators of Senior Living

One of the key differentiators of the senior living lifestyle is the opportunity to engage in a broad continuum of care—run by trained professionals with the ability to provide services and coordinate specialized care with third-party services and partners as needed.

Brookdale communities offer the gamut of services needed by seniors in all areas of their well-being. Our residents appreciate having options for:

- independent living (an active and independent lifestyle);

- assisted living (additional care for activities of daily living and chronic health conditions);

- memory care (a higher level of care with specific programs and environments designed to support those living with dementia);

- skilled nursing (specialized medical care and therapy services in a supportive setting);

- respite care (short-term arrangements for families in need of support while they tend to personal affairs);

- home healthcare (licensed clinical care in the comfort and privacy of your own home);

- private duty services (ranging from dog walking to letter writing to supportive care services);

- resident engagement (personalized to support the resident being the best, defined by them);

- outpatient therapy (rehabilitation that enables a patient to return home between sessions);

- telehealth (virtual visits with licensed medical professionals); and

- hospice services (for those in need of pain management and compassionate nurturing care at end of life).

> ## Seniors Find Value in Living within a Community of Friends.

The predictable nature of the senior living lifestyle is one of the key factors that attracts many seniors to our communities. The vast majority of the residents living at Brookdale pay for our services directly from their retirement income or savings (that is, private pay rather than Medicare or Medicaid), and they value the fact that pricing for our services is fair. Our care rates are based on the health needs of an individual.

The relationship between residents and our associates is critically important. Retaining our community leadership is a high priority for Brookdale, because it helps facilitate our residents' feelings of stability and security within a given community. Steady community leadership translates to greater predictability for residents and provides an opportunity for deep relationships to develop.

HERO HIGHLIGHTS FROM RON RABEN

Joined Brookdale Senior Living as a resident of Brookdale Hoffman Estates in Illinois in May 2018; currently member of Brookdale's National Advisory Council

ENGAGING AND MOTIVATING RESIDENTS EVERY DAY

I don't ever—ever—want to go through a pandemic again. But if I have to, I want it to be with Brookdale.

My wife and I are actually second-generation Brookdale residents. We live on the same floor that my mother did, just down the hall from where her apartment had been. We knew when Mom moved in that Brookdale was a nice place, but now we see all the other, equally important aspects of the Brookdale lifestyle—even beyond the pleasant atmosphere.

When I worked in education (for forty years!), I learned how important it was to engage students and motivate them every day. I thought about these experiences a lot during the long days of lockdown in our community. My fellow residents and I understood and appreciated that our Brookdale associates were trying to keep us as safe as they could by closing our doors to visitors, shifting to room service instead of using the dining room for meals, and other changes that provided for social distancing.

At first it was a novel experience. We were glad to see restrictions lighten up as conditions and local guidance allowed, but it was hard as we experienced the lockdown. My wife and I have what we call a pandemic grandchild: we didn't get to see her until six months after she was born, and even then, we couldn't hold her. We had to wave to her through a mask.

One thing our Brookdale team did that made a big difference for us was to communicate frequently! Executive Director Mike Ratchford and his team were in touch all the time, leaving updates in residents' in-house mailboxes—sometimes more than once a day. Through these messages, they shared information on the pandemic as it related specifically to our building and also provided updates related to corporate guidance and what was happening in the state of Illinois. We felt like we knew what was going on, and that helped make us feel better about the situation. It kept us engaged.

Our director of resident programs, Dan Roeder, went above and beyond to attend to the well-being of residents. Because the live entertainment we usually enjoyed was paused, he did everything he could to create activities to keep us engaged, including creating in-house scavenger hunts, new word puzzles delivered to our mailboxes, and arts and crafts supplies available for use in our apartments. His creativity and caring meant so much.

In addition, our director of dining, Sam Yerandi, did an epic job changing an entire dining experience from communal to room service for every resident, which included meals and often snacks and food items. You can only imagine the logistics and strategies it took to convert an entire program of food service to individual deliveries on eight floors in two separate building wings—250 apartments! I imagine it was a massive, exhausting, and frustrating job at times. But it was done seamlessly—with concern, empathy, cheer, and kindness—and residents appreciated every effort.

When vaccines became available, that became a party! And the positive experience we had, complete with a superhero theme, was the result of every department in the community working together—from marketing to activities to custodial and housekeeping. It was truly a team effort!

Out of everything that happened, it was the kindness and compassion from our Brookdale associates that really helped. I know they had their own concerns, but they continued to smile and engage in conversation as they delivered meals, and they appeared to be as cheerful as possible under the circumstances.

I can't help but think that this kindness came from Brookdale's top leadership and not just our community's staff. As a member of Brookdale's National Advisory Council (NAC), I had some Zoom˙ meetings with corporate leaders, and they were actively involved in our discussions, listening closely to our feedback and concerns. I felt like they deeply cared about what we were all going through, and it meant a great deal to all of us as we kept hope alive for our return to a new normal.

Demand for Senior Living Is Growing

Demand for senior living is growing as baby boomers enter their later years. In addition, the increasing prevalence of chronic conditions and higher acuity needs for seniors—particularly hypertension, heart disease, and Alzheimer's or other dementias—means that specialized care will continue to attract prospects to senior living communities.[25]

At the same time that the population of seniors is growing and their needs are increasing, there are fewer people to help support them. A significant drop in the ratio of unpaid caregivers to seniors (family members willing and able to work for free) is also expected to occur over the next decade—further fueling the demand for senior living as an important option to support seniors and their families.[26]

An Aging Population Leads to New Growth.

25   "Social Isolation and Loneliness among Older Adults in the Context of COVID-19," Global Health Research and Policy, June 2020.

26   Donald Redfoot, Lynn Feinberg, and Ari Houser, "The Aging of the Baby Boom and the Growing Care Gap," AARP, published August 2013, https://www.aarp.org/home-family/caregiving/info-08-2013/the-aging-of-the-baby-boom-and-the-growing-care-gap-AARP-ppi-ltc.html.

All of this is to say, in spite of the previously unimaginable challenge we experienced in having to respond to a global pandemic, the senior living industry is expected to recover, grow, and flourish. Seniors who opt into this lifestyle (and the families supporting them) will enjoy being part of our vibrant communities with an expanding assortment of social activities and resident engagement programs.

Through October of 2021—during the recent months leading up to the publication of this book—Brookdale has experienced growth in occupancy percentage for eight consecutive months.

We continue to enjoy our position as the senior living operator with the highest brand awareness (among unaided mentions) by twice the amount of our next largest competitor.[27] Furthermore, our customer service marks are higher than ever: in a separate study, Brookdale Senior Living received the highest score among assisted living/memory care communities in a tie in the J.D. Power 2020 U.S. Senior Living Satisfaction Study of resident/family member/ friend's satisfaction with senior living communities. (Visit jdpower. com/awards for more details.)

We are very proud of the exceptional leadership demonstrated by our executive directors and associates within our communities and with the high quality of service offered across the entire Brookdale organization, and we couldn't be more thrilled that our residents agree!

Ultimately the pandemic didn't dampen our enthusiasm for our industry. On the contrary, it strengthened our resolve and our position as an essential service provider in the modern landscape— and it heightened public awareness of the role of senior living in the healthcare continuum.

---

27   Based on online surveys sent to national survey panel participants in top-ten markets, including senior living prospects and their influencers from May 22 to June 1, 2021.

Honoring Seniors in American Society

There is no question that COVID-19 deeply affected all of us. We mourn the loss of loved ones and continue to honor their memory.

Perhaps the greatest silver lining in the pandemic is the silvery, sparkly spirit of the seniors who have touched our hearts. We are so grateful for the residents who faced the challenges of the pandemic with such grace and strength while living within our communities.

Our seniors are all truly remarkable individuals worth celebrating.

I'd like to honor the lives of American seniors by highlighting a few of the events that helped shape them. Our residents have overcome so many tragic events in their lifetimes as they actively participated in the transformation and progress we have made as a country. They possess great wisdom from lives well lived and a resilience that inspires us.

> ## Seniors Have Overcome Adversity—and Improved Life for All of Us.

Before 1920, women didn't even have the right to vote. Today, approximately 70 percent of our residents are women. During my community visits, so many residents have reached out to tell me how much it means to them to see a woman leading Brookdale. I am so honored by their support and pleased to carry the torch.

In 1929, Wall Street crashed and caused the Great Depression, which led to tremendous suffering and hardship. Many people experienced hunger. Today, our residents are served nutritious meals daily—and enjoy these meals with friends.

In 1941, the Japanese bombed Pearl Harbor, pulling our country into World War II. Our residents lived through or served in a number of wars or other conflicts, including World War II, the Korean conflict, and the Vietnam War. Others supported our wartime efforts, including at least one Brookdale resident who served as a "Rosie the Riveter." Today we honor the veterans and their spouses who have chosen to live with us by sharing their photos (past or present) on a Wall of Honor within our communities.

Our residents experienced or participated in the American Civil Rights Movement. At Brookdale, we have increased diversity at the highest levels of the organization, including on our board of directors.

Our residents have also participated in medical breakthroughs, cared for others in need, and created tools that have enabled so many people to live healthier lives—including contributing to the development of cancer treatments. Most recently, our residents led the way in receiving COVID-19 vaccines to help protect themselves and society.

We are constantly amazed by the accomplishments and great character of our residents, and we are so pleased that they have chosen to call their Brookdale community home.

Lessons Learned

We made it a point to engage in dialogue with our extraordinary residents, who amazed us with uplifting perspectives every step of the way. Importantly, they offered key insights that shaped for us a new understanding of the senior living industry: by fulfilling our mission of enriching their lives, we also served the greater good of society.

Having learned and processed so much from the challenges of the pandemic, I am filled with confidence that we can overcome any obstacle that comes our way as a company—and as individual leaders, associates, husbands, wives, mothers, fathers, daughters, and sons.

If we live long enough, it's inevitable that we'll experience adversity, heartbreak, or tragedy during a lifetime. The important thing is how we respond: Will the next challenge break us, or will we take it as an opportunity to learn and grow?

My belief is that the biggest challenges create the greatest opportunities for growth—growth that expands our potential for even greater success in the future. Because of this, I am filled with hope.

CHAPTER 12

Beyond Senior Living

Translating the Transcendent Lessons to Your Business

T
he senior living industry sits at the intersection of healthcare, hospitality, and real estate.

At Brookdale, our services are delivered in hundreds of locations in more than forty states across the country, and our business operates around the clock, twenty-four hours a day, seven days a week, 365 days a year.

We never close—we are the quintessential "essential" business.

Because of the broad continuum of services we provide, the number of residents we serve, and the sheer volume of associates we have, the lessons we learned from the pandemic are transferrable— whether in retail, telecommunications, or other businesses that rely on people to bring their vision to life. Whenever a business requires the coordination of such a vast network of employees, the challenge is to ensure your associates—the true front lines of any organization— are fully trained to execute on your campaign, motivated to fulfill your mission, and sufficiently nimble to pivot as necessary in order to accomplish what you need to achieve as a company.

I strongly believe the lessons we learned in leading through the greatest public health crisis in over a century are applicable to every industry and every business in some way, shape, or form.

Intense Focus on the Customer Experience

We are a mission-driven organization with an intense focus on the customer experience—in our case, residents, patients, and loved ones. We accomplish our mission one relationship at a time. The only way that we can be successful is by attracting, engaging, developing, and retaining the best associates. We know our associates want to be part of something that is bigger than themselves; they want to do work that really matters—and to have an impact on the communities they serve.

We are so grateful they can have a big impact at Brookdale.

Our associates are responsible for providing high-quality, personalized services to help our residents better manage the challenges of aging. Thus, we spend a lot of time and effort studying, innovating, and testing how best to help our residents improve their lives. As we pilot new technologies or processes, our residents and their loved ones are always at the center of our focus. Their feedback matters!

Regardless of the products or services being offered, every business needs to understand as much as it can about their customers and their needs. What problem are you solving? What promise are you fulfilling for your customers, and are you delivering on that promise effectively? If you aren't delighting your customers by delivering on the promise you make and satisfying that need, you won't be in business very long.

In today's market, it's not enough to offer a minimal level of service and call it a day. The quality of your products and services matters. In healthcare, we recognize that quality goes beyond clinical concerns and extends to quality of life. In senior living, that translates into a renewed focus on the social and emotional well-being of our residents.

Work Hard to Delight Your Customers!

To apply this lesson to other industries, quality depends on the needs of the customer: if your customer is interested in making a purchase quickly and easily (for example, a cup of coffee), the elements that create a quality experience vary greatly compared to a fine dining experience where customers want to spend more time savoring the meal.

In either case, the definition of quality depends on the needs and desires of the customer. But in both cases, you have an opportunity to deliver above and beyond your customer's expectations. Think of how it feels when you hear a barista ask, "Can I pour you a cup of happiness today?" That's the kind of quality delivery that can occur when associates are aligned with a higher mission and focused on meeting—and surpassing—the needs and expectations of your customers.

Every customer service transaction matters, no matter how minor in the grand scheme of a customer's life. Every associate has the potential to become a leader when aligned with a company's mission, committed to performing high-quality services, and focused on ways to improve the customer experience and the company's performance.

Developing leadership qualities is as simple as making small changes to stand out.

Extraordinary leaders appear at every level of an organization. Leaders should always strive to be well rounded, and they can provide even greater value when they do something special to stand out. As noted in Chapter 9 (A Culture of Caring), Board Member Vicki Freed introduced us to the qualities that set apart a leader from their fellow team members. She calls it the SUMS approach: (S)imple, (U)nexpected, (M)emorable, (S)ignature.

1. *Simple*: do something simple, so you can do it consistently.

2. *Unexpected*: make people stop and say, "Wow."

3. *Memorable*: make it memorable by making it personal.

4. *Signature*: develop your signature mark; only *you* do it!

HERO HIGHLIGHTS FROM MARC BROMLEY

Joined Brookdale Senior Living Board of Directors July 2017; currently a member of the advisory board of Nancy Creek Capital Management, LLC

LEADERSHIP STARTS AT THE TOP

As I think about Brookdale's response to the COVID-19 pandemic and what we can glean from it in a context broader than just senior living, I can boil it down to two leadership lessons that I think apply to any industry or organization:

1. *The CEO must lead. Certainly, various decisions and tasks can and should be delegated, but the top leader has to assume ultimate responsibility for the success*

---

or failure of a business during a crisis and otherwise. At Brookdale, I witnessed the incredible leadership of Cindy Baier as she took charge of an unimaginable situation, addressed early warnings from a former board member quickly and seriously, and prompted decisive action before we had clarity about the threat or guidance from CDC on COVID-19 protocol at senior living communities, public places, etc. She took responsibility for getting ahead of the situation and leading the charge. This early lead served Brookdale's residents and associates well.

2. *Share all news—not just the good news. While it's natural to want to put one's best foot forward, personally and professionally, avoiding sharing bad news is just not good for business. Company leaders need to have a clear picture in order to contribute meaningfully to the decision-making process. I was pleased to see that Cindy was candid, factual, and earnest in her communications with the board about Brookdale's status throughout the pandemic. She took the same approach in sharing information with the investment community, and I think Brookdale has benefited greatly from her approach.*

Of course, leadership also requires keenness in identifying the strengths of your organization; evaluating dynamics within the broader industry; creating a workable, strategic plan; and building a team that will do all that is necessary to succeed.

> Brookdale, the largest senior living operator in the nation, could not have operated as well as it did without Cindy at the helm. *As a result of her take-charge reputation, I believe other senior housing operators looked to Brookdale for direction and to Cindy specifically for guidance during the pandemic.*

Cultivating Empathy and Inspiring Loyalty

At Brookdale, our business is centered on people taking care of people. Passion, courage, partnership, and trust are the cornerstones of our culture; every other business has its own unique culture, but in all businesses, your culture should illustrate in various ways how you care for the people who care for you—the associates responsible for executing a company's mission on the front lines of any business.

As President Teddy Roosevelt first stated and business leaders like John Maxwell have emphasized, "No one cares how much you know until they know how much you care." Caring means cultivating the empathy to understand what people are going through. It's difficult to move forward as a team when individual members of the team fall behind because they are unable to find the support and resources they need to perform at capacity.

Maslow's hierarchy of needs was first introduced in the 1940s and still applies today.[28] Physiological needs (air, water, food, sleep, clothes, and shelter, for example) are the most basic human needs.

---

28   "Maslow's Hierarchy of Needs," CFI, accessed November 16, 2021, https://corporatefinanceinstitute. com/resources/knowledge/other/maslows-hierarchy-of-needs/.

Safety needs (health, personal, financial, and emotional security) come next, and the pandemic impacted both.

Leaders in many industries developed strategies to help meet these two levels of basic human needs, because they empathized with the struggle, even if they themselves were not experiencing financial or job insecurity to the same degree.

As the pandemic became a harsh reality for so many, the world seemed to shift focus away from nurturing higher-level needs like love, belonging, esteem, and self-actualization to helping support the basic needs of our most vulnerable citizens.

Leaders who empathized with the challenges of their associates and followed through with action—targeted bonuses and flexible programs addressing specialized challenges—inspired the loyalty of their associates in return. These were the leaders most able to pivot their businesses while keeping the organization focused on their core mission.

Empathy for Your Associates Inspires Loyalty.

Leading with an empathetic heart is the key to enrolling your associates in the mission of your business, regardless of your industry. If you hold your associates in high regard—if you can show them you *care* by supporting their basic needs, especially when times are tough—they will return the favor by pledging their loyalty to your organizational goals.

PERSONAL PERSPECTIVE FROM DAVE BAIER

Husband and unpaid advisor to CEO since May 1999

GUIDING PRINCIPLES TO LEAD ACROSS INDUSTRIES

Before I retired some years ago, I was a corporate vice president and a principal officer of General Dynamics

(GD), a Fortune 100 aerospace/defense company. I had people reporting to me around the world. There were certain guiding principles that I wanted embedded in the DNA of my organization. These principles eventually became known as "Baierisms." A partner at GD's outside auditor once remarked that I had trained my organization very well, as these so-called "Baierisms" were repeated almost verbatim all across my organization. They were also practiced.

The following are a few of my favorites:

1. *Don't be an ostrich. When a problem is small, people will willingly help to fix it. When it's permitted to get out of control, no one wants to be associated with it.*

2. *Play well with others. Teamwork is essential.*

3. *Hire eagles and teach them to fly in formation. (This is my modification to D. Wayne Calloway's quote about his management philosophy.)*

4. *When talking with business unit management, don't tell them what you do. Tell them how you are contributing to the unit's financial objectives.*

5. *Cash is king, because it is the only thing you can spend.*

I am honored to have led an incredible organization at GD. I was blessed with an extremely talented group of people whose dedication, competence, and hard work made our organization successful.

While GD faced many challenges when it was in a turnaround stage, I never had to deal with the existential crisis that Brookdale has faced with COVID-19. It made me appreciate my amazing wife even more. I have been awestruck by her unyielding commitment to do whatever it takes to help protect the residents, patients, and associates of Brookdale. Her unwavering belief in Brookdale's mission has released an almost inexhaustible supply of energy to keep Brookdale strong (#BrookdaleStrong) through the pandemic. She is in the right place at the right time. She brings the perfect combination of competence, command, and compassion that the moment requires.

Cindy also put some of the above Baierisms into practice. For example, she directed Steve Swain's focus on cash and his first, second, and third priorities on maintaining liquidity. Cindy has never been an ostrich. From the moment that Jim Seward alerted her to the potential threat of the novel coronavirus, she moved heaven and earth to help protect her residents, patients, associates, and her company. I like to say, "Play well with others"; Cindy says, "Teamwork makes the dream work." From her early days as a leader, she adopted the philosophy that "Leaders take eagles and teach them to fly in formation." Her focus on the financial objectives is a focus on both mission and margin.

Cindy often says to me, "We are in this together." This is a fundamental truism of marriage. In this case, Cindy also gets a partner who has experienced the dynamics that take place in a corporation in crisis mode. She can lean on me when she needs a trusted sounding board.

We can discuss strategy, communication, office politics, COVID-19 updates, etc. I am there for her whether she needs to talk through an issue or just needs a hug, a warm smile, a silly joke, or to just go out for pizza.

Eleanor Roosevelt once said, "[W]e do not have to become heroes overnight. Just a step at a time, meeting each thing that comes up … discovering we have the strength to stare it down." By any measure of the word, my wife is a hero.

Today's business environment is incredibly complicated, and no one person can have the breadth and depth of skills to make every decision independently. It is critically important to build robust teams that are equipped to leverage the diverse experiences and specialized skill sets of team members at every level of the organization. This allows a leader to help make the best decisions for a company and govern appropriately.

The success of any business depends on its people—they are hands down your most important resource.

At Brookdale, one of our founders, Dr. Thomas F. Frist Sr., introduced the concept that "Good people beget good people," and we still believe this is true today. It is critically important to build diverse teams that trust and complement one another so they can work together effectively. Every time a new team member joins us or departs, it takes time for the group to adapt to the change, realign with their operating principles, and establish trust in order to move forward together.

Teams that take time to build a solid foundation that includes new members can move more quickly when it's time to pivot. A single teammate who is out of alignment with the values and mission of the company or with others can create significant challenges (i.e., increased costs, low morale, failed execution, increased turnover, disengaged employees, and other suboptimal outcomes).

The long-term result of such dysfunction creates a ripple effect, like a stone thrown into a pond. Where the stone hits the surface, a small splash indicates that the water has been displaced, but the consequent ripples move out in every direction.

> ## A Single Teammate out of Sync Can Disrupt an Entire Organization.

That's the importance of alignment within the team around the mission—it ensures smoother sailing for the entire organization and leadership.

Balancing Cohesive Teams and Diversity

Brookdale operates in the best of times—and the most challenging. Because we can never truly close our doors, we must remain vigilant in our efforts to prepare for crises so we can operate effectively in incredibly challenging conditions. Many of our management techniques are transferrable across industries and can help other leaders defend against threats and capitalize on opportunities to create a bright future for their organizations. One of the best lessons for organizations: leaders have to show up even—and especially—when times are tough.

The pandemic highlighted how important it is to be aware of what's happening in the external environment and to understand the potential business impact of potential crises within a given industry's landscape and the wider world—even as trouble is brewing.

As previously discussed, every company benefits from a team characterized by a diversity of experiences and backgrounds, because these qualities increase the likelihood that you will be able to identify possible threats to your business coming from the external world. The first step is to ensure you have a board of directors and a leadership team composed of individuals with a wide range of diverse experiences, differing backgrounds, and critical skills.

> ## Gauge the Value of a Leader by Their Ability—and Willingness to Serve.

You can evaluate the competencies of the members of your board using a skills matrix and apply the same technique to your leadership team. In such an exercise, you list experience and expertise, or attributes (like critical industry experience, functional expertise, key roles, race, gender, etc.), across the matrix to ensure that nothing critical is overlooked. Using the board as an example, the members are listed in the columns, and the industries, functional expertise, or key roles are listed in rows. Checks are placed where the board member satisfies the specified criteria. This allows you to confirm that every row has adequate coverage by a member of the board.

Be sure to consider all leaders for both their abilities *and* their willingness to prioritize your company's mission in order to address the unique needs of your customer. Many leaders possess the qualifications and capacity to lead, but far fewer people are willing to make personal investments—sacrifices for the greater good—at the level necessary for the leadership team to rise to the challenge when crisis hits. As Bob Chapek, current CEO of the Walt Disney Company, says, "The greatest power is willpower."

The role of diversity is to eliminate "group think" and to identify opportunities, threats, and creative solutions that wouldn't be so effectively detected with a homogeneous team.

Leaders should remain vigilantly aware when a team is settling into the comfortable rhythm of the status quo and take decisive action to refocus the team's attention from a group-based consensus by reminding team members of their uniquely valuable, diverse perspectives. If everyone is thinking about the problem the same way, then it isn't necessary to have as many people focused on the issue.

It's important for leaders to balance the need for a cohesive team with the necessity for a vast array of team members who contribute independent-minded, forward-thinking insights to inform the company's strategy. Without a diverse and well-considered leadership team, a company is prone to missing critical warning signs or key opportunities for growth.

Communication Brings Your Vision to Life

As you leverage diverse perspectives from your leadership team, it's important to establish two-way communication in order to gather feedback and capture a wide variety of diverse perspectives. As management authority Stephen Covey counsels, "Seek first to understand, then to be understood."[29] I think this is the reason that we have two ears but only one mouth.

It's impossible to lead without effective communication and crisp messaging that keeps all associates in alignment with a company's overarching goals. Communication should be frequent, clear, and well distributed across a variety of formats (one-on-one or group meetings, emails, videos). People process information differently; some people are visual learners, while others rely on audible transfer to understand, so variety matters.

> ## Communicate Frequently, Clearly, and Meticulously.

Communications should be repetitive and comprehensive. You can be sure that associates who don't process the full message *as intended* will fill in the gaps with speculation and outside information that may not be accurate. Often a negative narrative is created to fill in information gaps, and this can create undue stress and disruption.

Brookdale tested the effectiveness of our communications loop by establishing listening systems, like skip level meetings (where a leader meets with an associate who reports to a direct report in order to solicit their direct feedback). This helped the leadership team to ensure that communication wasn't being distorted and helped us gauge the response to our messages at various levels within the organization.

It's equally important to communicate effectively with the wider world. Early in the pandemic, we built a website in order to

---

29   "Habit 5: Seek First to Understand, Then to Be Understood," Franklin Covey, accessed November 16, 2021, https://www.franklincovey.com/habit-5/.

disseminate our knowledge to others within our industry as well as to the general public, and we received numerous messages of gratitude from people who were able to leverage our knowledge in their business and personal lives.

Leadership means we have an obligation to help others—including a special role in providing accurate, updated information that can aid others in the face of a crisis.

HERO HIGHLIGHTS FROM HAYLEY HOVIOUS

Currently president of Nashville Health Care Council

RENEWED CLARITY AND A SENSE OF PURPOSE

As the president of the Nashville Health Care Council, I sit in a unique position within the healthcare industry. I interact daily with CEOs of organizations of all sizes, working across all aspects of the delivery system. Whether interviewing them formally in front of an audience or merely catching up over coffee or a call, I have the opportunity to learn about their leadership styles and tactics. These interactions gave an important perspective during the pandemic.

Over and over, I heard about CEOs communicating more often and differently, and I heard about their efforts to practice rigorous authenticity with their boards, employees, and patients. They also described the intense focus they brought to their organizations and the renewed emphasis on collaborations outside of their organizations.

Leaders realized the benefits of focusing completely around their mission. In healthcare, patients are at the heart of everything, and organizations that focused on keeping their patients and employees safe were able to move mountains. In a matter of days, initiatives that would have taken years to bring about were up and running. Previous barriers—whether real or imagined—fell as entire organizations worked toward specified goals. The focus brought clarity and a sense of purpose for everyone in the organization.

Communicating that focus became critical. With employees scattered and working at home or tirelessly serving patients in a clinical setting, leaders communicated far more often with their employees using all the tools at their disposal. In certain parts of the industry, that communication also included finding new ways to communicate with residents and their loved ones.

For Brookdale, this meant creating and disseminating content around safety to everyone that the organization touched in an effort to help keep the vulnerable populations they serve as safe as possible. This also included Cindy giving her time and energy (and those of her staff) to efforts that the council had developed for sharing best practices.

Leaders recognized that they could not do it on their own. While all great leaders know that their teams are critical to their success, the pandemic highlighted the need for collaboration with organizations outside of their own. The recognition that the challenges were more significant than any one organization's ability to meet them permeated leadership at all levels. Brookdale provided a wonderful example of this type of leadership, part-nering with Omnicare˙ (a CVS Health˙ company) through the federal government's Pharmacy Partnership for Long-Term Care Program to deliver vaccination clinics within their communities.

From my thirty-thousand-foot view of the healthcare industry, it is clear to me that we are better equipped to address future challenges thanks to the renewed focus on authenticity, communication, and collaborative lead-ership that emerged during the pandemic.

Every one of us may be affected by the healthcare delivery system at some point, whether in managing our own health or that of a loved one, and we all benefit when leaders develop more effective ways of leading. Having had a front seat to the incredible leadership that developed over the course of the pandemic, I can attest we are fortunate to have so many outstanding people working in healthcare.

Lead, Follow, or Get Out of the Way

The mission of a company is often steady and unchanging over time, but the vision is set by the company's leaders to illustrate how the mission plays out five, ten, or fifty years from now. At Brookdale, our mission is "enriching the lives of those we serve with compassion, respect, excellence, and integrity." Our vision is "to be the nation's first choice in senior living." Through our vision, we narrowed our focus to the United States and specified our intent to excel in one sector. The vision is how we plan to bring our mission to life.

Leaders must create and build support for the company's vision for the future in order to align their teams (including corporate leadership, local leaders, and associates) around it and execute effectively. Every individual team member must believe in the leaders' vision if they're going to make meaningful contributions to the organization. The more compelling the vision, the harder people will work—and the more sacrifices they will make to bring it to life.

Your vision must be clear and compelling in order to attract the people who will ultimately make it a reality.

HERO HIGHLIGHTS FROM FRANK BUMSTEAD

Joined Brookdale Senior Living Board of Directors August 2006; currently principal shareholder of Flood, Bumstead, McCready & McCarthy Inc.

TIMELESS LESSONS IN LEADERSHIP

Leadership matters—whether you're on a mission in the jungles of Vietnam or fighting to keep COVID-19 out of over seven hundred senior living communities. In any situation, leadership is best learned through experience.

I was taught about leadership in the navy, but I learned it in combat. I learned that the single most important thing I could do was make sure my sailors—the reports working directly for me—understood what I understood. If they had as defined a picture of the situation as I did, then they could continue the mission even if I was injured or killed.

I remember so clearly, all these years later, the search for live enemy mines. We swept the Cua Viet River, six miles south of what at the time was the North Vietnamese

---

border. We did this from 4:30 until 8:00 in the morning, seven days a week—traveling slowly so we could trick the pressure-sensitive mines into exploding without harming American boats.

We kept that river clean for seven months. After we accomplished our mission, the supply boats were then able to get safely upriver to their destination. Two of them had been blown up with total loss of occupant sailors' lives before I was called to the job.

Convincing my team to buy into such a dangerous campaign took more than just directing them to load up the boats with our equipment. Things move quickly in combat, and I soon realized that if they didn't comprehend the significance of the mission, they wouldn't respond in the way I wanted. So I sat them all down and explained exactly what we were after and why. I witnessed the recognition of danger and the importance of our mission dawning on their faces; from then on, I felt confident we were all pulling in the same direction.

That was an important lesson to absorb: It taught me the value of communication with the people you lead— and how it makes all members of a team perform even better at what they do. This lesson has remained at the forefront of my approach to business for my entire career, and I was so pleased that Cindy Baier agreed with my definition of leadership as she led Brookdale during the greatest public health crisis in over a hundred years.

In our conversations, Cindy asked me how I managed under extreme pressure. I shared with her, and I'll share here that I simply had to move beyond fear. At first I was scared every night, staring out from my hooch (the hut in which we slept and dressed) and the top of the double bunk where I slept. I had to process my fear over a period of days to realize that in order to be effective, I had to move beyond it. If I died, then I died—but I would certainly improve my chances of staying alive if I had the clarity of thought to make good decisions.

The lesson is the same for any good business leader during crisis: once you set aside your fear of the unknown, then you can think more clearly and lead more effectively.

This idea was discussed many times in strategic planning sessions among Brookdale's board of directors during the COVID-19 pandemic—and something that all business leaders should understand and enact, especially during difficult times.

Narrowing your focus increases the chances of accomplishing your objective. I have always believed that an organization should have five or fewer top priorities at any given time. The priorities are the key items that a company needs to focus on in order to achieve its vision.

When I became the CEO of Brookdale, we reduced our focus to the top three priorities and realigned our organization around them. The priorities I introduced were 1) attract, engage, develop, and retain the best associates; 2) earn resident and family trust by providing valued, high-quality care and personalized service; and 3) win locally and leverage our scale effectively.

When the pandemic hit, we needed to be clear about our overarching priority, which was even more important than the three priorities that we had been focused on. So we simplified our communications efforts to clarify that the most important focus was our North Star—the health and well-being of our residents, patients, and associates.

Although we had always relied on our North Star to guide us, we needed to focus almost exclusively on this priority during the pandemic. In normal times, this remains a part of our day-to-day operations; during the pandemic, things were changing so quickly that it had to become our primary focus. It helped us align our organization and reinforced the role of prioritization for Brookdale—a lesson that translates to any business.

> ## Learn to Survey the Landscape with an Independent Mindset.

Leaders must dedicate themselves to honing their skills as independent thinkers and capable surveyors of the threats and opportunities that can impact a company's growth. They must learn to integrate the views of a wide variety of people and foster an environment that encourages teamwork.

As you assess events that can impact your business, brainstorm possible outcomes (scenario planning), develop creative responses (including contingency plans), and evaluate the potential for impact. Take time to consider each potential solution based on the business objective, resources required, timeline for implementation, and criteria for measuring results as well as the expected impact. Entertain all ideas—even some of the "bad" ones—so you can feel confident you have found the best solution.

Once a decision is made, the goal is to ensure everyone on the team aligns for effective implementation. The message is lead, follow, or get out of the way. When it comes to executing, take the no-nonsense approach exemplified by many great leaders, including General George S. Patton, Ted Turner, and former Chrysler executive Lee Iacocca.

After implementation comes assessment: gather feedback, use key performance indicators to track progress, make data-driven decisions about outcomes, and then make adjustments to improve processes.

In most cases, it's better to move quickly and adjust as necessary once implementation is underway. If the consequences of failure are potentially harmful, then take time to carefully consider any dangerous effects of rapid implementation and proceed with caution. Develop sufficient protocols to test and evaluate the results of any meaningful decision, particularly actions taken during a crisis—when tensions are high and nerves slightly frayed.

At Brookdale, I can attest that the pandemic truly stretched our leaders to perform at a higher level than many realized was possible. Many understood that standing alongside me at the helm of an enormous organization during an unprecedented crisis was an opportunity to endure a unique growth and development crucible: the challenges we faced were once-in-a-career opportunities to prove one's merit and make a difference when it mattered most.

For those who rose to the challenge, duty required tremendous sacrifice but often positively impacted their career trajectories. Our tremendous success in navigating the treacherous waters of the pandemic was a credit to the leaders who answered the call when the sirens rang out; we were quick and agile not only because we were prepared but because we were willing to lead.

Crisis Efforts and Cross-Functional Teamwork

Every company has an obligation to provide their best and brightest associates with opportunities for upward mobility by offering projects that enable associates to expand their minds and capabilities outside of their day-to-day responsibilities—particularly opportunities that involve cross-functional teamwork. During a crisis, temporary assignments open the door for associates eager to illustrate their unique leadership capabilities or exercise untapped skill sets.

Additionally, clarifying decision rights at various levels of the organization helps organizations move more quickly and efficiently: it sharpens the focus of the corporate leadership team and enables localized leadership to inject a much-needed dose of enthusiasm for their local customers.

When strong execution is important, the leadership team is responsible for ensuring resources are available—and sometimes centralized—in order to get the job done. During the pandemic, Brookdale created a multidisciplinary command center (with leaders spanning critical functions within the company) to lead our response to the pandemic. Businesses across all industries can apply this concept to their own challenges, particularly when faced with an urgent need to consolidate decision-making powers across a broad slate of verticals, aggregate data, and secure financial resources in order to take decisive action and move forward effectively.

HERO HIGHLIGHTS FROM JEFF BALSER, MD, PHD

Currently president, CEO, and dean of Vanderbilt University Medical Center

BALANCING CENTRAL COMMAND RESPONSE TO EMPOWER LOCAL LEADERSHIP

At Vanderbilt, we've been building new muscles. As healthcare providers, we are ordinarily trained to wait for all the data to arrive before analyzing and then take action. Like most healthcare centers (including Brookdale Senior Living), Vanderbilt Health established a Crisis Command Center early in the pandemic, and we can attribute countless successes to this cross-disciplinary team's deft coordination and judgment through tidal waves of change.

Our associates had to tolerate an unfamiliar level of ambiguity—gathering whatever data was available, trusting their gut, and making decisions on a constantly changing playing field.

While there are countless examples of this phenomenon across the country, one particular example at Vanderbilt is telehealth. While Vanderbilt is a world leader in healthcare informatics—having performed the earliest system-wide deployment of an electronic health record in the mid-1990s—more than a quarter century later, telehealth was still a fringe capability. The technology had plenty of promise, but deployment was progressing at a glacial pace due to an array of obstacles. Few were technical, and most were grounded in process inflexibilities (i.e., insurance preapproval) and generalized anxiety about change (i.e., patient acceptance of virtual care).

Everything changed when the pandemic led to widespread clinic closures, and we realized the potential cost of our inertia—if it continued—was the discontinuation of our healthcare services for thousands of patients with chronic diseases requiring our constant support. Creativity and energy abounded, and healthcare teams from countless verticals with their own distinctive cultural norms—from health informatics, clinical operations, and finance to legal affairs, human resources, and health equity—all worked feverishly to identify barriers and assemble solutions.

Rather than a centralized command-and-control effort, this grassroots activity pooled the intelligence and resources of highly capable groups from across the medical center— each with deep knowledge and diverse expertise—to build new levels of trust while finding practical solutions at a breathtaking pace. Within a few weeks, Vanderbilt was able to provide nearly half of its ambulatory visit volume through telehealth, avoiding untold emergency room visits and hospital admissions and saving countless lives in the process. Anxieties about patient satisfaction with virtual care were rapidly debunked as surveys showed our patients generally had even higher satisfaction due to the benefits of receiving care while staying at home (i.e., no risk of COVID-19 exposure, no driving, no parking, no need for childcare, etc.).

Whether assembling homemade COVID-19 lab testing platforms when typical supply lines were exhausted or testing new models for horizontal redeployment of clinical teams to support overextended critical care staff, our organization saw thousands of associates managing their own controlled experiments—leveraging decades of their own personal expertise at a rate and pace never before seen.

The occasional failed experiments were overshadowed by countless successes that built new levels of confidence and resilience across the organization. Mirroring what happened at Brookdale when decision-making was moved closer to the customer (a.k.a. resident), people across the medical center were amazed and proud of what they accomplished—and forever changed by the experience. It's been a valuable lesson that translates to organizations across many fields and industries.

Cross-functional projects are a terrific development opportunity for leaders at all levels and even outside of an organization.

> ## Cross-Functionality Strengthens Decision-Making—and Gives Individuals an Opportunity to Lead.

Brookdale found tremendous value from peer networks as we connected with a broad cross section of leaders in the healthcare industry and with government officials. Leaders in all industries can benefit from leveraging their peer networks and taking early action to develop relationships with government contacts and within the broader industry.

People who are unified around an issue are a force multiplier, and relationships (as I've emphasized) are as good as gold.

Celebrate Shining Stars

Make a point to recognize rising stars or promote aspiring leaders as they prove themselves through challenges. Pay close attention to associates who appear hesitant to embrace additional responsibility when all hands are requested on deck: if they're feeling unsupported, they may be experiencing financial or professional insecurity, and it's the leadership team's job to shore up resources if possible so associates can perform at an optimal level. If they're simply unwilling to contribute to the higher mission at a similar level to the other hands on deck, they might be too inflexible to meet your mission and better suited for a different opportunity.

Taking time to acknowledge outstanding contributions invigorates team members at every level of the organization. Expand recognition efforts during a crisis by highlighting contributions through multi-tiered awards or meaningful gestures that honor efforts specific to the moment.

Brookdale's response to the pandemic was very visible. Because of this, we were honored to receive a great deal of recognition and industry awards from top-tier organizations. In turn, we prioritized internal recognition for our Brookdale associates through a vast array of awards, recognizing more contributions—at more levels of the organization—than ever before.

In any company, recognition is an important component of success for boosting motivation and shining a light on the culture of the organization. Recognition should amount to much more than a token gesture, and it should never be limited to a single category of associates (i.e., Employee of the Month).

As a leader, taking time to say thank you goes a long way, whether it's a phone call, a personal email, or—especially—a handwritten note. The personal touch often means a great deal to the recipient, and this is true across every industry.

Solutions, Solutions, Solutions

Many challenges seem insurmountable when you first approach them. Don't let the magnitude of the effort overwhelm you.

Triage the situation and focus on the most important priorities first. It is often helpful to set daily goals, because they help you focus on the small steps that will ultimately lead to success—and measurable milestones you can celebrate along the way.

> ### Solve Big Problems by Dividing Them into Achievable Tasks.

Divide the work; a burden that is shared is immediately lighter.

Leverage your professional networks to find solutions used in other situations that can be adapted to meet your needs. The SOAP process used in hospital systems (subjective data, objective data, assessment, and plan) is a great process we have been able to apply to the senior living industry.

Be creative. We found many new solutions by reimagining how we could redeploy capabilities that already existed within our network. This included looking at both our own internal capacities as well as our vendors' abilities. These lessons apply universally.

If you're in business long enough, you will undoubtedly experience various disappointments and setbacks. Don't let them discourage you. Instead take the opportunity to learn from them. Maintaining a quality of resilience—relentless commitment to problem solving—is an important part of success as leaders (and in the culture of a company).

These characteristics are helpful regardless of your business or industry.

Prepare for the Long Game

Despite the difficulty of short-term challenges, it's important to maintain focus on your strategy over the long term. Businesses that take advantage of opportunities on the horizon—before their competitors are ready—gain market share quickly.

Sometimes a team's success depends on how quickly the team can develop new skills or acquire new capabilities—but remember, acquiring new capabilities can be achieved by "buying" or "building." When time is of the essence, hiring experts or creating partnerships with established expertise can accelerate your response.

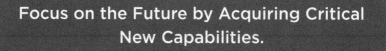

Focus on the Future by Acquiring Critical New Capabilities.

Every business depends on cash flow and liquidity, and every member of the leadership team needs to be able to grasp the items that influence the cash flow of the business and how changes are likely to affect it.

Maintaining cash liquidity for your company is required for your business to remain operational in normal times and especially through a crisis; it enables you to pay your employees, purchase supplies, and so on. This is one of the reasons businesses borrowed against their credit lines early in the pandemic; they needed to ensure they had enough cash to weather the storm.

Capital markets tend to vary in terms of the amount of risk they'll accept. Sometimes investors are more willing to take risk ("risk on"), and other times they believe it's prudent to be more conservative ("risk off"). In times of uncertainty, capital markets tend to tighten quickly. Thus it's important to take action to bolster liquidity when there's significant uncertainty. It's easier to get financing when you don't need it; staying one step ahead by identifying possible threats to your company's cash flow is the key to remaining financially stable throughout a crisis.

HERO HIGHLIGHTS FROM LEE WIELANSKY

Joined Brookdale Senior Living Board of Directors April 2015; currently chairman and CEO of Opportunistic Equities

OPERATING FROM A POSITION OF STRENGTH

If I've learned anything in business over the years, it's that you have to operate from a position of strength—Brookdale worked hard in the early days of the pandemic to do just that.

In the real estate industry (which includes senior living), the first key to operating from a place of strength is to ensure you remain well capitalized. If you are, then other organizations will want to work with you, regardless of the state of the economy. If you don't have access to cash and capital, you're operating from a position of weakness, and that will affect your ability to survive the bad times and grow in the good ones. Bankers, lenders, and other parties interested in joint ventures want to work with the companies they think will survive.

In the early days of the pandemic, Brookdale maintained its focus on cash liquidity and capital structure improvements, and this focus enabled us to remain in good stead as we confronted the most challenging crisis we had seen. The lessons we learned apply to many other industries beyond senior living and real estate.

Secondly, it's important for every company to review its business periodically to assess where money is made and lost, then proceed to make changes—structurally if needed—to bolster cash flow. Fortunately, Brookdale had already started this process by the time the pandemic began, moving toward a structure that favored ownership (versus leasing) of the buildings it operates wherever feasible.

The third business principle that the pandemic reinforced is the importance of enhancing a company's operational efficiency across the entire organization—scanning for inefficiencies company wide ensures that robust budgetary improvements can be made as needed.

This is a critical step when looking to secure a company's foundation for the future.

As we evaluate the post-pandemic environment for the senior living industry, we have to review where we've been as well as where we're going. Brookdale operated from a position of strength through the crisis, and it positioned us well as we reassess our priorities going forward. We are able to leverage new opportunities even as other companies continue to face challenges, and we are leading the industry into the future from a place of hard-earned wisdom.

I am so proud of the success we achieved as a company, and I feel confident that the tide will raise all of the senior-living industry boats that survived the COVID-19 storm over time.

Regardless of your leadership role, learning the basics of finance is an essential part of your leadership foundation. This is true across all industries.

Lessons Learned

Attitude is everything.

Negativity drains energy, and positivity creates it. The more serious the situation, the more important it is to be calm and positive—even the most challenging situation has a silver lining.

Leaders who operate businesses that make a difference in people's lives must operate within environments that are beyond our control.

We can't control our circumstances when crisis descends, but we most certainly can shape our reactions.

There is no doubt that sometimes circumstances beyond our control create previously unimaginable challenges. When times are tough, leadership matters more than ever. Step up, stay focused, and inspire those around you to work hard as a team to overcome the obstacles that you are facing. When you have amazing, dedicated people working together, many things that initially seem impossible are, in fact, possible.

The best way to have the future you want is to create it!

A Call to Action

Inspiring the Next Generation to Lead with a Servant's Heart

A s we considered our strategy for fighting an invisible enemy, I was constantly reminded of the parallels between our journey and the Apollo 13 mission rescue. During an early phase of this space mission to land on the moon, the loss of a service module resulted in the inability to provide water, oxygen, and power—the basic elements for sustaining life. If everyone involved in the mission hadn't worked together quickly to solve the issue—both among the various verticals of the command center and those on the "front line" within the module—the brave astronauts wouldn't have made it home. Solving the problem—from quite a distance, no less—was a matter of life and death. The bottom line for Brookdale and for the Apollo 13 crew was this: failure was not an option.

* * *

The feeling was a familiar one—I was reminded of my youth, when I experienced the trauma of my mom's car accident that nearly took her life. Nothing can prepare a child for the pain and heartache of helping a parent rebuild her life and home after a near-fatal car crash.

You don't question whether it's possible to come out on the other side—you just do what is necessary. You survey the landscape of the destruction around you, and you dig deep in your heart and look up to the sky in search of guidance from the highest-possible source of intelligence you can find.

* * *

Maintaining focus on our North Star kept us connected to a higher purpose when Brookdale faced the unthinkable. Looking back, we never would have imagined we could overcome so many obstacles and operate at the intensity we did for as long as we did. But we did.

Every day, our associates marched forth boldly—willingly walking into the front lines of the pandemic war. Our residents and patients waited patiently in the trenches as we worked to help hold off, contain, and mitigate the effects of a hostile enemy.

We knew that we could no longer tread down many familiar paths we had walked before, and we sought counsel for traversing the unknown. We banded together; and if someone was struggling, we'd lend a helping hand to our fellow servicemen and women until they were equipped to return to the battlefield again.

We did it again and again and again, often running our engines on fumes but, primarily, on that spirit of grit and determination that can only be found in a servant's heart. It was something that came from the deepest recesses within—a well of purpose and meaning that even the most seasoned veterans among us were unaware it existed until we were forced to excavate it. It was the human spirit taking flight.

In years to come, when people look back on their COVID-19 experiences, they'll likely feel a mix of strong emotions. People will surely recall the uncertainty and recognize how much things have changed. But mostly, I think we'll all remember the people with whom we shared this experience.

One of the heartwarming aspects of Brookdale's response to the COVID-19 pandemic was how we came together—like a family, focused on helping to keep everyone as safe as possible. We'll look back with love in our hearts, even as we grieve for the ones who were lost. What we must do is continue to support each other. If we share our thoughts and feelings, we can better process our reactions to what happened. We'll be able to look back with strength and courage and look forward with a smile, bittersweet though it may be. We will always remember those we have lost; may their memory be a blessing, and may we all find comfort as we fill this new world with caring and hope.

* * *

The lesson of the Apollo 13 mission has always held personal meaning to me, because Captain James Lovell opened a restaurant called Lovell's in Lake Forest, Illinois, in 1999, and it had been one of my favorite restaurants to visit—an inspiring setting for a quiet meal with my husband when we lived there before moving to Tennessee to join Brookdale.

The walls of the restaurant featured memorabilia from the flight as well as an "Apollo 13" movie poster signed by Tom Hanks, who portrayed Captain Lovell on screen. Most notably, the restaurant featured an impressive mural spanning twenty feet by eight feet called "The Steeds of Apollo." The Apollo 13 mission patch had been designed after this mural, which features horses in flight, high above the earth. Tom Hanks and his family bought the mural for Captain Lovell in honor of his distinction as the first person to fly in space four times.

The success of the Apollo 13 mission has always inspired me, because it demonstrated how to stay focused when the stakes are the highest imaginable: by solving the most important problems first, keeping calm in a crisis, and working together as a team to succeed.

It was a heroic effort that captivated a nation, because it captured the potential of humankind to overcome against all odds.

* * *

When COVID-19 reached the US, Brookdale was steering the course of our own unique module, crippled by a black-swan event. Our odds of success were uncertain as we faced off against an enemy we quite literally could not see.

We knew that not everyone would agree on certain decisions we made; we knew we needed to operate in ways we had never before contemplated; and we knew it would cost a lot of money to help protect lives. Yet we had a higher purpose that mattered more than anything else: we called it our North Star.

I've always felt an enormous weight of responsibility regarding the health and well-being of our residents, patients, and associates, and that feeling was magnified when the pandemic hit.

I made a personal commitment to do everything humanly possible to help protect precious lives—and to ensure Brookdale as a company would weather the storm. As the leader at the helm, I was willing to pay whatever it would cost me personally in terms of time, energy, and focus in order to help protect our people and business.

I was the captain of the battleship in an unprecedented war, and I knew we couldn't control our circumstances, but I knew we could do absolutely everything in our power to batten down the hatches and secure our ship for the bumpy ride.

* * *

At its core, Brookdale's mission is about people helping people. As we age, physical changes make it more difficult to manage the normal activities of daily living, including maintaining a home, preparing meals, tending to personal hygiene, managing medications, and in some cases, coordinating specialized care for chronic ailments.

By balancing the six key dimensions of wellness—the purposeful, emotional, physical, social, spiritual, and intellectual—our Optimum Life® programs are designed to create a lifestyle that promotes health, wholeness, and fulfillment.

Our story is unique because we support the daily lives of those who were among the most vulnerable to the virus due to age and chronic conditions. Residents live with us twenty-four hours a day, seven days a week, 365 days a year. Ordinarily, our residents eat together with friends in our dining rooms, exercise with one another in our Brookdale B-fit programs, and attend educational and social outings as a group. Connection to community is at the very heart of our business model.

Yet the risks of COVID-19 forced us to rethink everything: we had to reimagine engagement options as we set out to help keep our residents safe from an enemy we couldn't see.

We knew we would do what we had to do to help protect our residents from danger; what we didn't know was that we would also do … so … much … more.

* * *

Jonas Salk, who developed the polio vaccine, said, "The reward for work well done is the opportunity to do more."

As I look to the future, I am optimistic. Supply and demand are both in our favor. We will continue to build on our leadership position with our clinical and operational expertise, and we expect to benefit from many external factors that are aligning and creating a tailwind to aid in our journey.

Now that we're focused on post-pandemic recovery, I'm so pleased and encouraged by the progress we've made over the last year and that we're consistently welcoming new residents into our communities to help them with the challenges of aging, and that's really the point: people helping people to improve their lives.

We call our buildings "communities" for a reason. We're in the business of building relationships. I have heard so many seniors say that they have never had more friends in their life.

Life is even better for our residents now that they're plugged into digital technology that enables them to attend events virtually like never before—events that may have never been possible—and communicate more closely with grandchildren and great grandchildren who live at a distance. However, technology can never replace genuine social interaction.

Senior living meets this need through daily companionship and engagement with the heart-centered contributions of our associates.

The silver lining of the pandemic was that we proved we could meet that need even with our doors closed to the outside world.

* * *

For about two years, we've endured the toughest battle in Brookdale's history. The fight against the COVID-19 virus isn't over, but we've helped contain it, and the storm is less intense now than it once was.

This book is a testament to that: after working together with an outstanding crew of board members, leaders, associates, and partners, and collecting the heartwarming stories shared by our wonderful residents, patients, and their loved ones, we are so pleased to share this journey and the lessons we learned along the way.

If we can be of service to you in your own mission, please let us know.

I am so proud of my Brookdale family and the impact they make each and every day. It's such an honor to lead them all, and I hope this story can inspire and encourage others as you follow your own dreams.

I came from a small town of 2,750 people in central Illinois, I grew up dirt poor, and I was the first person in my family to go to college. However humble your beginnings, know that you can make an impact when you decide that failure is not an option.

Even if you fall short of the moon, be grateful—for you are among the stars.

JANUARY
2020

Awareness is raised of an unknown virus spreading in China.

Brookdale issues a preventative action plan to our communities. This includes available information about the virus and reinforces our strong, established flu and infectious disease prevention and control protocols as well as environmental cleaning precautions.

FEBRUARY

The WHO* identifies the novel Coronavirus and names it COVID-19. Brookdale establishes its Emergency Command Center to increase our level of preparedness, including monitoring our supply chain for PPE and increasing communication frequency with associates, residents, patients and their families.

MARCH

The CDC recommends restrictions on gatherings. Brookdale announces limiting community access and launches a website dedicated to COVID-19 updates including educational videos and downloadable content for the public to use.

APRIL

As unemployment spikes across the nation, Brookdale begins actively recruiting to fill more than 4,500 positions, including newly created roles.

Facebook features Brookdale as a resilient business for our COVID-19 response.

*World Health Organization

MAY

Resident engagement practices adapt quickly to community life with COVID-19 restrictions, incorporating the latest technology to help residents stay entertained and socially engaged.

JUNE

Using guidance from the CDC, state and local health departments, and our own clinical experts, Brookdale begins planning a phased approach to reopen communities.

JULY

The company achieves a testing milestone — more than 100,000 COVID-19 tests administered to residents and associates.

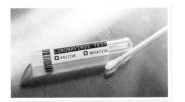

AUGUST

Brookdale completes baseline testing of residents and associates at all of our communities across more than 40 states.

SEPTEMBER

Brookdale continues to lead fundraising to fight Alzheimer's disease. Across the nation, Brookdale's associates, vendor partners, residents and their families take part in a virtual Walk to End Alzheimer's. They collectively raise almost $1.2 million[1] for the Alzheimer's Association in 2020.

OCTOBER

Brookdale partners with CVS Health for future COVID-19 vaccines within the Pharmacy Partnership for Long-Term Care Program.

NOVEMBER

Brookdale ranks highest in Customer Satisfaction with Assisted Living & Memory Care communities according to J.D. Power. [2]

DECEMBER

COVID-19 vaccinations start at our communities one week after the federal government granted Emergency Use Authorization for the first vaccine.

[1] Funds raised by associates, residents, families and business partners.
[2] 2020 J.D. Power U.S. Senior Living Satisfaction Study; tied in 2020

JANUARY
2021

The company hosts its 500th community COVID-19 vaccination clinic for residents and community associates. More than **40,000 vaccinations** are administered in just over four weeks.

FEBRUARY

Brookdale completes 100% of its first community vaccination clinics.

MARCH

Brookdale completes the second round of vaccine clinics at all communities.

Brookdale residents and their loved ones are showcased in a *Dateline NBC* special featuring families reunited after a year of COVID-19 restrictions.

APRIL

Brookdale completes at least three rounds of vaccine clinics at all communities.

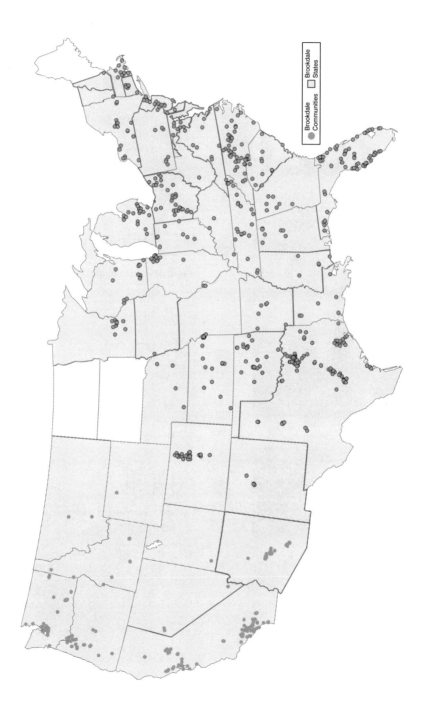

The can-doers
The make-it-greaters
The above and beyonders

These are Brookdale's Everyday Heroes.

Before the world was threatened by the COVID-19 outbreak, we created the Everyday Heroes program for associates who excelled in serving our residents and patients. They embody our selfless spirit.

And now, more than ever, you continue to raise the bar. You're on the front lines helping to maintain the health and safety of our residents and patients. And we're so proud of you all.

To Our Frontline Associates

Thank You

(Print ad) Featured in:

The **New York Times** · THE **WALL STREET JOURNAL** · The **Washington Post**

©2020 Brookdale Senior Living Inc. All rights reserved. BROOKDALE SENIOR LIVING and BRINGING NEW LIFE TO SENIOR LIVING are the registered trademarks of Brookdale Senior Living Inc.

Bringing **New Life** to Senior Living®

BROOKDALE
——— SENIOR LIVING ———

brookdale.com

353

We take care of our exceptional people, because they're taking care of your exceptional people.

Real messages of gratitude sent to our associates and caregivers during COVID-19
See more at brookdale.com/thanks

INDEX

About the Author

From her humble childhood on a rural farm in Illinois to leading the nation's premier operator of senior living communities, Lucinda ("Cindy") M. Baier is the president, chief executive officer, and a member of the board of directors of Brookdale Senior Living. As of year-end 2020, the $3.5 billion company has the ability to serve approximately sixty thousand residents through its independent living, assisted living, Alzheimer's and other dementia care and continuing care retirement communities, as well as its comprehensive network of services. Brookdale's forty-thousand-plus employees are taking care of America's seniors, and in 2020, *Fortune* magazine ranked Brookdale as one of the top two hundred largest publicly listed employers in the country.

Cindy became Brookdale's top leader on February 28, 2018. As CEO, she led the company through the COVID-19 pandemic, the largest public health crisis in a hundred years, by aligning the company on the priority of the health and well-being of its residents, patients, and associates. She helped focus Brookdale's efforts on increasing diversity, resulting in the board achieving gender parity during 2018. Since she became CEO, Brookdale has increased people of color in leadership roles and on the board.

Within the second year after Cindy became CEO and introduced the "winning locally" strategy, the company's Net Promoter Score* increased 20 percent. In her third year as CEO, J.D. Power recognized Brookdale as #1 in customer satisfaction in assisted living/memory care communities.

Cindy has led significant transformation efforts at Brookdale, including changing most aspects of Brookdale's senior living business to help protect its residents, patients, and associates against COVID-19 virtually overnight; restructuring leases; and unlocking significant value through the sale of assets.

Prior to joining Brookdale, Cindy served almost a decade as a board member of public and private companies and organizations. Cindy has always felt a strong desire to make a difference.

Cindy has been recognized by a number of professional organizations, including being named one of the CEO Forum Group's 2021 Top 10 CEOs Transforming Healthcare in America; she is a recipient of the Corporate Citizenship 2020 Award from the Committee for Economic Development of The Conference Board; and for the fourth consecutive year, she was named to the *Nashville Business Journal*'s "Power 100" list and has twice been named to their "Most Admired CEO" list.

Cindy has been quoted in the *Wall Street Journal* and *Modern Healthcare* and has appeared multiple times on CNBC's *Power Lunch*.

Prior to becoming CEO of Brookdale, Cindy served as the company's chief financial officer from December 2015. In addition to experience as a seasoned chief financial officer in several companies, she has been responsible for multi-billion-dollar operations, worked as the CEO for a publicly traded retailer, and served as an executive officer of a Fortune 30 company.

Cindy is a certified public accountant and a graduate of Illinois State University, with both bachelor and master of science degrees in accounting.

Family has always been important to Cindy. She is eternally grateful for the life that she shares with her husband, Dave, and the love of her sister, Lisa, and brother-in-law, Mitch. She enjoys spending time with her three stepchildren and their spouses, and she appreciates the energy and spontaneity of her five wonderful grandchildren.